REASON, MORALITY, AND BEAUTY

200 Years of Immanuel Kant

REASON, MORALITY, AND BEAUTY
Essays on the Philosophy of Immanuel Kant

edited by
Bindu Puri
and
Heiko Sievers

GOETHE-INSTITUT
MAX MUELLER BHAVAN
NEW DELHI

OXFORD
UNIVERSITY PRESS

OXFORD
UNIVERSITY PRESS

YMCA Library Building, Jai Singh Road, New Delhi 110001

Oxford University Press is a department of the University of Oxford.
It furthers the University's objective of excellence in research,
scholarship, and education by publishing worldwide in

Oxford New York
Auckland Cape Town Dar es Salaam Hong Kong Karachi
Kuala Lumpur Madrid Melbourne Mexico City Nairobi
New Delhi Shanghai Taipei Toronto

With offices in
Argentina Austria Brazil Chile Czech Republic France Greece
Guatemala Hungary Italy Japan Poland Portugal Singapore
South Korea Switzerland Thailand Turkey Ukraine Vietnam

Oxford is a registered trade mark of Oxford University Press
in the UK and in certain other countries

Published in India
by Oxford University Press, New Delhi

© Oxford University Press, 2007

ISBN-13: 978-0-19-568393-6
ISBN-10: 0-19-568393-5

Typeset in Aldine401 BT 10.5/12.5
By Star Compugraphics Private Limited, Delhi
Printed in India at Ram Printograph, Delhi 110 051
Published by Oxford University Press
YMCA Library Building, Jai Singh Road, New Delhi 110 001

Contents

Foreword   MRINAL MIRI   vii

Preface   HEIKO SIEVERS   xiv

Introduction   BINDU PURI   1

Section 1
MORAL PHILOSOPHY:
TOWARDS A PURITY OF MORALS

Kant and the Revival of Virtue Ethics   SHARAD DESHPANDE   11

Autonomy of Reason and Ethics of the Face: Imagining
a Civil Society in Kantian Lineage   GOUTAM BISWAS   26

Necessity, Universality, and the
A Priori in Ethics   JONATHAN DANCY   40

Kant on Happiness, Friendship, and Inclination:
An Aristotelian Critique   BINDU PURI   55

From Kant's Methodology of Pure Practical Reason
to a Novel Ethical Education   HÜLYA YETIŞKEN   76

Respect for Morality and Value Judgement:
From Kant to Neo-Kantianism   XIE DIKUN   85

Section 2
SELF AND AUTONOMY:
ISSUES OF FREEDOM AND SELF-LEGISLATION

The Difficulty of the Subject   GOENAWAN MOHAMAD   103

Autonomy and the Virtue of
Self-Legislation   BIJOY H. BORUAH   118

Krishnachandra Bhattacharyya on the Unknowability
of Self in Kant: Problematizing the Programme of
Indian Remedies to Western Problems   A. RAGHURAMARAJU   134

Section 3
RELIGION

'Religion and Public Reasoning': Enlightenment and
Critical Deliberation on Religion in Western and
Islamic Societies Today   MATTHIAS LUTZ-BACHMANN   155

Section 4
AESTHETICS

Kant, Adorno, and the Dynamics of
Artistic Appearing   MARTIN SEEL   169

Symbolizing Permanent Desire: Kant's Aesthetic Judgement
and Duchamp's 'Painting of Precision'   ANDREA ESSER   179

Notes on Contributors   189

Foreword

Kant, Modernity, and Beyond

Mrinal Miri

Ours may be the most hospitable of ages in endorsing the theme of the flux. That is, it may be the most inclined to embrace in a spontaneous, quotidian, even expert and specialized way the following doctrines: (i) the world is cognitively intransparent; (ii) attributions of real structures indissolubly implicate the tacit collective bias and collective resources of inquiring societies; (iii) the cultural diversity and non-convergence of conceptual schemes, 'styles of reasoning', horizontal prejudice and blindness and the like are ineluctable features of the natural history of human inquiry; (iv) there is no principled division between intra and intersocial conceptual diversity, communication and understanding of both sorts are, like the world itself, subject to an incompletely penetrable intransparency; (v) discourse and intelligent behaviour function effectively within the flux, without any assurance of their being, or of our being able to discern, essential, invariant, universal exceptionless structures grounding, enabling or confirming knowledge, truth, validity, proof, rationality, the interpretation or application of formal principles of consistency or coherence and the like; (vi) the distinctly cultural nature of linguistically apt human persons is itself radically alterable through historical change sui generis, not obviously expressible in the terms of the supposed regularity of the physical world; (vii) the very existence of persons or selves is an artifactual evolution uniquely embodied in the biological uniformities of homo sapiens; and (viii) attributions of real structures in both the physical and cultural worlds are radically underdetermined by any and all testing conditions, which are themselves tacitly constrained by the transient conceptual horizons within which particular claims are made.
There you have a strenuous tally of the largest philosophical saliences of our own day... the focus of the most important current debates... They are all committed, one way or another, to the doctrine of the profound plasticity of the world; and, taken together, they yield a uniquely popular and ubiquitous disposition to favour protagoreanism.'—Joseph Margolis[1]

If Margolis is right about 'the philosophical saliences of our own day'—and there is good reason to believe that he is—then clearly we have moved a long way away from Kant in the last 200 or more years of European thought. Kant believed in (1) the complete transparency of the structure of the knowable world—a transparency guaranteed by what he called the *categories*; (2) the unitariness and universality of rationality; (3) the ahistoricity and culture-indifference of the conditions of knowledge or indeed cognition; and (4) the transcendental unity of apperception as the essential core of the human self.

I do not wish here to trace the route through which European thought has travelled in the last 200 years or so. In any case this would be an extremely difficult task and much beyond my competence. Instead, I would merely like to point out some of the aspects of Kant's thought which have both influenced modern thought and been subjected to very searching criticism. Also I consider very briefly, Kant's account of aesthetic value, which, perhaps for sound enough reason, seems altogether to have escaped the attention of the modern mind.

Let me begin by saying something about Kant's philosophical method. Perhaps the best description of the method is 'methodological solipsism'. The question that Kant begins his philosophical enquiry with is: 'Given that I have experiences of various kinds, what is it that makes this possible?' This is *not* a question about a causally satisfactory (scientific) account of what makes experiences happen, as it were. It is a question, in the language of twentieth century analytical philosophy, about *concepts*: 'Given that I am an experiencing being—am a being capable of wielding the concept of experience, am minimally capable of having thoughts such as "I am in pain", "I see something red", what other concepts must I be capable of wielding?' So an engagement with philosophical enquiry requires no more than the assumption that I, as a subject of experiences, exist. Kant shared this methodological solipsism with his empiricist predecessors, for example, Hobbes, Locke, Hume, and others, although their views about what else exists in the world may be very different, including their views about what the 'I' really refers to. This was, of course, very famously, also the philosophical method of Descartes. It is interesting that methodological solipsism leads to a position, which is anything but solipsistic—a position that is at the very heart of the Enlightenment project. And this is the position that even if the world is filtered through my mind, my knowledge of it is objective, that knowledge and rationality are unitary and universal notions and that they cannot, therefore, be a function of historical and cultural contingencies. This is also, of course, the singular epistemological stance of modern western science from roughly the seventeenth century onwards. One way of seeing Kant's philosophy is to think of it as articulating the foundational conceptual framework of modern science. Kant of course mistook it for the universal, eternal framework of human thought.

While methodological solipsism remains the accepted stance of much of contemporary European intellectual self-awareness, there has been, even from Kant's own time, a steady erosion of its hold. For the solipsist, the mind and its ideas are the primary epistemic tools in man's possession—this is the famous 'way of ideas'. It is by the 'correct' procedural manipulation of the ideas that the mind puts itself in touch with the world outside it. Kant's deviation from 'the way of ideas' consisted in his powerfully argued assertion that some—even if very few—among our ideas have a very special status. They, only they, among all our ideas determine the form in which the real world must present itself to us. These of course are the so-called categories of the understanding. But the cornerstone of Kant's philosophy remained his uncompromising commitment to the universality and objectivity of authentic knowledge. And this has also been the core commitment of modern European thought although it has by now conceded much to what Margolis calls the hospitality of our age to the 'theme of flux'. The primary locus of the universality-objectivity commitment has of course been modern science, but it has, chiefly because of the great success of modern science and its spectacular and unprecedented technological spin-off, successfully permeated all the so-called human sciences—politics, sociology, psychology, economics, linguistics, and so on. While the 'theme of flux' has invaded these disciplines—think of Marxism and contemporary French structural functionalism (Levi-Strauss, Lacan, Barthes in their very different ways), and Ferdinand de Saussure of linguistics—they remain committed to an ultimately objectivist account of man and society. While thus Kant remains a significant presence in European thought of our times, it would be instructive to look briefly at the erosion that I mentioned of the objectivity-universality-stability (permanence) standpoint of Kant and of the 'way of ideas' of his immediate predecessors.

Perhaps the biggest and the most persistent challenge to the 'scientific outlook' has come from the "linguistic turn" that European thought took at the turn of the twentieth century. Some of the salient aspects of the linguistic turn are: (1) language becomes a central focus of theoretical attention; (2) the idea that language is an instrument that humans devise in order to (a) convey thoughts, ideas which take place in the inner arena of the mind and (b) marshal these ideas by following the correct 'rational' procedure so that they then can 'represent' the world authentically is gradually abandoned; (3) the solipsist vision that the language user can be in complete command over his language and can use it in total solipsistic isolation gives way to the view that the inalienable home of language is the linguistic community; (4) there is a veering away from the view that meaning consists in a relationship between discrete units of language (for example, words, sentences) and bits of the world that is extra-linguistic to the view that language constitutes the human world and the very specific way in which humans become aware of the nonhuman world (that is, as permeated by meanings); (5) there is a wide acceptance of the idea that language is an organic whole which is to say that the whole is as much in the parts as the parts are in the whole; another way of putting it (that of Humbolt's) is to say that language is a web in which the human world, the world in which humans have their being, is inalienably entangled and, when for example in speech, we touch any part of the web, the whole reverberates; (6) language is a capacity that comes to be realized primarily in speech and, therefore, 'it is open to being continually recreated in speech, continually extended, altered, reshaped. And this is what is constantly happening. Men are constantly shaping language, straining the limits of expression, minting new terms, displacing old ones, giving language a changed gamut of meanings.'[2]

There is much more to the linguistic turn than this. But this is sufficient to show how far we have moved away from the Kantian positions mentioned above. If language is constitutive of the human and the knowable world, then the latter cannot be transparently present to us; it must forever be open to differentiated articulation; since rationality is not extra-linguistic, it must be subject to similarly variegated articulation; also, since the community is the primary locus of language, it is doubtful if the self—whether the empirical self or the so-called 'transcendental unity of apperception'—can any more be regarded as the real subject of knowledge. This puts an end to methodological solipsism as a viable starting point for philosophical enquiry. If language is a whole and its parts are organically related to each other and to the whole, then different languages might have to be regarded as distinct organic wholes and this will raise desperately uncomfortable questions about the ideas of the universal and the objective and the ahistoricity and culture indifference of man's epistemic enterprise.

Of course, the univeralist, objectivist stance has far from disappeared, as I have already indicated. But the challenges posed to it by the 'linguistic turn' are formidable and in most cases we have an incredibly diminutive version of it compared to the strident vision of the enlightenment.

Let me turn now to Kant's moral philosophy. The challenges posed by the linguistic turn are equally daunting here. But inspite of the great proliferation of moral 'systems' in our times, the Kantian universalist moral philosophy seems still to be a going concern. Specific Kantian ideas have a central place in the articulation of influential theories like liberalism, in defending what is supposedly a universal concern for human rights and in clarifying the centrality of the idea of the individual human being in our modern self-consciousness—Kantian ideas such as the autonomy of the moral self, morality as consisting in following universalizable, rational rules, the very concept of a person as setting a limit to utilitarianism. To my mind, the most telling blow to Kantian moral philosophy comes from a combination of the linguistic turn and a return to Aristotelianism. The rule-centric, universalist moral theory per force ignores the great variety and subtlety of moral language. The universal rule, which does not admit of exceptions, is more suited to the enforcement of justice, which is supposedly blind, and to effective bureaucratic management than to the life of morality. Impartial bureaucracy and equality of all before law seem to be two central guiding thoughts of modernity, and insofar as this is so, modern civilization has an unquestionably Kantian shape. But morality must be distinguished from bureaucratic adherence to rules applicable across various kinds of human contingencies just as it must be distinguished from 'blind' justice; this represents a powerful line of criticism of Kantian thought. Crucial to this line of thought is the Aristotelian idea of the faculty of 'judgement' which enables one to perceive a human situation in the great density of its moral complexity and specificity. This is then expanded into the idea that moral language, which is necessarily expressive of the life of morality, is enormously subtle with the possibility of multiplicity of articulations embedded in it. Thus we have the very impressively argued view that it is in the highly dense, complex works of fiction that moral ideas find relatively adequate articulation: the best texts in moral philosophy are the most powerful works of fiction of all times. The requirement of judgement and the focus on the particular do not, however, throw the door open for relativism in moral matters. Neither would be intelligible unless morality were an inter-subjectively debatable and binding phenomenon.

The third major area of interest for Kant was our judgements of beauty. Correct judgements of beauty, like correct moral judgements must be universally valid—this is Kant's starting position. The question to which he seeks an answer is: 'How are such judgements possible?' Once again, this is not a scientific question demanding an answer in terms of causation. This is a question, if you like, about the concept of beauty itself: given that we wield the concept of beauty in the way that we do—that is, as intersubjectively available and objectively binding—what else, conceptually, must be the case for this to be so? The difficulty here is compounded by the fact that for Kant beauty is not a perceived feature (like colour or shape) of the object that is judged to be beautiful; to see something as beautiful is to derive a special kind of *pleasure* from it. The peculiar character of the pleasure consists in the fact that it is disinterested, that is, it is not dependent on considerations of the class to which the object that is judged to be beautiful belongs, nor on considerations of what its possible uses are. The pleasure springs from the contemplation of the *form* of the object alone. These two features of a judgement of beauty are, according to Kant, sufficient to guarantee its objectivity and universality. Kant's arguments here show neither the rigour nor the seriousness of his arguments in the *Critique of Pure Reason* or *The Groundwork of the Metaphysic of Morals*. Besides, in *The Critique of*

Aesthetic Judgement, Kant is primarily concerned with the beauty of *natural* objects. Although artistic objects, for example, buildings and paintings, do come in for consideration, it is cursory at the most and the great variety of artefacts, which can be the subject of aesthetic judgement, is not even acknowledged. It is not surprising therefore that Kant's views on aesthetic value have received very little philosophical attention, nor have they been found particularly useful in the construction of contemporary theories about artistic value. This is in sharp contrast to Kant's influence in the areas of philosophy of knowledge and moral philosophy. It is a pity therefore that this neglect of *The Critique of Aesthetic Judgement* has also meant that some extraordinarily pregnant ideas in the book have not caught the attention of theoreticians of later times. To mention just two such ideas: in considering the beauty of works of art, Kant suggests that the judgement of beauty, besides being an expression of disinterested pleasure in the form of the object, also expresses an aesthetic idea—an idea that induces much thought but cannot be brought under any concept—that is an idea that is ineffable. The second idea is that a judgement of taste emanates from the free and harmonious play of the imagination and the understanding. It seems to me that both these ideas can be unpacked in a way that could throw much light on the entire phenomenon of the aesthetic.

To conclude, it is undeniable that Kant's thought played a pivotal role in the unfolding of the intellectual self-awareness of what we call modernity; but this self-awareness is in the process of being transformed—and this transformation is also a movement away from Kantian preoccupations and predilections.

Notes

1. Joseph Margolis, *The Truth About Relativism*, Blackwell, Oxford, 1991.
2. Charles Taylor, *Human Agency and Language*, Cambridge University Press, Cambridge, 1988, p. 232.

Preface

Heiko Sievers

Around the globe, the year 2004 was marked by seminars, conferences, and publications on the occasion of the 200th death anniversary of Immanuel Kant, the great German Enlightenment philosopher who died on 12 February, 1804, in the East Prussian city of Königsberg (now Kaliningrad). Eighty years earlier, on 22 April, 1724, Kant had been born in this city, which he never left during his lifetime, apart from the occasional excursion to the vicinity. Throughout 2004, countless international scholars of philosophy, ethics, epistemology, political science, aesthetic theory, and history examined Kant's wide-ranging cosmopolitanism and focussed on specific aspects of his relevance in the twenty-first century. Conferences initiated by the Head Office of the Goethe-Institut in Munich and organized in more than twenty-five cities across the world featured prominently during the commemorative year.[1] After all, Kant had revolutionized philosophy: his thinking has shaped 'the modern face of the landscape of Western thought'[2] beyond the boundaries of his discipline.

* * *

According to Kant,[3] there were two things that filled the mind with ever-new admiration and awe: 'the starry sky above me and the moral law within me'.[4] Throughout his life, Kant's philosophical reflections were challenged by the questions of the experience of nature and moral action. Based on his childhood memories, of which few records survive, it was his mother who opened 'his heart to the impressions of nature' and sowed the first 'seed of good' in him.[5] She died when Kant was thirteen. The other stages in his life—university, lectureships, a professorship in philosophy—were all in his native city: a 'peaceful situation precisely suited to my needs, with work alternating with speculation and social intercourse'[6] that proved so fruitful for his inner life.

Although Kant never left Königsberg, he was always in touch with the latest academic debate. Far from being an isolated and brooding genius, he maintained close contact and indulged in intellectual exchanges with the protagonists of the Enlightenment (for instance, Moses Mendelssohn), before becoming one himself, and with contemporary Enlightenment critics such as Johann Georg Hamann and Johann Gottfried Herder. The major influences on his philosophical work came mainly from France (Jean-Jacques Rousseau) and England (David Hume). However, it was not until 1781 that the *Kritik der reinen Vernunft* (*Critique of Pure Reason*) was published—a work that forged his reputation as the greatest German philosopher, and which changed 'if not the world, then at least philosophy'.[7] It was followed by works including *Grundlegung zur Metaphysik der Sitten* (*Foundation of the Metaphysics of Morals*) in 1785, *Kritik der praktischen Vernunft* (*Critique of Practical Reason*) in 1788 and *Kritik der Urteilskraft* (*Critique of Judgement*) in 1790.

Kant's theme was reason, which can address both the theoretical questions of knowledge ('What can I know?'), as well as the practical questions of action ('What should I do?'). Kant examines it from both perspectives. A key term here is 'critique', by which he does not mean criticism of his subject, but rather examination, differentiation, and justification. It is in this sense that Kant addresses the question 'What can I know?' in his *Critique of Pure Reason*. He holds that the basis for reason is an objectively valid knowledge of nature, but also contends that the area in which theoretical reason can justifiably speak of a knowledge of nature is limited—in other words, all knowledge entails a priori concepts and sensations (that is, which do not appeal to experience). This was a new idea, as theoretical philosophy (metaphysics) had traditionally dealt with questions about God, immortality, the human soul, and the origin of the world. Human beings have no experience of God, the soul or the world as a whole, therefore such 'objects' may be conceived, but cannot, in principle, be experienced. Any debate on such metaphysical objects is devoid of experience and applies to empty concepts. Consequently, theoretical reason can have nothing to do with them.

While the *Critique of Pure Reason* shows that reason has certain limits, Kant aims to show in his practical philosophy that morality is the exclusive domain of reason. In response to the question 'How should I act?' he replies first by referring to moral consciousness. This highest principle on which all action should be based is derived exclusively from the use of practical reason, which is simply the ability or the will to determine one's action oneself, independent of external factors. The only key to action is the moral law, which presents itself to reason in the form of a categorical imperative: 'Act as if the maxim from which you act were to become through your will a universal law.'[8] As a free autonomous person, a human being can choose whether or not to act in accordance with this law. That also means, however, that neither a priest nor a king nor God can set down the moral law; rather, it lies within human beings themselves. Moral action is thus a question of man's self-determination.

Kant's contemporaries were divided in their reaction to his philosophy. Some hailed him as the new founder of philosophy, while others considered him dangerous. His reputation as an atheist extended beyond his native city. Kant, the 'pulveriser of everything' (Moses Mendelssohn), had not just fallen victim to traditional metaphysics, but his thinking questioned all authority by calling upon the power of reasoning—a call that had a lasting impact. Eckermann, for example, records Goethe as saying in 1827 that Kant was 'undoubtedly' not only the 'most excellent' of modern philosophers, but also the one 'whose teaching has continued to prove itself and has penetrated our German culture most deeply'. 'He has,' continues Goethe, 'had an effect on you even without you having read him'.[9]

Goethe's statement is still valid today. It may well be concluded that it is Kant's 'mode of thought' in 'subversive affirmation' (Otfried Höffe), systematically criticizing what it values most highly, what continues to influence contemporary thinking rather than his philosophical positions. His eighteenth-century voice may also sound strange to our ears today, however, as the contributors impressively show in these two volumes, he can be an enormously stimulating conversation partner even in the twenty-first century.

* * *

Kant's ideas and demands, such as how to achieve and sustain the peaceful coexistence of states—for example the supposition that peace is based on confidence—can easily be applied to present-day international conflicts. This was the premise of the seminar '200 Years of Immanuel Kant: An Examination of the Notions of Enlightenment, Autonomy, and Terror', the only such conference in South Asia during the anniversary, initiated by Bindu Puri and organized by the Goethe-Institut/Max Mueller Bhavan, New Delhi at Neemrana from 7–9 October, 2004.

In the traditions of ancestor worship, the rationale behind celebrating a death anniversary is quite obviously to keep 'alive' a relationship severed by death; or else to celebrate an *enduring* relationship between the deceased and his descendents which death is unable to destroy. It is quite astounding to see Kant's towering presence in many of the current crucial political and ethical debates. Indeed, he seems to be anything but dead. On the contrary, he is sometimes treated as a contemporary. In the context of the second Gulf War, for example, Antje Vollmer, the then vice-president of the German parliament and a prominent leader of Germany's Green Party, entered into a controversy with Roger Scruton on the open Democracy website literally about the question of whether or not Immanuel Kant 'could have supported the US-led war in 2003 to overthrow the Saddam Hussein regime in Iraq'.[10] The manner in which Vollmer referred to Kant's principles while scoring her points against this war was virtually like drawing support from an old friend or a former teacher who is momentarily unavailable—perhaps down with fever or with the cell phone switched off:

-   'It is hard to see Immanuel (…) giving his consent to an initiative based on such bad faith, inaccuracy and misjudgement.'
-   '…spreading the idea of republicanism by means of war is emphatically not something which Immanuel (…) would have supported.'
-   '…but war itself, waged from abroad, cannot bring democracy and lasting peace. Of all thinkers, Immanuel (…) would have understood this.'
-   '…the Middle East and the world today are not truly safer, more democratic or more peaceful than before the Iraq war.

I think this runs contrary to all Immanuel's (...) expectations of the successful application of human reason.'

In her essay, Vollmer drew on one of Kant's most popular texts, namely his sketch on *Toward Perpetual Peace*, written late in his life on the occasion of a treaty forged in Basel in 1795 between Prussia and revolutionary France which he qualified merely as the 'suspension of hostilities, not a peace'.[11] This short treatise is indeed one of the best examples of Kant's extraordinary vision and contemporary relevance. Here are some of its central arguments:

- *'Standing armies shall in time be abolished altogether.'* Why? *'For they incessantly threaten other states with war by their readiness to appear always prepared for war...'*[12]—an appeal for disarmament, as relevant today as ever before.
- *'No state shall forcibly interfere in the constitution or government of another state. For what can justify it in doing so?'*[13] This is one of the founding principles of the UN charter, which continues to be constantly violated even in the twenty-first century. The extent to which, for example, US President George W. Bush has imbibed Kant's 209-year-old principle is apparent in the following remark made during a television debate with the Democrat John Kerry: 'I have been to a lot of summits. I have never seen a meeting that would depose a tyrant or bring a terrorist to justice.'[14]
- *'No state at war with another shall allow itself such acts of hostility as would have to make mutual trust impossible during a future peace (...) For some trust in the enemy's way of thinking must still remain even in the midst of war, since otherwise (...) the hostilities would turn into a war of extermination...'*[15] Although this principle was enshrined a long time ago in the 1864 Geneva Convention and in The Hague Land Warfare Convention of 1899 and 1907, both conventions are still a long way from successful enforcement.

And finally there are Kant's three 'definite articles':[16]

    a) *'The civil constitution in every state shall be republican'*;
    b) *'The right of nations shall be based on a federalism of free states'*; and

c) *'Cosmopolitan right shall be limited to conditions of universal hospitality'* (a harsh criticism of the colonial powers of his
   time).

These bear witness to Kant's conviction that it is the establishment
of the *rule of law within* a state and in the relations *between* states that
forms the essential precondition for durable peace.

In an article on the relevance of the treatise today, the German
political scientist Herfried Münkler observes that

the Organization for Security and Cooperation in Europe (OSCE), the
European Union and possibly the European part of NATO can justifiably be
considered (...) as embodiments of a federation of states as Immanuel Kant
might have envisaged them. (However,) to apply this concept on a global scale
to the United Nations (...), would be a daring step.[17]

Yet another indication of Kant's enormous contemporary
relevance comes from different quarters. Robert Kagan, the prominent neo-conservative protagonist of the *Project for the New
American Century*, starts his controversial article 'Power and Weakness'
on the incompatibility of European and American world views, with
the following provocative reference to Kant:

Europe is turning away from power, or to put it a little differently, it is moving
beyond power into a self-contained world of laws and rules and transnational
negotiation and cooperation. It is entering a post-historical paradise of peace
and relative prosperity, the realization of Kant's 'Perpetual Peace'. The United
States, meanwhile, remains mired in history, exercising power in the anarchic
Hobbesian world where international laws and rules are unreliable and where
true security and the defence and promotion of a liberal order still depend on
the possession and use of military might. That is why on major strategic and
international questions today, Americans are from Mars and Europeans are
from Venus.[18]

While David Held, with reference to this equation, quipped that
the 'US-strategy is best perceived as *pre*-Hobbesian because it is a
return to the state of nature',[19] one could also argue that, in fact,
Kagan's reference to Kant seems quite appropriate. If, therefore,
Europe would also like the US to move from Mars to Venus, it will
have to muster substantial support to wage a truly Kantian struggle
for the global realization of what he called 'the civil law of men in a
nation', 'the law of nations in their relation to one another' and 'the

law of world citizenship'—in other words, the global victory of reason and the rule of law.

* * *

The editors are deeply indebted to the contributors in these volumes and to all Goethe-Institut colleagues from around the world who were involved in the commemoration year and who selected and suggested papers presented at the conferences that they had organized. Our particular gratitude and appreciation go to Berthold Franke, former Head of the Department of Culture and Society at the Goethe-Institut Head Office in Munich, to Simone Lenz, who was responsible in this department for the commemorative events in 2004 and liaised from Munich with the German Kant experts, and to the Goethe-Institut online team for the very informative website created for the occasion. Our thanks also go to the academic community in Germany that wholeheartedly supported the Goethe-Institut's initiatives and played a vital role in the success of the debates and events. We would particularly like to mention the Kant-Gesellschaft in Mainz and the Kant-Archiv Marburg, as well as Otfried Höffe, Martin Seel, and Volker Gerhard, among many others, for their valuable contribution and advice. On behalf of all the colleagues, we extend our sincere thanks.

The editors are equally grateful to the staff at Oxford University Press, for their unstinting support and invaluable help in bringing out these two volumes.

Notes

1. Between February and December 2004, conferences were held in Oslo, Copenhagen, Stockholm, Bordeaux, Tunis, Rome, Amsterdam, Kaliningrad, Dhaka, Porto Alegre, Lisbon, Genoa, Beijing, Moscow, Wellington, Curitiba, Bogota, Bucharest, Istanbul, Sarajevo, Zagreb, Vilnius, Osaka, Athens, Ankara, Jakarta, and in September 2005 in Sao Paulo. In addition, numerous lectures by German and international scholars were held throughout the world.
2. Otfried Höffe, *Kants Kritik der reinen Vernunft. Die Grundlegung der modernen Philosophie*, Munich, 2003, p. 11.
3. I am grateful to Antonia Loick from whose text I have drawn in this part of the preface: "'The Starry Sky Above Me and the Moral Law Within Me"—

The 200th Anniversary of the Death of Immanuel Kant,' Goethe-Institut website, 2004.

4. Immanuel Kant, *Kritik der praktischen Vernunft*, Hamburg, 1990, p. 186.
5. Hermann Schwarz (ed.), *Immanuel Kant. Ein Lebensbild nach Darstellungen der Zeitgenossen Borowski, Jachmann, Wasiansik*, Halle, 1907, p. 169; quoted in Steffen Dietzsch, *Immanuel Kant. Eine Biografie*, Leipzig, 2003, p. 23.
6. Ludwig Ernst Borowski, *Darstellung des Lebens und des Charakters Immanuel Kants*, Königsberg 1804 quoted in Manfred Kühn, Kant. *Eine Biografie*, Munich, 2003, p. 259.
7. Manfred Kühn, Eine Biografie, p. 280.
8. Immanuel Kant, *Grundlegung zur Metaphysik der Sitten*, Hamburg, 1994, p. 42.
9. Fritz Bergemann (ed.), *Johann Peter Eckermann: Gespräche mit Goethe*, Leipzig, 1968, p. 222; quoted in Steffen Dietzsch, *Immanuel Kant: Eine Biografie*, Leipzig, 2003, p. 156.
10. Antje Vollmer, 'Immanuel Kant and Iraq: A Reply to Roger Scruton', in *openDemocracy*, 1/4/04, http://www.opendemocracy.net/faith-iraqwarphiloshophy/article_1821.jsp.
11. Immanuel Kant, 'Toward Perpetual Peace: A Philosophical Project', in Mary J. Gregor (ed.), *Practical Philosophy*, Cambridge, 1996.
12. Ibid., p. 318.
13. Ibid., p. 319.
14. *The Hindu*, 3/10/04.
15. Immanuel Kant, 'Toward Perpetual Peace: A Philosophical Project', in Mary J. Gregor (ed.), *Practical Philosophy*, Cambridge, 1996, p. 320.
16. Ibid., p. 322.
17. Herfried Münkler, 'Kant's "Perpetual Peace": Utopia or Political Guide?', in *openDemocracy*, 27/5/2004, http://www.opendemocracy.net/faith-iraqwarphiloshophy/article_1921.jsp.
18. Robert Kagan, 'Power and Weakness', in *Policy Review*, No. 113, June 2002, http://www.policyreview.org/JUN02/kagan.html.
19. David Held, 'Return to the State of Nature', in openDemocracy, 20/3/2003, http://www.opendemocracy.net/faith-iraqwarphiloshophy/article_1065.jsp.

Introduction

Finality Without an End: Morality, Autonomy, Religion, and Art in Kant

Bindu Puri

This, the first of the two volumes on the philosophy of Immannuel Kant, examines (1) Kant's rationalist universalism in the face of the increasingly persistent presence of particularistic forces and (2) the Kantian position that in the funda-mental postulates of morality, freedom and religion; and in the appearing of the object of art there is an essentially unfinished character. This is because the three postulates of practical reason—the freedom of the will, the immortality of the soul and the existence of God—are ideas of reason. No object adequate to the transcendent idea can ever be found within experience. Therefore morality exists in a struggle between reason and inclinations, freedom needs to be reconciled with the other as an end in himself, and to have religion is a duty of the human being to himself, human beings should act as if moral laws are divine commands. Again, in the perception of the appearing of the object of art, there is the suspension of epistemic determining, there is harmonious play of the faculties of imagination and understanding with no attempt to fix a definite meaning, just a disinterested experience of pleasure. The judgement of beauty expresses an idea that necessarily cannot be conceptualized, that is an idea that is ineffable. So that the idea represents something possible but necessarily unfinished. Yet this essentially unfinished character of the moral striving, religious belief and artistic object somehow produce the moral and aesthetic judgement, which is not private but universal and necessary.

The volume addresses this problematic of the universal rationalism in Kant alongside the character of moral striving, religious faith and the aesthetic judgement as approximations to an essentially unfinished end. This is done across the four sections, which articulate concerns, across cultures and continents, about, Kant's ideas of morality, freedom and self, religion and aesthetics. Section 1 discusses issues in moral philosophy. In the context of the age in which we live, which, as Mrinal Miri argues in this volume, endorses the theme of the flux, this examination of Kant's rigorous universalism becomes urgent. So that it is the case that the *philosophical saliences of our own day* have moved in the direction of particularity, undeterminacy, plasticity, fluidity of the world and of our experience of it. This is obviously a move away from Kant who believed that human experience in all its forms has a judgement character and there is no human experience, which does not conform to that structure. The Kantian subject of experience then is a hypostatized and autonomous rational subject who functions as the agent of the judgements. Moral and aesthetic judgements are universalizable. The essay by Jonathan Dancy in the first section challenges this fundamental Kantian position. Dancy argues that the Kantian rationalist universalism in morality makes an inference from the fact that moral truths are known a priori, to the conclusion, that they are therefore necessary and universal in form. Dancy takes a position, which has now come to be called particularism in ethics. The particularist maintains that moral facts are particular facts about what is a reason in a particular case. Basic moral facts are contingent and not necessary, nor universal in form. And yet, some contingent particular moral truths can be known a priori. Just like, as Dancy argues, judgements about similiarity and relevance are known a priori but are particular and contingent judgements. Again Dancy challenges the great Kantian connection between rationality and morality itself. As also, the exhaustive distinction between experience and reason. He questions whether all failures of morality are indeed failures of rationality. According to him, moral failures need not be failures of sense experience or of rationality but failures of quite a different kind. Moral knowledge may then be located in between the extremes of experience and reason, somewhere in the intermediate space or simply in a capacity that rational beings have, which in itself, is not based in experience or reason, though it might presuppose, both, experience of life in the world and reason as an interpretative faculty. The essay then challenges Kant's universal rationalism in morality as also the very connection between morality and reason, which was the spirit of enlightenment morality. This is done to make room for the particularity of moral reasons. An increasingly pressing and dominant need in our world where a sense of the indeterminacy of human experience prevails.

Gautam Biswas articulates the problematic of Kantian morality, resting as it does, on a notion of freedom, which is essentially limited by the self as committed to the other in a moral community, which underlies the civil society. Freedom legislates its own limitations. For Biswas, the problem is to locate the transcendental idea of freedom in the context of a civil society and the reality of life between man and man. He argues in his paper that the Kantian tradition has a certain continuity with Levinas and *ethics of the face* where the idea of an autonomous self is equivalent to the idea of the moral equal of the self, the other. This has a precursor in the same tradition with the *dialogical ethics* of Martin Buber, which requires a horizontal placing of moral equals. The genuine community here is the goal and culmination of the I–Thou relationship. This is the community of the others, a community in which the 'I' does not bring any closure for the other in the community. In terms of this tradition, argued for, by Biswas, the Kantian notion of freedom as a transcendental idea of pure reason is never actually arrived at in totality. It cannot, as an idea, do that at all. It self legislates its own limitations and must do so, as commanded to by the categorical imperative, which legislates both, that the other should always be treated as an end in himself and that moral agents make up a community of ends, a kingdom of ends. Freedom essentially does not have a finality with an end, there is no closure, it is in a dynamics of adjustment to the other as a moral equal. Freedom remains essentially in this kind of evolution and does not ever reach an adequate expression in experience. Indeed as a transcendental idea it is clear that nothing can be found in experience at all, which is adequate to the idea. In quite the same tone, the essay by Bindu Puri talks about the fact that the rationalistic and universalistic character of the enlightenment morality in Kant, suffers from the serious lacuna that it has no place for characteristically human elements like desire, inclination, friendship and happiness. Kant cannot admit any heteronomous principles in human goodness. For the universality of moral law makes it clear that it cannot be based in the special constitution of human nature or the accidental circumstances in which it is placed. Happiness then cannot be part of a moral maxim and with it also stand removed other capricious and accidental things like love, friendship, human inclinations and desires. The essay, by offering an Aristotelian and Kantian comparison on the concept of friendship, tries to argue that these characteristically human things need not only be seen as disruptive of human goodness. They can also be constitutive of human goodness for in them lies the strength to make man commit himself and extend himself far beyond what he ordinarily can do. Kant of course sees morality as essentially consisting simply of this struggle with inclinations and desires. Moral theory, which takes note of them, however, can then harness these elements and make them powerful sources of moral motivation through moral education and training to build a world where, instead of being generated through impulses, moral atrocities are actually rendered impossible because of the same feelings and emotions. Shifting from this kind of argument, the essay by Hulya Yetisken explicates Kant's views on moral education and demonstrates the significance of this method in his philosophy as a whole. The section then traces, in this and other essays, the problems of Kantian universalism vis-à-vis the persistent particulars whether moral reasons, the other as a contentious presence, or simply inclinations and desires that defy rules and principles. It is in this kind of problematic that one of the important challenges to Kantian morality comes from the Aristotelians in the present century. For with Aristotle it is possible to construct an ethics, which makes room for the practical faculty of judgement, or phronesis that implies a particular person's judgement in a specific situation. Also such an ethic allows the presence of factors that make for the vulnerability of the ethical life and the fragility of human goodness, factors like human happiness, love and friendship. Such a moral theory, while it seems closer to human goodness, is also closer to the spirit of the age where change, flux and difference are as real as principles and there seem to be no rules that can prepare a moral agent for all the differences and peculiarities that the flux generates.

Section 2 moves to the issues of the human subject and its autonomy, issues, which are of course closely related to those of the previous section. The Kantian subject is the rational subject with an essential freedom, both to make law and follow it. His own subjecthood dictates to him as a rational agent to follow his self-legislated laws and thus limit his autonomy. Again here, in Kant, there seems no final realization of a rational, free subject. Human subjects can only approximate the rational autonomous subject in a striving with heteronomous principles and experience of frailty of the will. The essay by Raghuramaraju discusses the problematic of the self, which as the source of knowledge is essentially unknowable. Raghuramaraju sees the Kantian self as disguised divinity, in continuity with a theological tradition, which it is seemingly a radical departure from. He also, in this context, examines and critiques Krishnachandra Bhattacharya's attempted solution to the Kantian problematic. Bhattacharya has used the Advaitic approach to solve the unknowability of the Kantian self, breaking open the equivalence between knowing and thinking assumed by Kant. Raghuramaraju resists this attempt to create solutions across cultures and traditions because of a general point about the failure of such attempts to understand internal aspects of the tradition in which the problem has been initially located. Philosophical problems are located in a certain tradition, history and culture. These build a complex interiority, which is structured into the philosophical problem itself so that solutions across cultures are not able to delve into that complex interiority. In his essay, Barua articulates another aspect of the problematic related to the Kantian subject—the problematic of freedom and determinism. In the positive sense, human autonomy means that the will is able to act on the basis of self-legislated principles and further that these are not heteronomous. So that autonomy implies complete freedom from one's needs as a sensuous being. The autonomous self is, both master of, and, mastered by, the self. The essay raises the question of the justification of the harmonization of the two dimensions of the human self—being in deterministic grip of nature and being as able to govern herself as a rational agent. Barua sets this important reconciliatory task against the background of the relation between nature and morality and locates the moral life as always a life of trying to be moral in the struggle between reason and inclination. Morality then exists in a sort of elbow room and man begins his moral life when he leaves the sphere of causality. Yet morality is in the struggle and for the holy will there is no moral law as a categorical imperative. So that, morality also must be essentially a set of principles or imperatives self-legislated by the rational subject, which involves that subject in a struggle with inclinations thereby, contemporaneously, also creating the sphere of the moral. Goenawan Mohamad, the Indonesian poet, tries to articulate the anxiety of the Kantian subject, ridden, as autonomy is, with self-suffering and melancholy. In this context, he discusses Adorno's critique of Kant for making the whole moment of freedom rationalistically narrowed. The paper proceeds to interestingly identify the Kantian subject as the basis of the twentieth-century Muslim revivalist movement, concluding that perhaps the emancipation of the self targeted in revival discourse, is to be found by incorporating a notion of a fluid self. The self is to be found in a continuous act of generating subjecthood, rather than in a hypostatized self, a solidified idol, to be consecrated. The self then is like a desire, which is never fulfilled, always to be reached and created.

Section 3 examines the issue of religion in Kant. Given the structure of Kant's epistemology, the legitimacy of belief in the existence of God and of religious discourse generally becomes problematic. For Kant, belief in God and religious truth claims cannot be validated by a notion of revelation, as revelation finds no place in the rational faculties of man. God, freedom and immortality are ideas of pure practical reason, which, in their practical function, are involved in determining the will and in providing principles of moral conduct. Kant argues that human beings self-legislate their moral principles but act as if their moral principles were divine commands. Neither the validity of moral principles nor the legal order of the state is to be based on reason and revelation. Further, within particular religious traditions, Kant spoke of the possibility and necessity to examine the truth claims of religion in an open and unlimited process of public reasoning by which alone, Kant believed, the legitimate authority of religion could come to light. The essay by Matthias Lutz-Bachmann in this volume traces the programme of such public reasoning in the western liberal tradition and traces it to Kant's predecessors in early Christian philosophy and theology. He would like to see the same programme taken forward by means of a new epistemological approach to the specific logic of religions in philosophy, located in a public debate to be carried out within particular religious traditions between their interpretors and representatives. Yet, as discussed, it would be in the character of belief in God and the nature of religious discourse to be essentially an approximation, for the transcendent idea can never be seen in actual experience, the pure concepts can only be approximated, never completely arrived at.

Section 4 examines the dynamics of artistic appearing in Kant. In aesthetic judgement, according to Kant, the subject suspends the epistemic activity and in the interplay of the faculties of imagination and understanding, takes a disinterested pleasure in the appearing of the aesthetic object. While the aesthetic judgement is not a judgement into which we can be persuaded by the use of principles and reasons, yet it has a universal voice and claims the agreement of every one else. Both the papers in this volume examine aspects of the claim of modern art, as voiced in the readymades of Marcel Duchamp, that art should have nothing to do with the sensuousness of the art object. Marcel Duchamp, in many interviews and statements, claims that what is to be avoided in art is precisely aesthetics and aesthetic pleasure. He refuses art as pleasing only to the eye. The work of Duchamp then seems to produce evidence against Kant and demonstrate the limits of his aesthetics. Martin Seel, sees Duchamp as against Kant, and argues that in his ready-mades, for example, the snow shovel, Duchamp does not really succeed in rejecting the sensuousness of the art object. It is precisely because there is an attempt to see in the *snow shovel* something other than the ordinary, that it is an artistic operation. In artistic operations, it is then impossible to escape the dynamics of artistic appearing and the experience of the disinterested pleasure in that appearing. In sharp contrast, the second paper by Andrea Esser builds a surprising analogy between Kant and Marcel Duchamp. Duchamp's *Large Glass* is in fact read by Esser as a Kantian symbol. Duchamp himself called it a *marriage of intellectual and visual reactions*. According to Esser the *Large Glass* and Duchamp's readymades are defying any fixation of definite meaning, just as the erotic partner remains unavailable to the other—this is to be so—if he or she is to continue to be an object of desire. There is an analogy between Duchamp's mundane objects and Kant's art objects—both need to be essentially out of reach and both need to retain a certain resistance against our will. They are symbols retaining a structure of infinity, an infinity that always has to be produced anew, representing something possible but necessarily unfinished. Further, Esser also makes an interesting point that Duchamp's readymades demonstrate the limits of Kantian aesthetics. For they show clearly that art is not only an aggregate of things to be judged aesthetically valuable, but also a system, which develops in a historical process. Kant's analysis of the aesthetic object does not take this dimension into account.

The four sections then articulate reflections, across cultures and continents, 200 years after Kant, on his universalism in diverse areas of man's rational quest. Despite the differences of concern and interest they all seem to explore the relationship between the rationalistic universalism and the need to acknowledge the existence of flux, change, particularity and difference. Further they also explore the relation between Kantian universalism and the essentially unfinished character of the Kantian postulates of freedom, morality and religion, as also the appearing of the object of art.

SECTION 1

MORAL PHILOSOPHY:
TOWARDS A PURITY OF MORALS

Kant and the Revival of Virtue Ethics

Sharad Deshpande

The revival of virtue ethics over the last few decades is a major contributing factor in taking a close look at Kant's moral philosophy
once again, this time in terms of issues that surround the concept of
virtue. The range of issues that are involved in this revival is vast
and varied. The issues pertaining to the relationship between Kant's
moral philosophy and virtue ethics are significant in this context
because of historical and conceptual reasons. The revival of virtue
ethics, one may say at the outset, completes the historical circle, from
the centrality of virtue in moral discourse to that of obligation and
again from the centrality of obligation back to virtue. The first half
of this circle illustrates how Western moral philosophy in its
modernist phase reversed the question, 'How should I live?' to 'How
should I act?' by privileging the notions of (moral) obligation and
(moral) duty. This reversal, it is alleged, amounts to a reduction of
the pre-modern conception of moral life as that which is 'worth
living' to the modernist conception of action that is 'obligatory'. Kant
(the deontologist) and Mill (the utilitarian) are the central figures
in this historical process. The other half of this historical circle illustrates how, within the domain of moral philosophy, several pre-
suppositions and distinctions that are held to be typically modern
underwent a thorough critical examination in the post-analytic phase
of Western philosophy. The post-analytic critique of several concepts
in modern moral philosophy such as reason, rational person, duty,
good, and obligation may have some affinity with the post-modernists
in this respect. The revival of virtue ethics is not complete as yet; it
is still an ongoing process to which a number of contemporary moral
philosophers have contributed. As per the general consensus that
has emerged by now, it is Elizabeth Anscombe's essay 'Modern Moral

Philosophy'[1] that has focused sharply on the inadequacies of the deontological and utilitarian versions of modern moral philosophy. This essay has opened up almost a new era of re-examination of deontological and utilitarian ethics from various perspectives. Anscombe charges both Kant and Mill for reducing norms of action either to moral law (the Kantian option) or to the idea of good (the utilitarian option). Kant is especially charged with introducing (moral) legalism without presupposing a divine lawgiver and for instituting the notion of 'self-legislation' that is held to be highly problematic. Whether the ideas of moral obligation necessarily require a legislative model and what exactly Kant means by 'self-legislation' and why this concept is not acceptable to the proponents of virtue ethics are the points that need close attention. In fact, a number of issues—both conceptual and historical—arise in making explicit several contexts in which Kant's ethics and consideration of virtue are put together.

One such context emerges out of the very distinction that some have made between virtue ethics and virtue theory.[2] Virtue ethics, it is said, consists in the advocacy of virtues and hence is prescriptive, whereas virtue theory views virtues in a more general manner by explicating the content and the function of virtue. Sometimes the intended difference in these nomenclatures is minimized by saying that both these expressions at times refer to the form of inquiry in which the considerations of the nature and value of virtues is of prime importance. But at times these nomenclatures simply refer to the neglect of virtues in modern ethical theories. Given the distinction between virtue ethics and virtue theory, it would be generally agreed that Plato and Aristotle were both virtue ethicists and virtue theorists. But Kant's position vis-à-vis this distinction is problematic because, as per the received opinion, Kant does not talk about virtues in the Aristotelian sense—virtue as a stable state of character. Second, Kant's discussion of virtues is couched in the framework of his doctrine of the categorical imperative that is supposed to stress reason against emotions or pleasure, which are founded in human psyche. This makes Kant an antagonist of virtue ethics of the Aristotelian kind. The issue of the relationship between Kant and virtue ethics acquires an important dimension in which the Aristotelian conception of virtue and the associate issues become significant.

The growing corpus of literature in the area of virtue ethics confirms the feeling that virtue-based ethics has become a strong alternative to deontology and utilitarianism. However, whether the overall postmodernist outlook prompts the revival of virtue ethics is a matter of considerable speculation and detailed argument. For instance, given the distinction between virtue ethics and virtue theory, it is not easy to distinguish whether the current interest in virtues is merely theoretical in the sense that it is influenced by the growing dissatisfaction with the 'modern' ethical theories or the interest in virtue-based ethics is prompted by the general dissatisfaction about some basic features of modern western society and thereby, on the positive side, 'opting ultimately for a different kind of society and for different kinds of relationships among its members'.[3]

The current dissatisfaction with modern ethical theories is felt on various grounds. As the proponents of virtue ethics often stress, what matters in the moral discourse is the person rather than the process of arriving at some solution in a conflicting situation. What matters is the person and the sort of life that she leads, the character of a person and her 'morally relevant traits' rather than 'moral principles' or the laws of moral obligation. Iris Murdoch[4], in conformity with the general spirit of the postmodern critique of rationality, questions the Kantian notion of the Rational Person, which is held to be the central notion around which the entire edifice of modernity is built. The ideal of the rational person was to ensure the progress of science and the consequent decline of religion. This in its turn gave rise to the particular conception of the universe, which is supposed to be devoid of purpose and is mechanistic but at the same time the rational person is supposed to possess free will and free choice. The Kantian rational self is alienated from the universe since the laws of mechanics do not govern it, but as a maker of choices that are not governed by external forces, the rational person has to be endowed with free will. Many critics of modernity are uneasy with this modernist conception of the rational person, which is supposed to be autonomous in the sense of not being governed by any external authority. Murdoch argues for a self that recognizes external authority. As in the case of learning language, one must respect the structure of language which is already there, so also in the ethical sphere the same kind of respect is found 'in the exercise of love and justice, where again it exemplifies a response to demands which are not themselves chosen'.[5]

The virtue ethicists' dissatisfaction can be further spelt out with reference to the underlying assumptions that deontology and utilitarianism share in common. Despite the differences, both these versions of modern ethical theory believe, for instance, that humans are bound by some 'universal' duties, that moral reasoning consists in applying 'principles', that the foundation of virtues is psychological and hence derivative from some a priori notions of *right* and *good*.[6] The dissatisfaction is also about such distinctions between 'justification' and 'motivation' of action that seem to be based on the peculiar notion of reason which in its own turn is under attack on various counts. Another important issue on which the proponents of virtue-based ethics criticize deontological and utilitarian theories pertains to the possibility and the role of principles and rules in moral discourse. As per the received view, the function of a moral theory is to formulate principles or rules to guide human action that can be termed as rational. Such principles or rules must be sufficiently abstract to cover the variance factor. When a person faces a situation of conflicting interests, she is supposed to consult the principles and 'apply' them. The deontologists as well as the utilitarians both insist on some principles or rules as necessary to guide human behaviour though they differ on the content of such principles. The proponents of virtue-based ethics raise serious doubts about the very possibility of the formulation and the consequent application of a principle or a rule that will determine what is right in practical matters, or in conflicting situations. All such programmes have essentially failed because of the inbuilt tension between the abstract character of a principle and the specificities of given practical situations. As against this, the proponents of virtue-based ethics emphasize the role of character in moral discourse. The principles or rules in moral discourse have to be integrated with a person's character that is the primary focus of morality. Saying that the basic judgements in ethics are judgements about character has summarized this. The primacy of character thus becomes a focal point for virtue ethics. The primacy of character thesis asserts that (1) the judgements about character (aretaic judgements) are independently valid from the judgements about the rightness of action (deontic judgements) and (2) the concept of virtue is explanatorily prior to that of right conduct.[7] The primacy of character thesis thus goes against the deontologist and the utilitarian views on the relationship between virtue (that is, traits of character) and rightness (of action). According to the deontological and utilitarian views, the concept of right action is theoretically prior to that of virtue since there has to be an independent criterion for the evaluation of the character traits.

The proponents of virtue ethics have questioned the importance given to the concept of moral duty or moral obligation in the deontologist and the utilitarian theories directly or indirectly. Alaisdair MacIntyre[8] and Richard Taylor[9] along with Anscombe, have raised doubts about the notion of moral duty on conceptual and historical grounds. It is argued that the notion of obligation presupposes that there be some authority that promulgates the law. It is in terms of a law that certain acts become obligatory. But it is argued that unlike the religious laws or the laws of the state, moral obligation does not seem to spring from any authority whether personal, impersonal or divine. This makes Philippa Foot and Taylor say that the notion of moral obligation or of moral 'ought', with its alleged superiority over other types of obligations, is, as a matter of fact, a 'free floating and unsubscribed'[10] or 'an empty concept'.[11] This raises a historical question of the origin of the notion of moral obligation. It has been observed that the notion of moral obligation as an overriding concept did not exist before the beginning of Christianity. In the Greek tradition, the moral obligation was not independent of the legal (state) obligation, nor was it independent from the notion of *good*. The notion of law as overriding and universal has its basis in the Christian notion of a divine lawgiver. It has been observed that in the historical process, the notion of the 'universal character' of obligation, that is, an obligation being valid for everyone irrespective of her/his individual desires or ends survived even after 'the religious belief was abandoned by most of Western society. People still regard moral obligations as universally valid and as overriding, although they deny the very frame of thought that gave sense to this view. Hence the emptiness of the concept'.[12] This leaves two alternatives open: either one accepts that a divine command theory is essential to hold the idea of moral obligation or as Taylor argues, one simply rejects the very connection between the religious framework and moral obligation and 'opts for' a new approach to ethics.[13]

Kant has advocated the non-derivative concept of duty as the central concept of morality. He has advocated the universality criterion to rule out the consequentialist measure of the moral worth of action. He is the major philosopher representing the Enlightenment efforts to construct an ahistorical and universalistic conception of morality ignoring the traditions and local communities.[14] Because of these moves on his part, Kant's ethics is usually labelled as 'rigidly rule governed', 'not accounting for the differences between persons (as moral agents) and cases (in which moral considerations become relevant)', offering the 'unconvincing account of the self, freedom and action', being full of 'excessive individualism based on the notion of right', and failing to give adequate account of virtues. Kant is also held responsible for causing the 'analytic philosophers neglect of virtue'[15] and for 'treating persons in abstraction from character and thus... guilty of misrepresenting not only persons but morality and practical deliberation as well'.[16] Whether these and allied charges are applicable to Kant is a point of dispute and the Kant sympathizers have indeed disputed it. For instance, it has been observed that some of these charges are true not primarily of Kantian ethics, but of some recent theories of justice that are 'conveniently labelled' as Kantian. In fact, the liberal theories of justice do not talk about virtues.[17] That they are labeled as 'Kantian' is due to the fact that they advocate the universal standards of justice. Some of these theories view justice 'as continuing the social contract tradition' while others view justice as grounded in an 'agreement' arising out of 'subjective conceptions of good'.[18] This raises the question of linking the considerations of justice with those of virtue. Since Kant's *Metaphysic of Morals* is an attempt to give an integrated account of justice and virtue, the question is how to read his account in the light of the present-day theories of justice that in fact deny the alleged link between justice and virtue.

Some exponents of virtue ethics emphasize, or overemphasize, the importance of human nature in such a way that the differences between Aristotle and Kant begin to appear as total. But whether this is so cannot be stated in a straightforward 'yes' or 'no' fashion.

In deciding this issue a great deal of analysis is required. Considerations of human nature vis-à-vis virtues appear at two levels, namely, the psychological and conceptual where one conceptualizes some idea of 'human flourishing' or 'human good'.[19] It has been suggested that providing a psychological foundation for virtues might turn out to be a dubious programme if one identifies virtues with certain psychological states. Virtues (that is, virtuous behaviour) cannot be without consequence. Hence, 'a moral virtue is a character trait which produces good consequences for others'.[20] Psychological states only facilitate those consequences. Given these two aspects, that is, virtue as certain psychological traits and virtue as having consequence in the form of human good, the notion 'human nature' becomes central in our reading of Kant and Aristotle. Both Aristotle and Kant give accounts of virtuous agents. For virtue theorists, these accounts are incompatible with one another on the issue of what psychological states are necessary for virtue. As is well known, for Aristotle, virtue consists in 'cultivated inclination' and therefore, pleasure is the proper accompaniment of virtuous activity. Satisfaction of 'cultivated inclination' leads to pleasure. As Aristotle puts it, 'Actions which conform to virtue are naturally pleasant' meaning thereby they are not pleasant only to those who perform virtuous actions, but 'pleasant in themselves'. For Kant, on the other hand, virtue is not an 'aptitude' and a 'habit of morally good actions acquired by practice'. Kant's insistence is on the *ground* or the *basis* from which this aptitude springs. Unless a moral principle (such as categorical imperative) is evoked, virtue as an 'aptitude' or 'a habit of morally good actions acquired by practice' will not be 'armed for all situations nor adequately secured against the changes that new temptations could bring about'.[21] In other words, inclination (be it cultivated) cannot serve as a ground for virtue, unless the inclination is backed by something unchanging. What is unchanging for Kant is the sense of moral duty or 'fortitude'. For Kant the crucial factor in defining virtue is the ability to master oneself. Aristotle and Kant viewed human beings differently. For Aristotle, the excellence of human beings is best realized in a harmonious well-ordered trait of character. For Kant, human beings inevitably experience base inclinations. Given this difference, both Aristotle and Kant hold that the restriction they put on virtue is justified since the condition makes the trait 'more reliable'. It has been observed that at least for some virtue theorists; Kant, despite the alleged antagonism between him and Aristotle, is as appealing as Aristotle, if not more so. Deciding to act well in spite of one's inclination would be a case of acting well irrespective of everything else. It would be far better a case than that of a person whose motives may be accompanied by pleasure. It is observed that even though a person may get pleasure in acting well, what motivates the action is still the motive of duty and thus 'virtue does not require pleasure'. Virtue theorists, thus, are divided on whether there is any necessary relation between virtue and pleasure. Here, a good deal can be said in favour of both Aristotle and Kant. And to recognize this is to overcome the alleged conflict between Kant and the proponents of virtue ethics. This is vindicated by the fact that there are some virtue theorists who are Kantians (of a sort!)

The other way to look at the alleged opposition between Kant and virtue ethics is to recognize explicitly that there are two (and not just one) types of virtue—Aristotelian and Kantian. This recognition is a step towards a possible dialogue between Aristotle and Kant. Kant's conception of virtue is of course different from that of Aristotle. Kant discusses the notions of autonomy and respect that typically belong to modernity. Recently it has been suggested that one can see a possible link between Kant and Aristotle via the Stoics impact on Kant.[22] Usually, casting Kant as a 'harsh duty philosopher' emphasizes the Stoic impact on Kant. But this reading might be misguided. It is argued in this connection that Kant's effort to develop an 'anthropology of morals' brings him closer to Aristotle. But all the same, Kant's moral anthropology rests on 'pure' morality, on a conception of the autonomy of reason as independent from the human condition. The Kantian project is to establish reason alone as the source of moral authority. For Aristotle, on the other hand, there is nothing but the 'human case and its inescapable finitude'. However, the dialogue between Aristotle and Kant addresses such issues as the place of rules and procedures in an account of morality, the role of external goods in the conception of what is morally worthy, the place of emotion in moral character, the relation of justice to virtue, the value of friends in the best human life. These issues are well indicative of the continuity of concerns of Western moral philosophy at two different points of history.

II

Before going into the charges that are levelled against Kant's ethics, it is necessary to have a brief outline of Kant's exposition of virtues and the space it occupies in the overall Kantian project. A systematic exposition of Kant's conception of virtue appears in the second part of *Metaphysic of Morals* under the heading *Doctrine of Virtue* (Tugendlehre) wherein he delineates and justifies duties of virtue or the ethical duties. In the first part of *Metaphysic of Morals*, Kant discusses the *Doctrine of Right* (Rechtslehre) wherein he speaks about juridical duties. Both the types of duty are grounded in the categorical imperative but their difference is due to the nature of constraint or legislation that is appropriate for both. Juridical duties (For instance duty to keep contract) are legislated externally and an agent can be compelled to fulfil them. Duties of virtue or ethical virtues (for example, the duty of beneficence) by contrast are self-imposed or are enjoined by 'inner legislation' and the only kind of constraint they involve is 'self-constraint'. Juridical duties can also be performed from inner legislation, that is, from the spirit of duty rather than out of fear of external sanction. In this sense, all duties are 'ethical' at least indirectly. But ethical duties, in particular, cannot be legally enforced. Ethical duties, thus, have to do with 'character' in terms of the strength of will, or fortitude in obeying internal sanctions. For Kant, fortitude in relation to the forces opposing moral will in us is virtue. So the doctrine that brings inner freedom under laws is a doctrine of virtue.

This brief outline of the *Metaphysic of Morals* provides a point of textual inquiry. As Kant himself declares, the *Critique of Practical Reason* was to be followed by a 'system' which he termed as the *Metaphysic of Morals*, the question may be raised at the outset, namely, (1) how are *Rechtslehre* or the doctrine of rights and *Tugendlehre*, or the doctrine of virtue related to one another in the light of Kant's own general framework as outlined in *The Critique of Practical Reason* and (2) how the *Tugendlehre* that is, the Kantian doctrine of virtue is to be read against the virtue ethicists' and virtue theorists' various accounts of virtue. Similarly, a close textual reading of the *Metaphysic of Morals* will have to be carried out in terms of raising questions about the pivotal concepts that Kant uses that is, maxim, good-will and emotion.

Defenders of Kant suggest that a re-reading of these concepts may help clear the charges against Kant. Onora O'Neill and Louden have proposed re-readings of the Kantian text in this direction.[23] Louden for instance, points out that the very opening of Kant's *Grundlegung* highlights the unqualified goodness of good-will and not of the supreme value of duty or principle.[24] Louden suggests that Kant's position on the nature and status of good-will can be interpreted in the framework of virtue ethics which takes the agent's character as basic. Most Kantian scholars have emphasized that good-will is not pleasure (a psychological state) nor is it duty (an act performed in accordance with principle). From the virtue ethics perspective, it can be taken as 'a state of character which becomes a basis of all of one's actions'.[25] But more importantly, the good-will and the life that is lived by the agent are internally related since the consistency requirement demands that an agent 'cannot exhibit a good-will one moment and an evil on the next. Steadfastness of character must be demonstrated'.[26] Louden takes this internal connection between good-will that Kant says is good without qualification, and the life that an agent actually lives. Kant's statement about good-will is not a statement about a principle but it is a basis for a moral judgement on the agent's character as such. It is less important to raise the question, 'Is my will good?' in connection with every single act that an agent performs than to raise it in connection with the whole life that is lived by the agent. The suggested shift from linking the good-will that is supposed to accompany a given act to the life that the agent lives is important. But what is the relation between good-will and virtue? Virtue for Kant is, as noted above, 'Fortitude in relation to the forces opposing a moral attitude of will in us.'[27] What exactly does Kant mean by fortitude? On virtue ethics interpretation fortitude exhibits the ability to 'resist urges and inclinations opposed to the moral law. Kantian fortitude is strength (*starke*) or force (*kraft*) of will, not in the sense of being able to accomplish the goals one sets out to achieve, but rather in the sense of mastery over one's inclinations and constancy of purpose'.[28] Kant at this point seems to be saying something similar to what Aristotle is saying about human nature. Both Aristotle and Kant recognize that humans are natural beings in the sense that they possess inclinations, urges, propensities which are simply 'given' and hence natural. But humans also possess the faculty of reason. However, since Aristotle views all inclinations at par, that is, there is nothing good or bad about the inclination as such, the tension between two opposite inclinations has to be resolved by some other faculty like reason. Kant on the other hand locates the tension not between inclinations but between inclinations and reason. This makes him give a different solution than the one given by Aristotle. Aristotle's solution lies in arriving at the 'mean' between two extremely opposite inclinations through the use of reason. Man's rationality consists in this. But for Kant, since the tension is between inclinations *and* reason, and since acting on inclinations is not totally eliminable in the case of human beings, not every good-will is 'holy will'. For Kant, 'human morality in its highest stage can still be nothing more than virtue'.[29] Virtue is only 'approximation' of holy will. From this reading of Kant, Louden suggests that 'if virtue is the human approximation to the good-will and if the good-will is the only unqualified good, this does imply that moral virtue, for Kant, is foundational and not (as one would expect in a deontological theory) a concept of derivative or secondary importance'.[30]

The status of maxims as opposed to rules or principles is another grey area in the reading of Kantian texts. In the present context, the question is what precisely Kant means by a maxim of action. For Kant, a maxim is a subjective principle of volition. This statement of Kant can be interpreted by saying that a maxim is a specific policy for action that prescribes a particular course of action in a given situation. A maxim thus turns out to be a rule or at least a *quasi* rule. But a 'rule' (especially in the context of action) in the full sense of the term, is supposed to be independent of specific intentions or even the general intentions. But a maxim, to the extent it is a subjective principle of volition, must have some connection with the intentions of the agent as far as the specific situation is concerned. But then, given the multiplicity of situations in which we never know for sure (1) what our intentions are going to be and also (2) the cases of agent's acting without any specific intention, what we are to look for, is not a specific intention but the cluster of underlying intentions. Onora O'Neill suggests a distinction between a maxim that is based on a specific intention, and, a maxim based on the cluster of underlying intentions. This distinction enables, it is claimed, the virtue–ethics or the agent-centric reading of Kant since the concept of underlying intention is internally linked to the idea of the character of a person. It is not the specific intentions that make the kind of persons that we are, rather, what characterizes us is the whole of the underlying intentions.

The contrast that Kant is making between the 'inner' and the 'outer' legislation has been interpreted as making virtue an individual, inward and private affair. By driving the virtues into the self and specifically into the will, Kant is said to be providing a ground for one general criticism often levelled against his ethics, namely, he rests too much upon the 'fragile structure of the voluntary, and specifically of introspection'.[31] There is no unanimity amongst the advocates of virtue ethics as to how much they are 'willing to rest on this fragile structure'. Most Kantian critics deny that the locus of virtue is the inner self. For them shared practices, traditions and the ways of life of a community serve as the locus of virtue. Both the alternatives, it is observed, provide the basis for a closer look at Kant's claim that duties of virtue are inner. Kant's examples of 'perfect duties to oneself' (like refraining from suicide out of self-love or from damaging one's body by self-mutilation) raise the issue whether they could be treated as full duties of virtue. 'Duties of virtue in the full sense are unenforceable not because they are self-directed; but because they are *imperfect*, which makes them structurally unsuited to enforcement, even owed to others.'[32] They are imperfect because, in Kant's scheme of things, they are duties 'to adopt certain ends' and they involve the prescription of ends as broad policies, 'wide in requirement'. Duties that are wide in this sense are imperfect in contrast to perfect duties that more narrowly obligate or prohibit specific types of action. The most general ends or the duties of virtue are the ends of one's own perfection and the happiness of others. Within the Kantian framework, this provides for the separation of 'self-regard' and 'other regard' in a way that is not sharply drawn in Aristotle. With regard to such duties, external legislation and enforcement fail for the reason that we can be forced to do acts but not to adopt ends or purposes. External compulsion would generate an outward show of virtue by enforcing action that would express a certain maxim of ends. If duties of virtue are expected to pursue ends, such ends will have to be objective. Kant in fact argues in this way saying that since human action is intrinsically purposive, that is, undertaken for certain ends which are usually, though not always, subjective—there is a ground for the application of the categorical imperative. Accordingly, the first principle of the doctrine of virtue is: 'Act according to the maxim of ends that it can be a universal law for every one to have.' The difficulty with this form of legislation is that it confuses between demanding that the principle which specifies action be adopted by all with the virtue that demands that the broader strategies and policies on which purposive beings base theirs, also be adopted by all.

Kant's classification of imperfect duties, that is, of virtue proper is based on the assumption that there are two sorts of objective ends—the natural and the moral.[33] Our wider principles and projects may refer to either of them. Kant further characterizes both these ends in terms of happiness and perfection. However, it is alleged that the 'relation of these two ends to duty is asymmetric in our own case and in others. Our own happiness can hardly be a matter of duty and others perfection can hardly be a matter of duty since it is something which we cannot provide for others'.[34] This reverses the order of ends which we ought to have a duty to adopt, that is, others' happiness and one's own perfection. In each case, these ends keep open the course of actions; since we cannot do everything 'that is needed to achieve either end; what we can do will vary with circumstances and nearly in all circumstances there will be many ways of meeting the demands of imperfect duties'. But in spite of this 'openness' of duties of virtue, they will obviously have a bearing upon what we ought to do in particular circumstances.

The issues, such as, whether Kant adopts 'too psychological and inward an account of virtue', does his insistence that 'virtue is a matter of adopting certain ends such that they are variously expressed and that virtues cannot be enforced,' that their pursuit needs 'moral strength of will', tend to raise a further question, that is, does Kant necessarily see virtue as 'inner orientation' that is to be ascertained by introspection, or, does he deny the connection between virtue and its actual practice in a given context? This question is at the core of virtue ethicists' criticism of Kant.[35]

Notes

I am thankful to Mangesh Kulkarni of the Department of Political Science, University of Pune, for helpful comments and a careful reading of the earlier version.

1. Elizabeth Anscombe, 'Modern Moral Philosophy' first appeared in *Philosophy*, Vol. 33, 1958, pp. 1–19. It has subsequently appeared in numerous anthologies.
2. The distinction is made by Roger Crisp in his Introduction to *How Should One Live?: Essays on Virtues*, Clarendon Press, Oxford, 1996.
3. Ruth Anna Putnam, 'Reciprocity and Virtue Ethics' in *Ethics*, 1988, pp. 379–89.
4. Iris Murdoch, *The Sovereignty of Good*, Ark, London, 1985. This reference is from the Introduction by Roger Crisp and Michael Slote in *Virtue Ethics*, Oxford University Press, 1997.
5. Crisp and Slote, *Virtue Ethics*, p. 10.
6. Daniel Statman, 'Introduction to Virtue Ethics' in Daniel Statman *Virtue Ethics*, Edinburgh University Press, 1997, p. 3.
7. Ibid., p. 7.
8. Alaisdair MacIntyre, *After Virtue: A Study in Moral Theory*, Duckworth, London, 1981.
9. Richard Taylor, *Ethics, Faith and Reason*, Englewoods Cliffs, New Jercy 1985; and Richard Taylor, 'Ancient Wisdom and Modern Folly', *Midwest Studies in Philosophy*, vol. 13, University of Notre Dam Press, 1988.
10. Philippa Foot, *Virtues and Vices and Other Essays in Moral Philosophy*, University of California Press, Berkeley, 1978.
11. Taylor, 'Ancient Wisdom'.
12. Statman, 'Introduction to Virtue Ethics', p. 4.
13. Taylor, 'Ancient Wisdom'.
14. Robert Louden, 'Kant's Virtue Ethics' in Daniel Statman (ed.), Virtue Ethics p. 286.
15. Foot, *Virtues and Vices*, p. 1.
16. Bernard Williams, *Moral Luck: Philosophical Papers 1973–1980*, Cambridge University Press, 1981.
17. Onora O'Neill, 'Kant's Virtues' in *How Should One Live?* p. 77.
18. Ibid., p.78
19. Julia Driver, 'The Virtues and the Human Nature' in *How Should One Live?* p. 111.
20. Ibid., p. 113.
21. Kant, *The Doctrine of Virtue*, James W. Elligton (trans.), Hackett Publishing Company, Indianapolis, 1983.
22. Nancy Sherman, *Making a Necessity of Virtue: Aristotle and Kant on Virtue*, Cambridge University Press, 1997.
23. See Onora O'Neill, 'Kant's Virtues' in *How Should One Live?* pp. 77–97; and Robert Louden, 'Kant's Virtue Ethics', pp. 286–99.

24. Louden, 'Kant's Virtue Ethics', p. 289.
25. Ibid.
26. Ibid.
27. Kant, *The Doctrine of Virtue*.
28. Louden, 'Kant's Virtue Ethics', p. 289.
29. Kant, *The Doctrine of Virtue*.
30. Louden, 'Kant's Virtue Ethics', p. 290.
31. Onora O'Neill, Louden, 'Kant's Virtues', p. 85.
32. Ibid.
33. Ibid.
34. Ibid.
35. Ibid., p. 88

Autonomy of Reason and Ethics of the Face

Imagining a Civil Society in Kantian Lineage

Goutam Biswas

Kant's concept of moral autonomy brings about an impasse between Kant's distinction between 'is' and 'ought'. Scientific discourse about phenomena and moral discourse founded upon pure practical reason is a landmark in the history of philosophy and it shaped the basic contours of many celebrated thinkers including the critics of Kant in different domains like philosophy of science, social science and ethics. It is interesting to note that even the critics of Kant's *Critiques* considerably owed their thought to Kant and thereby knowingly or unknowingly became more or less Kantian in creating a lineage and heritage, if not legacy in an absolute sense, of Kant. Few recognized it in terms of developing their thought-structure with a contrast between Kant and his critics. As Richard Bernstein rightly observed, Max Weber is one of them. In Bernstein's observation, 'Kant emphasized this absolute distinction to justify the autonomy, objectivity, and universality of moral judgement. He certainly was not dubious about the possibility of rationally justifying the categorical imperative. But one of the strains in Nineteenth-century thought was an increasing skepticism about the autonomy and objectivity of moral judgement and its presumed rational foundation. No critic is the equal of Nietzsche in his searching and profound criticisms of the moral or normative half of the Kantian dichotomy. Weber, as philosopher and social scientist, accepted the logical absoluteness of the Kantian dichotomy and felt the full power of Nietzsche's critique of moral judgement. Weber insisted on the "absolute heterogeneity" of facts and values, and recognized that sciences, including the social sciences, can only deal with the factual side of the dichotomy.'[1]

But this 'absolute heterogeneity', besides being a methodological stance in sciences, is also a characterization of what 'fact' *vis-à-vis* 'value' is. Can facts be completely purged of the values in a social space? The only possible answer to this seems to be in terms of a *value-telos* of all sciences; the objectivity thus acquired in an unmixed and pure fashion through scientific investigations, in Bourdieu's term, is ultimately for a social, cultural and communitarian profit, for a better state of affairs and for a better upbringing of everything, provided such profit is not monopolized by some along with a monopolization of the economic and social conditions of the profit. It is interesting to read Bourdieu in this context: 'Most of the human works that we are accustomed to treating as universal—law, science, the fine arts, ethics, religion, and so forth—cannot be dissociated from the scholastic point of view and from the social and economic conditions which make the latter possible. They have been engendered in these very peculiar social universes which are the fields of cultural production—the juridical field, the scientific field, the artistic field, the philosophical field—and in which agents are engaged who have in common the *privilege* of fighting for the monopoly of the universal, and thereby effectively of promoting the advancement of truths and values that are held, at each moment, to be universal, indeed eternal.'[2]

Struggle against this monopoly of the social and economic conditions to dispel the cleavage between the privileged and underprivileged in this regard is also a social task for Bourdieu to materialize the Kantian paradigm. Bourdieu proposes to be 'more Kantian than Kant' in this respect, and I presume, whatever he contends with reference to Kant's aesthetics is logically extendable to Kant's moral philosophy:

I am ready to concede that Kant's aesthetics is true, but only as a phenomenology of the aesthetic experiences of all those people who are the product of *skholé*. That is to say that the experience of the beautiful of which Kant offers us a rigorous description has definite economic and social conditions of possibility that are ignored by Kant, and the anthropological possibility of which Kant sketches an analysis could become *truly universal* only if those economic and social conditions were universally distributed. It means also that the conditions of actual universalization of this (theoretical) universal possibility is thus the actual universalization of the economic and social conditions, that is, of *skholé*, which, being monopolized by some today, confer upon this happy few the monopoly over the universal.[3]

From Bourdieu's point of view, the practice of universalization founded upon a concept of universalizability of all moral maxims in categorical sense and all aesthetic judgements itself becomes a moral practice if this universalizability of moral maxims and aesthetic judgement is put to a process of conscious and real programme. Bourdieu says,

Kant's test of universalizabiliy is the universal strategy of the rational critique of ethical claims (those who assert that others can be treated badly based on a particular property, for example, skin color, can be questioned with regard to their own disposition to accept similar maltreatment if their skin were the same color). To state the question of morality or the moralization of politics in sociologically realistic terms, we must consider in practical terms the conditions that would need to be fulfilled to keep political practices permanently subjected to a test of universalizability, so that the very workings of the political field force its actors into real universalization strategies.[4]

Bourdieu's position seems to lead us to an ambivalence for taking a strategic stand towards Kant's ethics, because Kant's contentions in his moral philosophy, particularly his stipulation of the concept of autonomy based upon pure practical reason resists a programme of Bourdieu's kind in which, as Bourdieu puts it, 'Only a realpolitik of reason and morality can contribute favourably to the institution of a universe where all agents and their acts would be subject—notably through critique—to a kind of permanent test of universalizability which is practically instituted in the very logic of the field.'[5] This seeming resistance arises from what can be called the *pseudo-thematic* of Kant's ethics, which is opposed to Bourdieu's *problematic*. The *thematic* is conceived here as bereft of any further possibility and without any problem so far as the essence of the concept is concerned. I call it the *pseudo thematic* because it hides the problematic of Kant's ethics. The problematic of Kant's moral philosophy lies in his deep-seated concern for a free and creative civil society in which every individual has a moral autonomy founded upon reason and no individual is an arbiter. Let us recall in this connection his view on perpetual peace:

We can say that establishment of universal and enduring peace constitutes not just a part but rather the entire final end of jurisprudence within the limits of mere reason. Peace is the only condition under laws guaranteeing 'the mine and thine' within a group of neighbouring persons living together under a constitution whose rules are not derived from the experience of those who have fared best under it and whose experience, therefore, might serve as a norm for others. Rather, the rules must be derived by reason a priori from the ideal of a legal association of men under public laws generally, because all examples (which only illustrate and do not prove) are deceptive. Such rules, however, require a metaphysics, the necessity of which is carelessly conceded even by those who make fun of it.[6]

Hence the public space was very much within the cognizance of Kant, but he presumed it to be resting on peace and reason. For him the examples may prove to be vacuous for the construction of a space of this kind. Hence the metaphysics of morals is a requirement. Bourdieu would go further by suggesting that an actual programme of demonopolization should run simultaneously alongside the construction of a public space founded upon reason alone.

Further, a correspondence between Bourdieu's programme and Kant's concept of autonomy or self-government in moral matters can be construed in the context of conceptualizing what a civil society should be. This imagination is legitimate as the concept of civil society itself is not *closed*, it is *open* and in a continuous process of framing and reframing the normative structure of democracy. This is imagining a civil society against the backdrop of a dichotomy of pure practical reason corroborating freedom and autonomy of the individual and practical reason subservient to ends that one tends to achieve in a public space, the ends that mostly determine the rationale of an action. The dichotomy is more than conceptual for the contradiction between pure practical reason and practical reason in terms of 'ends' is conceptually comprehended as well as experienced in a live context. This follows the general understanding that if something purely rational and/or conceptual is juxtaposed with something empirical, the former also becomes a part of an ex-periential whole, may be with certain alterations, for the reason that the juxtaposition itself ushers in a different perspective. Hence the dichotomy can be viewed in an experiential context, the context of members of a civil society consciously striving for moral perfection of their space and making a critique of themselves and their world. The realpolitik of reason converts this dichotomy into a dialectic in which the programme of Bourdieu's kind in the effort of being more Kantian than Kant himself becomes an ethical task by itself. But is such conversion possible without the face of the other? Both the problematic of Kant's moral philosophy and Bourdieu's attempt to transgress it in a different practical vein create the necessity of the other in a moral context that is at the same time supposed to retain the value of the autonomy of the individual. The history of continental moral philosophy can be viewed in a new perspective from this point.

The demand for an applied dimension of Kant's moral philosophy in the form of Bordieu's type gives rise to a pertinent question: 'Does the question of morality, always and inevitably, follow the pure practical reason?' Or 'does it necessarily involve an existential *other*, that is, the *face* confronting the self by virtue of which the self too becomes an *other*?' The second question about morality speaks of simultaneity of self and the other. By *face* I mean the psychophysical being of the other that holds me as a self horizontally within a space of relationship, the space that becomes the primary locus of morality for humans with the possibility of creating a civil society in the truest sense of the term. This meaning will be elaborated further in the course of vindicating my contention that the meaning of pure practical or moral reason becomes explicable with reference to this locus. There is a scope of misapprehending it to be an unnecessary strenuous exercise to relate two basically unrelated terrains of thought. But are they so unrelated? The following of pure practical reason in the form of categorical imperative or moral law is itself a command or an imperative in view of a critical assessment of what Kant called 'the popular moral philosophy' in his *Groundwork* and his emphasis upon the need for a *Metaphysics of Morals*. The emergence of the idea of *Pure Practical Reason* may be understood also in terms of a human demand and crave for moral perfection and in Kantian framework it is envisaged in terms of individual autonomy founded upon the unfaltering reason as pure practical reason. This is the autonomy of will that is free and rational. Therefore autonomy of will is in one sense freedom of reason. The conjunction of reason and freedom is significant in this context as it justifies the elevation of human reason in its practical employment above the sensible world for a better nurturing of the *otherness of the other as a moral equal* and a better governance of the human world.

Therefore 'freedom' is to be understood as 'free reason'. In the *Groundwork*, Kant opposes the autonomy of will to heteronomy of will that does not subscribe to moral law, which is the result of rational will. In Kant's words, 'Reason must look upon itself as the author of its own principles independently of alien influences. Therefore as practical reason, or as the will of a rational being, it must be regarded by itself as free; that is, the will of a rational being can be a will of his own only under the Idea of freedom, and such a will must therefore from a practical point of view be attributed to all rational beings.'[7] Reason, in Kant's meaning, is autonomous and therefore freedom is to be conceived with reference to this concept of autonomy. Moral worth of any action is determinable only in terms of this conjunction of reason and freedom, that is, autonomy. Truths of practical reason are therefore distinguishable from truths of ordinary moral facts, the truths that are susceptible to many distortions in assessment, examination, evaluation and interpretation because the autonomy of practical reason is not recognized there as the fundamental point of departure. Hence, reason as pure practical reason is unfaltering in a purposive way; it has to be unfaltering for the sake of retention of the autonomy or freedom of the moral agent in actual existential contexts where the presence of the *other* prevails, demanding moral treatment from the free, rational self.

The question of human autonomy is essentially concerning individual autonomy in the context of civil society where the tension between the coercive character of the collectivity and the urge for individual freedom continues. The concept of *autonomy* is thus explicable as a substitute of the concept of *freedom* as the latter has certain nuances beyond the limits of civil society; freedom here is more a derivative from the concept of autonomy that reconciles the two poles of a civil society or, if not a derivative, it is at least re-explicated in terms of the Kantian concept of autonomy. In either case the context of a civil society shows up its relevance for the correction and further refinement of practical reason that in its turn offers refinement and perfectibility to the civil society. It gets further vindicated in the context of what Kant meant by 'the state of peace':

The state of peace among men living side by side is not the natural state (*status naturalis*); the natural state is one of war. This does not mean open hostilities, but at least an unceasing threat of war. A state of peace, therefore, must be *established*, for in order to be secured against hostility it is not sufficient that hostilities simply be not committed; and, unless this security is pledged to each by his neighbour (a thing that can occur only in a civil state), each may treat his neighbour, from whom he demands security, as an enemy.[8]

The concept of civil society is a product more of a social imagination and therefore defies any definitional nitpicking. For our purpose, we may borrow the following description of it:

The exploration of civil society emphasized the basic experiences of individuals living in societies. It tried to take apart and explain the tensions that we all feel between what we want to do as individuals but what we are compelled to do, or restrained from doing, as members of society. Civil society is about this fundamental experiential and relational connection between individuals going about their own lives and members of society doing what they are told. The point is, of course, that those individuals and members of society were, and to some extent continue to be, actually one and the same.[9]

When reason intervenes into the mind of the individual, it tries to remain as pure as possible for avoiding the possibility of licentiousness because licentiousness alters the dignity of the *other* member of the civil society. As Tester comments further, 'To imagine civil society was to separate the internal from the external, the independent from the dependent, the achieved from the ascribed, the "Same" from "Other", the homogeneous from the heterogeneous, the active from the passive. Civil society meant to never again take the freedom of society and social relationships for granted.'[10] From Kant's point of view, the imagination of civil society is impossible without its rational, autonomous and free moral foundation. Kant left the clue for us to imagine further that this autonomy in the context of civil society is not of a closed type to disallow communication and mutual improvement of free selves.

While an upward or hierarchical elevation of consciousness and reason from its empirical placement and public abode to a metaphysical and transcendental realm signifies a negative look at the popular moral philosophy and the search for a metaphysics of morals was vindicated by Kant, one should not be oblivious of Kant's critique of the discipline of pure reason from a non-hierarchical standpoint. Let us recall Onora O'Neill's reading of Kant in this connection. According to O'Neill, the concept of discipline is explicable only from a negative stance, and Kant's contention that mathematics with its entire perfectness can offer no generalizable model for the use of reason is understandable with reference to his rejection of reason as a dictatorial authority akin to political dictatorship. She quotes approvingly from Kant's 'The Discipline of Pure Reason in its Practical Employment':

Reason must in all its undertakings subject itself to criticism; should it limit freedom of criticism by any prohibitions, it must harm itself, drawing upon itself a damaging suspicion. Nothing is so important through its usefulness, nothing so sacred that may be exempted from this searching examination, which knows no respect for persons. Reason depends on this freedom for its very existence. For reason has no dictatorial authority; its verdict is always simply the agreement of citizens, of whom each one must be permitted to express, without let or hindrance, his objection or even his veto.[11]

This concept of reason may be understood as the foundation of or at least as a necessary component of the 'community of others', that is, the community of *ends in themselves*. In the context of the first critique too, reason is free from all empirical and contingent aspects of knowledge, but it keeps all objects of human knowledge within the purview of sense intuition. Reason operative in understanding its conjunction with sensibility is necessary for producing knowledge, but in its practical employment, reason is carefully guarded against all empirical considerations. Hence, Kant's philosophy has been consistently characterized as 'transcendental', not without proper justification. But transcendentalism in his moral philosophy can be interpreted as a means of forming a community of moral agents and renewing the meaning of the mundane world with the values coming from the practical reason in the form of 'commands'. As K.C. Bhattacharyya pointed out, the certitude in moral willing has two forms:

The certitude has two forms—that free causality is being realized in internal sense as temporal or mental series and in external sense as causality in the spatio-temporal world. The first certitude is that free choice will be expressed as sensible *life* i.e., a necessary chain of mental appearances and the second is fulfilled in its objective as an objective rational *system* or nature. The former is time and the latter space (-time) to practical consciousness.[12]

Despite his idealistic proclivity and frequent reference to the *free self* in presenting Kant's thesis, it is interesting to note the clear mention of the importance of *sensible life* in Kant's moral philosophy and the clue for establishing the relation of practical consciousness in its elevated form with the world of sense. In this connection, Acton's observation is noteworthy:

> Although Kant considers morality is basically rational, he agrees with empiricist philosophers and with ordinary men that there is an element of feeling and emotion in it too. He identifies the moral feeling or emotion with what he calls reverence or respect (*Achtung*), a feeling which only a rational being aware of the moral law can have...Reverence, according to Kant, is analogous to fear, in that it is felt by relation to *the command,* of the moral law, and it is analogous to that in that it is "*self-produced* a concept of reason". But although this moral feeling is produced by reason, it could not be experienced by beings who did not also have irrational inclinations and desires. For the reverence which involves the abolition of my self-love is only felt when I compare my own irrational sense-given inclinations with the possibility of acting for the sake of moral law.[13]

This observation is good enough to ensure a link between the pure practical reason and the world of sense. Going somewhat beyond the ordinary morality is thus justified in terms of reverence for the law. One may as well conjecture that freedom or autonomy of self is a kind of achievement after a strenuous cultivation of reverence for the moral law rising above one's self interest leading towards an abolition of self-love. However, it is important to emphasize the idea of *free selves* to understand what the 'ethics of the face' could be from the lineage of Kant.

The idea of an autonomous self is equivalent to the idea of a *moral equal* of the self, that is, the *other*. When a civil society is imagined in Kantian fashion its basic tension between the collective or coercive force and individuals' caprices in the name of freedom is contested with a different meaning of freedom and by assigning autonomy to all its members. Every member of the civil society is then a moral equal without holding any power over one another. As Levinas pointed out, 'What Kant calls "kingdom of ends" is a plurality of free wills united by reason.' And he validly questioned, 'But is the freedom of one not, for another's will, the latter's negation, and thus at least a possible limitation? Is it not a principle of possible war between multiple freedoms, or a conflict between reasonable wills...?'[14] This question, however, cannot be treated as questioning the Kantian heritage in the history of continental moral philosophy or even the legacy of Kant. In fact, it may be argued that the existential meaning of *face* in the context of moral philosophy would not achieve its culmination in the philosophy of Levinas without the Kantian idea of abolition of self-love. This amounts to a kind of self-abolition through submission of self to the moral law; or, one may add, it is a self-surrender to the law for the sake of being just and moral to the other. The dialogical ethics, which requires a horizontal placement of the moral equals, owes not so less to Kant. Before Levinas, Martin Buber explicated the concept of 'genuine community' as the primary concern of all history, as the goal and culmination of the I-Thou relationship. This is the community of 'others', the community in which the 'I' does not bring any closure for the other in the community. It is not too far from the truth that Kant's detraction from dictatorship in a civil state is for the sake of retention of this autonomy of the other and his well-known categorical imperative for not treating the other as a means is in congruity with the dialogical existentialism that proposes the 'ethics of the face'. While this congruity does not make these two divergent philosophical trends identical, a Kantian and neo-Kantian legacy and lineage is reasserted for ushering in a new perspective in the history of European moral philosophy; the difference leaves the room for criticism and further progress in a culture. The emergence of dialogical ethics of Martin Buber thus grows on a fundamental similarity with and difference from Kant:

"Buber's concept of the responsibility of an I to a Thou is closely similar to Kant's second formulation of the categorical imperative: Never treat one's fellow as a means only but always also as an end of value in himself. But even here, when moral philosophies of Kant and Buber seem to join, there is an essential difference. Kant's sentence grows out of an *ought* based on the idea of human dignity. Buber's related concepts of making the other present and not imposing one's own truth on him are based on the ontological reality of the life *between* man and man."[15]

Levinas's stand is even more radical. But this radicalism in dialogical and existential ethics would not appear in the scenario without a Buber whose dialogical ethics emphasize *relation's own being* or the ontology of the dialogical space as prior to the subject, the space leading to an 'ethics of the face'. Kant's practical philosophy can thus be regarded as creating a lineage. If there is a question regarding the nature of immoral action, Lewis White Beck summarizes Kant's position in *Perpetual Peace*:

Actions whose maxims cannot be publicly exposed without thwarting the purpose of the action itself are not responsive to the rights of others, and are therefore immoral. Actions are right if they can be fully effective only when their maxim is known to those touched by the action, for in these actions the person is treated as an end in himself.[16]

The *other as an end in himself* thus becomes the central theme in Kant's moral as well as political philosophy. What is the 'ethics of the face'?

The 'ethics of the face' has its own nuances in a non-derivative sense. The *face* here does not mean the sheer physicality of the face or the appearance of someone before a perceiving self. The face has two meanings in this context. (1) It means the being of the other faced by the self in a horizontal way. The horizontality, of course, carries a reference to the physical appearance. But then its *logos* remains unfathomed. Therefore, 'horizontality' is conceived here as potential to negate its externality in separation from its *logos* and its internality completely cut off from its experiential perspective in an arbitrary fashion. This leads to its second meaning. (2) *Face* means a nexus of internality and exteriority of the being of the other. As the nexus presents the total being of the other carrying forth the internality of his/her being to experientiality, this experientiality cannot catch him or her finally in one snap. The experientiality can have aesthetic satisfaction with *profiles a* being in a creative sense admitting the possibility of many other profiles. The *face,* therefore, means the *otherness* of the *other* and an *alteriety*. With these two meanings, it is understandable that the *face* generates an unending and live moral stance—the self. Therefore, *self* means responsibility for the *other* by consciously nurturing a relationship with the *other* through a continuous and torturous negation of power over the *other*. As Levinas puts it, 'Possessing, knowing, and grasping are synonyms of power… The relationship with the Other is the absence of the other; not absence pure and simple, not the absence of pure nothingness, but absence in a horizon of future, an absence that is time.'[17] Contesting the idea that self-consciousness can affirm itself as absolute being, Levinas holds that self means responsibility that pre-exists any self-consciousness. In his words,

Responsibility for the other, for the naked face of the first individual to come along. A responsibility that goes beyond what I may or may not have done to the other or whatever acts I may or may not have committed, as if I were devoted to the other man before being devoted to myself. Or more exactly, as if I had to answer for the other's death before *being*. A guiltless responsibility, whereby I am none the less open to an accusation of which no alibi, spatial or temporal, could clear me. It is as if the other established a relationship or a relationship were established whose whole intensity consists in not presupposing the idea of community. A responsibility stemming from time before my freedom—before my (*moi*) beginning, before my present.[18]

This is an attempt to touch the moral reality or unveil a reality different from the physical or factual reality in the context of the relational. In Buber's terminology, the real is relational. While in Kant pure practical reason is presupposed for moral autonomy and freedom yielding perfect human relation that is potential to create a good and civil community or society, the dialogical ethics starts with relation and self-abolition on the basis of an existential conversion. Dialogical ethics of Martin Buber paving the way for a more radical ethics of the face, that is, leaving the clue for a more radical meaning of dialogue entrusts the posterity with a greater responsibility of reviewing the earlier traditional categories of ethics and morality for a further assessment of the source of moral (categorical) imperatives and the criteria for determining the moral worth of any action in relation to other humans and in the context of the dynamics of society and polity. While it is important to know the differences between the 'earlier' and the 'later' causing a shift in tradition, it is equally important to understand the tradition and the lineage that is always chequered due to intervention of criticality. Lyotard's observation on Levinas' ethics makes it clear that Levinas' primary concern to safeguard the specificity of practical discourse cannot be totally delinked from Kant's care in the second critique to make the principles of practical reason independent of those of theoretical reason. Also, as Lyotard says, 'The author of *Otherwise than Being* seems to agree with the author of the *Critique of Practical Reason* that in order for the principle of the will to be moral, it cannot be inferred from statements describing empirical context, whether psychological, social, or historical, and that it cannot be justified by the various interests of which it is made up.'[19]

We cannot conclude anything finally about the kinship between Kantian ethics and ethics of the face as long as Levinas's emphasis upon the specificity does not seem to care much to accommodate the idea of a *community* of others which, from the standpoint of Kant as well as Martin Buber would be an ideal characterization of a civil society devoid of dictatorship and hegemony. But we can re-explicate the Levinasian concept of specificity in practical discourse in terms of the idea of a *morally fulfilling life*, which is conceivable as the basic motto of the formation of a civil society. This concept of life from the standpoint of moral requirement brings about the relevance of Gandhi too in the context of continental moral philosophy, but at this juncture we shall not indulge in the details of it. In fine, this kind of life is impossible without an ethics of self-abolition, which is, a corroboration of and simultaneous with, the ethics of the face. But this self-abolition is always in favour of a dialogical self, which, as the morally fulfilling life demands, needs to be non-hegemonic and prepared to leave its centrepoint of power.

The centrepoint of power is morally degrading and Kant made it very clear that 'possession of power inevitably corrupts the untrammelled judgement of reason'.[20] Taking clue from Kant and the dialogical ethics of Martin Buber, it is possible to re-understand the ethics of the face and accommodate it within the context of imagining a civil society that is basically non-dictatorial and non-hegemonic consisting of individuals constantly engaged in renewing their freedom and autonomy in Kantian sense and in dialogue in the sense of Buber and Levinas.

The civil society that is imagined after Kant's ethics and 'ethics of the face' is a conscious creation, a rearing on the basis of a dialogical relationship among humans perhaps extendable further to the entire world in terms of the attitude grown out of the dialogical thought. This society is therefore not something readymade where an individual enters voluntarily or out of some external governance. Human beings perform 'willed action' in this world of others and extend the horizon of the other and the self. At the level of ideas, every idea is floated here for a discursive testing in the sense of Habermas. A discursive testing or what may be called 'argumentative decision making' is possible in the form of communicative action, the action that is impossible without a prior commitment to the *otherness of the other*. Kantian ethics is sometimes wrongly conceived as involving an element of coercive subordination of the subjective nature of self to self-given laws. It should be remembered that even if it is coercion, it is self-chosen and not superimposed from any external source; it is choice for a right cause. The same is true with Buber and Levinas; self-oblivion is a conscious programme in their philosophies. Kantian ethics and the autonomy that it vouches for nurtures an element of progression/transition from this self with blind surrender to unreasoned desires, inclination, and the like, to another self that is committed to a transformed reality and future dialogues in a civil society of its own kind.

Notes

1. Richard J. Bernstein, *The Restructuring of Social and Political Theory*, Methuen & Co Ltd, London, 1979, p. 47.
2. Pierre Bourdieu, *Practical Reason: On the Theory of Action*, Polity Press, Cambridge, (translated from the French *Raison Pratiques*), 1998, p. 135.
3. Ibid., p. 135.
4. Ibid., p. 144.
5. Ibid.
6. Immanuel Kant, *Perpetual Peace*, (White Beck trans.), The Liberal Arts Press, 1957, p. 58.
7. Immanuel Kant, *Groundwork of the Metaphysic of Morals*, (Paton trans.), B.I. Publication, Indian edition, 1979, p. 33.
8. Immanuel Kant, *Perpetual Peace*, p. 10.
9. Keith Tester, *Civil Society*, Routledge, London & New York, 1992, p. 5.
10. Ibid., p.11.
11. Onora O'Neill, *Constructions of Reason: Explorations of Kant's Practical Philosophy*, Cambridge University Press, Cambridge, 1989, p. 15.
12. K.C. Bhattacharyya, *Studies in Philosophy*, Motilal Banarasidass, Delhi, 1983, p. 667.
13. H.B. Acton, *Kant's Moral Philosophy*, The Macmillan Press Ltd, London, 1970, p. 14.
14. Sean Hand (Ed.), *The Levinas Reader*, Blackwell, Oxford, 1989, pp. 121–2.
15. Maurice Friedman, *Martin Buber: The Life of Dialogue*, 4th edition, Routledge, London, 2002, p. 235.
16. Lewis White Beck, 'Introduction' in Kent, *Perpetual Peace*, p. xii.
17. *Levinas Reader*, p. 51.
18. Ibid., pp. 83–4.
19. Andrew Benjamin (ed.), *Lyotard Reader*, Blackwell, Oxford, 1993, p. 288.
20. Kant, *Perpetual Peace*, p. 34.

Necessity, Universality, and the A Priori in Ethics

Jonathan Dancy

Kant held that moral laws are necessary truths, that they are universal in form and are known a priori. These three claims are interconnected. He believed that only universal truths could be necessary, and that if they are necessary they must be known a priori, if known at all. He also held that moral laws are synthetic practical propositions (Gr. 4.420). These various views are considered here. I argue that what I think of as basic moral truths are indeed known a priori, despite being synthetic. But their being known a priori does not require them to be necessary and universal in form. I not only reject the inference but also maintain that its conclusion is false: basic moral truths are contingent and particular.

Some of my arguments will be brief. This is because I have already laid out the relevant points in greater detail elsewhere.[1] The position from which I view all these matters is what has come to be called particularism in ethics. The particularist holds that the possibility of moral thought and judgement in no way depends upon a suitable provision of moral principles. Kant, by contrast, held that if there is no true Supreme Principle of morality, moral distinctions are null and void. There could not be a greater distance between his view and mine.

One important point of contrast is that the particularist starts by thinking about moral reasons, not about moral duties, moral obligations or more generally about what overall we ought morally to do. But Kant does not seem to operate with an idea of a moral reason. If one does think in terms of moral reasons, one will suppose that there can be reasons on both sides of the question. But Kant's whole approach to ethics is in terms of maxims and their ability to serve as universal laws. The maxim on which one acts, whatever its content—and the exact way to understand the sort of content that Kant supposed his maxims to have is hotly debated—does not specify a reason for doing the action one proposes to do. Or rather, if it does, there seems to be no 'opposing' maxim specifying the reasons for not doing that action. One might imagine that a maxim might include some such phrase as 'despite the fact that she does not want me to do this, I will do it in order to gain an advantage'. A maxim with such a 'despite clause' would have specified a consideration as a reason against. But how is it that what that feature stands as a reason against is left completely mysterious in Kant's philosophy. Contrary to the claims of some eminent Kantians, therefore, I am of the opinion that Kant was not trying to capture the idea of a moral reason. He went straight for the overall judgement that this is what I ought to do, understanding that in terms of the universalisability of a maxim of the form 'I will do an action of this sort, whenever I find myself in circumstances such as these'.

This contrast between Kant's top-down approach (though I have here suggested that he didn't get very far down) and the particularist's bottom-up approach is significant for our general topic. For Kant, it seems, facts about one's overall duty in this or that sort of situation are the basic facts of morality—and such facts are universal and necessary. For the particularist, basic moral facts are facts about what is a reason for what, case by case. What I mean by 'case by case' is that the particularist supposes that what is a reason in one case may not be so in another; it may even be a reason against. I call this view 'holism in the theory of reasons'. Particularism is built on this form of holism, which can be re-expressed as the claim that reasons do not need to be invariant. A reason is variable if the feature concerned is a reason in some circumstances and not in others. If moral reasons are like this, then even though moral thought and judgement is firmly based on reasons, it does not need to be based on the sort of invariable reasons that would be captured in universal moral principles. Moral principles, after all, can be thought of as specifying a feature and giving its moral relevance. A principle is nothing if not universal. So if a principle is true, the feature it specifies must be of invariant relevance; for the principle is trying to capture something invariant. The particularist, supposing that there may be no invariantly relevant features, does not deny that there are moral reasons but does deny that there must therefore be moral principles to hold those reasons in place.

For the particularist, the basic moral facts are facts about what is a reason in a particular case. This is what we all start from, and it is more or less all that we have to rely on when trying to come to an overall judgement about what course of action is most suited to the present situation. The particularist's moral epistemology has to fit that perspective. Are those basic moral facts necessary or contingent? A basic moral fact is such a fact as this; that you are dealing with someone in distress is a reason for you to go gently (here). There is no suggestion that distress (even the distress of *this* person, say) is always a reason to go gently, only that it is so here. On another occasion, things might be different. It follows from this that the basic moral fact is contingent, not necessary. It is a fact that might have been otherwise, and would be otherwise in situations that are relevantly different from this one. Basic moral facts are contingent, therefore, and they are not universal in form. Does it follow from this that they are not knowable a priori? I don't think so. After all, even when all the empirical information—that is, the information that we think of as ordinarily available to the senses—is in, we still have to determine which aspects of the present situation, as revealed to us in experience, count which way as reasons. That decision seems to take us beyond anything that the senses can inform us about. And this is so even if we allow that some a posteriori knowledge is the product of inference. Certain sorts of inference from sensory evidence are generally allowed to yield a posteriori knowledge— such as my knowledge, here in New Mexico where I am writing, that the weather will continue fine for at least the next minute. But the forms of inference that are involved in these cases, which take us from a posteriori knowledge to another, do not seem to be involved in the process by which we pass from recognition of empirical matter of fact to knowledge that (for example, her distress is here a reason for us to go gently). Even if we have the benefit of previous experience of such cases, the most we can get out of that is the recognition that her distress is *probably* a reason. Now this sort of knowledge would only be a posteriori if the evidence on which it is based is a posteriori. And that just returns us to the primary question here: in a case where we don't have the benefit of previous experience, is the 'process' by which we come to recognize that her distress is a reason, one that can be thought of as taking us from a posteriori knowledge (that she is in distress) to another a posteriori knowledge (that her distress is a reason to go gently)? And the answer seems to me to be no. If our decision that it is a reason is capable of counting as knowledge, then, it seems that it will have to be a priori knowledge that is at issue, since we only have two choices—a priori and a posteriori—and the latter is ruled out. So the particularist is left in the uncomfortable position of holding that some contingent and particular truths can be known a priori.

Now though this position is indeed uncomfortable, I don't think it is eventually untenable. But the present point is, of course, that it is flatly at odds with Kant's claim that only necessary universal truths can be known a priori. Something has to give, therefore, and my aim here is to show that it is Kant that has to give, not me. If that turns out to be right, we will have to find something to say about the discomfort I referred to just above. The problem is the old problem of the synthetic a priori, but intensified by the denial that what is a priori is universal and necessary. How could we know particular contingent truths a priori?

Particularism is at a dialectical disadvantage, because it sets its face not only against a long and influential tradition as well as against the supposedly untutored intuitions of ordinary folk. To topple that dominant perspective, it needs to provide impeccable argumentation. But in addition to that, it faces a tough explanatory task. Why is it that so many people are unshakeably attached to what particularism sees as an error? Some of the blame can be laid at the door of the Christian churches, at least so far as we are trying to explain habits of thought in Europe. But that cannot be the whole story. There are other ways in which one might come to think that basic moral facts must be universal in form.

Consider W.D. Ross. For him, basic moral facts are facts about our prima facie duties. Ross maintained that we know these facts with certainty, and we know them a priori; but he also maintained that their truth is revealed to us by what we know about particular cases. What we know about particular cases is epistemologically prior, then, but not morally basic. (For him, as for me, what is basic is a matter of moral metaphysics, not of epistemology.) The question for him, then, should have been what we can know about the particular case that would enable us to extract from it the kind of general moral knowledge of prima facie duties that he supposed we all possess. What could the particular case reveal? All that we can find there is a feature counting in favour of, or against, some response. How could such a thing manage to reveal to us the truth of a general moral principle to the effect that this feature must always play that role? Ross's answer was that the form of inference involved is 'intuitive induction'. This is induction because it takes us beyond anything present in the premises, but intuitive because the inductive process leads us to recognise the truth of the conclusion directly. ('Directly' here means that if the process is successful one's knowledge of the conclusion ceases to be inferential, if it ever was.) But what about our knowledge of the epistemically basic facts about features counting, in favour or, against, in particular cases? Is our knowledge of that sort of thing a priori or a posteriori? Ross did not address this question. He is clear that one's knowledge of the principle of prima facie duty is a priori. The question I am after is whether this requires him to suppose that one's knowledge of the premise (that this feature counts in favour here) is a priori too, or whether intuitive induction is a process that can take one from a posteriori knowledge to a priori knowledge. The paradigm instance of intuitive induction may be misleading in this respect. It is the way in which we come to know that a form of inference, *modus ponens*, say, is valid by being shown instances. How are we to conceive of the validity of an instance? It is presumably a necessary truth, and known a priori, but is it universal in form? It is possible to say that it is, because the validity is not potentially dependent on any other features of the context; the idea will be that these premises take one necessarily to that conclusion, and we move by intuitive induction to the realization that this is a matter of *form*. Now compare that paradigm case with the moral case that is our real concern. Is what is revealed by the particular case, when we discern that this feature is here, a reason, covertly universal in form? I suspect that Ross would say yes, because he is already supposing that these truths are context-independent—the very thought that the particularist denies. But why is he supposing that they are context-independent? The answer must be that the general principles of prima facie duty are known a priori, and this requires that what we see in particular cases that reveals the truth of those principles must somehow be the general truth itself, only clothed in a particular form. My suggestion then is that Ross rightly took it that moral knowledge is a priori, and wrongly supposed that if it is a priori, it must be knowledge of universal truths, that is, of true propositions that have universal form. This supposition he may be said to have inherited from Kant.

There is a fundamental Kantian argument to be addressed, then, which goes like this:

1. Whatever is knowable a priori must be necessary.
2. Whatever is necessary must be universal in form.
3. Moral truths are known a priori.
4. So moral truths are universal in form.

There is a simpler argument in similar style which does not mention the a priori.

1. Whatever is necessary must be universal in form.
2. Moral truths are necessary truths.
3. So moral truths are universal in form.

I will restrict myself for the moment to this simpler version, which does not mention the a priori. The main difference between the two arguments, as I see it, is that the first, though it entails that moral truths are necessary truths, does not actually use that as a premise. Now as I have said, particularism denies that basic moral facts are necessary truths. Why did Kant hold the opposite for *his* basic moral facts? Four things need to be mentioned in answer to this question.

The first point, the one most stressed by Kant, is that moral obligations bind all rational creatures, not just humans. Moral obligations, therefore, are not grounded in the contingencies of the human situation, but require a ground of a different sort so that they can apply to all possible rational beings. Kant wrote (Gr. 4.389):

> Everyone must grant that a law, if it is to hold morally, that is, as a ground of an obligation, must carry with it absolute necessity; that, for example, the command 'thou shalt not lie' does not hold only for human beings, as if other rational beings did not have to heed it ... that, therefore, the ground of obligation here must not be sought in the nature of the human being or in the circumstances of the world in which he is placed, but a priori simply in concepts of pure reason; and that any other precept, which is based on principles of mere experience—even if it is universal in a certain respect—... can indeed be called a practical rule but never a moral law.

Again (Gr. 4.408)

> [If the moral law] must hold not only for human beings but for all rational beings as such, not merely under contingent conditions and with exceptions but with absolute necessity, then it is clear that no experience could give occasion to infer even the possibility of such apodictic laws ... And how should laws of the determination of our will be taken as laws of the determination of rational beings as such, and for ours only as rational beings, if they were merely empirical and did not have their origin completely a priori in pure but practical reason?

These remarks are not perfectly clear. In considering them, I want to grant Kant, for purposes of argument, what seems to be his main premise here, which is a claim about who is subject to the moral law—the domain of application, as one might call it. The moral law governs all those who are even capable of responding to it (or, as Kant would put it, capable of acting in accordance with a representation of it; Gr. 4.412). But this does not entail that there cannot be laws that only really apply to humans, that is, to those subject to our conditions, liable to our failings, emotions and the like—and I do not really think that Kant supposed otherwise. There could be a law saying that if you have just been humiliatingly defeated at squash, and experience a strong desire to smash your opponent over the head with your racquet, you should walk off the court quickly and try to calm down. (I think this is Michael Smith's example.) This law governs the behaviour of all rational beings, but is only able actually to affect the behaviour of those liable to strong emotions of a certain sort.

Kant might however be thinking that since the moral law governs the behaviour of all rational beings, it governs our behaviour only as rational beings. But if so, his point can only be that it is as rational beings that we are capable of responding to those rules, of controlling our emotions in accordance with them. There can clearly be rules about the appropriateness of emotions.

Another possibility is that Kant is thinking that if the moral law governs the behaviour of all rational beings, and of ourselves only as rational beings, it must be possible for a purely rational being to come to know that law. Since a purely rational creature is restricted to a priori knowledge, the grounds for the law cannot be empirical. But even if we allow that those grounds cannot be empirical, this would do nothing to determine the possible contents of such laws; it rather addresses our ability to know that they are laws. The reason why the law is law (if there is such a reason) cannot be an empirical reason, but must be some feature that a purely rational creature could come to know.

Kant also makes a point about exceptions. There cannot be exceptions to a moral law; whatever the law says is true in all conditions whatever, that is, as we would now say, in all possible situations or worlds. It is therefore a necessary truth.

My question is whether there is anything here—anything true, that is—that a particularist could not accept. My general view is that so long as we do not assume in advance what sort of thing the moral law is to say, or the form of basic moral truths—and Kant is in no position to make any such assumption right at the start of the *Groundwork*—it remains perfectly possible that though all are subject to the law, the law itself is particularist, by which I mean that its basic pronouncements are truths about what is a reason for what, case by case. Differences between situations may affect what is a reason for what in them.

The last point above, the one about exceptions, is the sort of thing I mean to exclude by saying that we should not assume in advance what sort of thing the moral law is to say. If the moral law specifies *laws*, that is to say universal principles, those principles must be true, and for them to be true is for them to be exceptionless. Our basic moral principles could not, for instance, say that lying is *normally* wrong, if only because that would be no guide to someone trying to work out whether this case was one of the exceptions. The most that such a principle could tell him would be that it probably was not an exception, which, though it is of some help, is not really what was required. But this is just to specify a consequence of holding that the moral law specifies universal principles; it is not to give any reason to suppose that this is what the moral law is in the business of doing, which is what the particularist is wanting to deny. So it seems that we cannot extract the conclusion that the moral law specifies necessary truths from the claim that it specifies universal principles, because that claim is also in dispute.

Kant seems sometimes to give a different sense to the idea that moral laws hold with necessity. In this new sense, even if they do not express necessary truths, they *necessitate* us. They require us to act, and accept no excuse. Of course this sort of necessitation is different from causal necessitation, since one may well not do what one is necessitated to do in this sense, what one is required to do, while what is causally necessitated must happen, cannot fail to occur. The moral law, as Kant often says, concerns what ought to be done but very often is not done. Now there is here the special point that purely rational beings cannot fail to do what they are rationally required to do, because they have no non-rational motivation. So they will always do what they ought (and of course moral requirements are just one species of rational requirement, for Kant). But nonetheless the laws which they observe do not impugn their autonomy; they remain free to do the other thing—it is just that they will not do it, since their nature prevents them from having any incentive to act contrary to the requirements of morality, or of rationality more generally. So the crucial point is that Kant's second conception of necessitation allows that one is free not to do what one is necessitated to do. All this, however, is simply irrelevant to the question whether moral truths are necessary truths or universal in form. The particularist would happily say that we are necessitated by the constraints present in the case before us, seeing no need to think that anything capable of necessitating one in the way must be of a certain form, or a necessary truth.

What I take myself to have argued so far is that moral truths, though they necessitate, need not for that reason be necessary truths.

My next point is that they do not need to be universal in form in order to govern the behaviour of all rational beings. Kant's point about the domain of application, which I am allowing for the moment, really tells us nothing about the form of the things that apply in that domain. If the basic pronouncements of the moral law were claims about what is a reason for what in particular circumstances, those claims would apply to all rational beings without exception. Even if the claims contained some restriction on the sort of person, or even just the person,[2] for whom the reason is said to exist, this would not mean that their domain of application is thereby restricted. In logic, the domain of quantification is not itself restricted by the antecedent of a conditional. If the domain of quantification is all rational beings, the proposition that if one is a parent, one should care for one's child is a proposition to be assessed as true or false within that wider domain. One *could* say that there is a narrower domain, that of parents, and what the law says within that domain is that all should care for their children. But one need not say this, and there is a reason not to, which is that otherwise the notion of the domain of quantification would cease to have much of its point. Analogously with the moral law: the domain (domain of application, now) is that of all rational beings, and the law is that parents should care for their children. The particularist would see this rather differently: the domain is all rational beings, and the moral law pronounces that this person has a reason to care for that child, since s/he is the child's parent. (It may be that another person has a child which she has no reason to care for; but if so there will be some explanation of this fact.)

So far I have argued that the pronouncements of the moral law need not be necessary truths, even if they apply to all equally. But now there is the a priori to be considered. Is it true, as both Kant and Ross seem to think, that since moral truths are knowable a priori, they must be necessary and universal in form? If this were true, then though an empirical morality might be as the particularists suppose all morality to be, a morality knowable a priori would have to consist of necessarily true moral principles.

The connection between the epistemological distinction between a priori and a posteriori knowledge and the modal distinction between necessary and contingent has been loosened by Saul Kripke's 'discovery' of a posteriori necessities. But this does little to help us in the present case. The question is the reverse one about a priori contingencies: how something that is not necessary could be knowable a priori. The normal routes to a priori knowledge are the conceptual route and the semantic route, and both of these seem to be excluded in the moral case. Moral truths are not true merely in virtue of the concepts involved, and they are not true merely in virtue of meanings either. Conceptual and semantic competence, then, cannot be what explains our ability to know what is a reason for what in the moral sphere. Kant would, I think, phrase this question in terms of what synthesizes such judgements. If I understand this way of putting things at all, it amounts to asking how we know that the two terms of our judgement (subject and predicate) are connected, or, in more objective vein, what is it that connects the two terms. In the case of ordinary empirical judgements, the answer is experience. This does not mean that experience puts the terms together, but that it is experience that puts us in a position to see a connection between them. If I judge that Italian ice cream is nice, the connection between being Italian ice cream and being nice is entirely provided by experience, and therefore can only be contingent. So what is it that enables us to put the two terms together when we judge that her having asked me not to do it is a reason for me not to do it? It cannot be experience, because experience gives out before we get to this sort of judgement. Must it then be reason? Kant would say yes, and then insist that the primary object of reason cannot be something so particular, but must be something universal and necessary. But I think that this is too swift.

A truth is synthetic a priori if it is not analytic, and we can know it in a way that is not derived from our experience. What counts as being derived from our experience is somewhat vague, but I suppose that what is being ruled out here is being either provided by experience (presented as part of the surrounding scene) or being inferable from what is so provided. It is not that if something is a priori it cannot be inferable from experience, but only that it can be known in a way that does not involve such inference, even if it can be known a posteriori as well. Now it seems to me that there are quite a lot of truths that fit this recipe and which are neither necessary nor universal. An example I have given before concerns our judgements of similarity. Suppose that I am asked to judge of four things A, B, C, and D whether A is more similar to B than C is to D. Is Mahler's music more like that of Richard Strauss than Mozart's music is like Haydn's? I take it that I make such judgements, at least some of the time. And some of them will count as knowledge. Mozart's music is more like Haydn's than Beethoven's is like Bach's. Now such judgements are mediated by experience, in the sense that without the relevant experience I could not even begin. But they are not provided by experience, nor are they straightforwardly inferable from what experience does provide. Such judgements are much too nuanced for that; to make them, one has to have a sense of which similarities really count for something (for present purposes only, of course) and which are not very telling for those purposes. Therefore, we are dealing here with a priori knowledge, and it is particular, not universal in form.

It seems to me that it is also contingent rather than necessary; but this is a further matter, and needs further discussion. Mozart might have written different music, and if he had, his music might have been no more similar to Haydn's than Beethoven's is to Bach's. But still, one might say, it is a necessary truth that Mozart's music, given its actual empirical nature, is very similar to Haydn's, given its empirical nature. And this is what one is determining a priori, if anything. Perhaps, then, the example I gave in the previous paragraph is inadequate. It is an example of the a priori determination of a particular necessity, and not, as I suggested, of a particular contingency. So it does not serve to defend the particularist's suggestion that basic moral claims are particular and contingent but known a priori.

I don't think this challenge is sound. It is a necessary truth that Mark, given his actual height, is taller than Jonathan, given his actual height. But the necessity of that truth is compatible with its being a stubbornly contingent truth that Mark is taller than Jonathan. The necessary truth is a consequence of the contingent one, and, I would say, known only by knowing the contingent one. I maintain that the contingency of the fact that Mozart's music is so similar to Haydn's is not impugned by the fact that in all worlds in which Mozart wrote what he wrote in this world, and Haydn did too, Mozart's music will be just as similar to Haydn's as it is here. The matter is analogous to the situation with reasons. It is a contingent truth that this feature is a reason to go gently here, since in other circumstances this same feature might not have been a reason. It is a necessary truth that this feature is, in this context, a reason to go gently, since wherever that context recurs, this feature will be the same reason that it is here. But this necessary truth (which requires, of course, a suitable conception of 'this context'), is a consequence of the particular truth, and, I would say, known only by knowing the contingent one.

It may seem to be a mystery that a contingent truth can entail a necessary one. But that is not quite what is the issue here. What is really the case is that if we start from the contingently true proposition and ask how things would be in other situations in which everything possibly relevant to the question—whether that proposition is true or not is held constant—the answer will be that in all such situations we will get the same contingent truth. This is not the same as saying that the original contingent truth was not contingent.

So for a second example, consider judgements of relevance. Our judgement of what is relevant to what seems to me to be inescapably particular, though I understand that some people are working on principles of relevance.[3] Further, I would say that judgements of relevance sometimes amount to knowledge. But none of them seem to be respectably a posteriori.

Of course that leaves the question what synthesizes these judgements. At this point I want to say that we just have the capacity to judge these things. The relation of similarity is one that we would not be human if we could not track to some extent. Some similarities are perceivable and experienceable, but others are not. (Similarities between the views of Kant and of Aristotle would be of the latter type.) Is it reason that enables us to track such things? Not in any very restricted sense. (If reason is the capacity to track reasons, as some suggest, then knowledge of what is a reason for what will be rational knowledge of the bluntly particular and contingent, in my view. But this only shows that it does not help in this context to appeal to such a conception of reason.) We have the capacity to assess similarities, and it is a rational capacity if anything, I suppose; but calling it so does not advance the argument in any direction. So if the question is what synthesizes the two terms in our similarity judgements, I am tempted to suggest that the answer 'nothing' is as good an answer as we are going to get. (Another answer is 'we do'.) And the same applies to judgements about relevance.

So far I have been suggesting that Kant fails to establish, that morality must be based on necessary universal principles known a priori. I have not tried to argue that since particularism is true, Kant must be mistaken. My argument was rather that Kant's inferences, or associations, are mistaken, and that we can see that they are mistaken by considering an alternative conception of morality, the particularist one, and asking what Kant would have to say against it. If, as I suggest, the answer is nothing, or nothing effective, that is enough for me. The crucial question is whether Kant has given us reason to suppose that there must be moral principles if there is to be morality at all. I maintain that no such reason has been provided, and none can be extracted from the fact that basic moral knowledge is a priori.

There remains the great Kantian connection between morality and rationality. Does the fact that moral truths are not known empirically show that they are known by pure reason? Not if we restrict pure reason to the discovery of necessary universal truth. What then happens to the notion of pure reason if we extend its capacities to the discovery of the sorts of contingent particular truths that I have been talking about?

Suppose we do think of pure reason as the capacity to recognize and respond to reasons. This is not impossible; there are reasons for moral judgements, however we conceive of them. There are also reasons for judgements of similarity, and for judgements of relevance. Now the rational being will have to be aware of more than just what is a reason for what. She will have to be aware of whatever considerations can affect that sort of thing, and in my view that is a considerable expansion. As I take it,[4] there are features that enable other things to stand as reasons, without being reasons themselves. If so, our rational being will have to be able to be aware of these enablers—as of anything else that plays an analogous role. (There are disablers as well as enablers, and there are also intensifiers, which strengthen the reason given us by something else, and attenuators, which do the opposite.) All these things must come within the recognitional capacity of our rational being.

In a way, there is nothing wrong with thinking in these terms. The only reservation I have derives from Bernard Williams' characteristic question, what are we to say about someone who fails to recognize a reason, or even just an enabler. Are we to think of such a person as irrational, at least to this extent? Have we now retained the central Kantian idea that moral failures are rational failures? Of course there are two sorts of moral failures: failures to discern what is a reason for what, or how one ought (that is, *morally* ought) overall to respond to the present situation, and failures actually to respond in that way once one has recognized that one should. The latter are failures of rationality only to the extent that what one might call rational motivation should defeat whatever other forms of motivation there might be. Since I am not myself convinced that there is any such general rule, I leave this aside. What about the other sort of failure? Suppose, to adapt a well-known example whose author I cannot discover, I fail to discern that a child is alone in a crowd. Is this worth calling a defect of rationality? My own view is that to think in those terms would be to stretch the notion of rationality, and of failures of rationality, too far, and for no reason. For instance, often we fail to notice a reason because we are tired, or otherwise engaged. I do not think it is worth labelling such failures as marks of irrationality. We should not forget, after all, that what has been driving us in this direction is the supposedly exhaustive distinction between experience and reason. Whatever drives the thought that this distinction is exhaustive does little to unsettle one's sense that there are failures of many different types, and that it serves little purpose to maintain that all are signs either of blindness (as a general name for a defect of sense) or irrationality.

Notes

I am grateful to Mark Sainsbury and to Paul Woodruff for their comments on this essay.

1. Most recently in my *Ethics Without Principles*, Clarendon Press, Oxford, 2004.
2. I am thinking here of the possibility of agent-relative reasons.
3. I am referring here to the work of D. Sperber and D. Wilson.
4. I have argued for this view in many places, most recently in Chapter 3 of *Ethics Without Principles*.

Kant on Happiness, Friendship, and Inclination

An Aristotelian Critique

Bindu Puri

In Kant, there is an attempt to make a reconciliation, given the fact that human beings as appearances are determined by natural laws and yet, if they are to be responsible as moral agents, they must be presupposed to be free. Kant locates this freedom in laws of reason and in autonomy. This autonomy makes possible various activities central to the moral life. For instance, praise and blame presuppose autonomy. Again moral agency, the fact that a moral agent believes that he ought not to lie, even if given the course of the world at the time that lying was inevitable, makes sense only if a man is free from natural causality and determined as an agent by laws of reason. Agency is central to living a moral life. One cannot speak of *ought* at all if an autonomous agency does not exist. This essay attempts to look at other activities also seen as somehow necessary to the moral life. For example happiness, friendship and love, born of human inclination. In brief, all those complicated parts of human affairs that go by the name of human relationships. It would not be wrong to say that man's moral life and sense of himself as a moral agent at many times centralizes these relationships. Moral theory then could look on them as playing a role in moral life. Kant has paid a lot of attention to friendship. In fact, after Aristotle, it is Kant to whom friendship is so important a thematic in moral theory. This chapter attempts to articulate Kant's views on happiness, friendship and inclination and present a critique, somewhat Aristotelian in spirit. The reasons for looking at friendship and happiness together is that where friendship is clearly seen as a part of that very fascinating thing called human happiness, the view that one would take about friendship would very much depend, on the role assigned to happiness, in moral goodness. Also if happiness has no role to play in making men good, it is difficult to say that friendship, which has certain complex but decisive influences on happiness, can be constitutive of that human good.

Kant and Human Happiness

We must first take a look at the Kantian understanding. In the case of human will, the laws of reason become categorical imperatives for they involve necessitation, as there is a struggle with desires and inclinations. For a holy will there would be no necessitation and hence no categorical imperative. Under human conditions this categorical imperative bids us to act in accordance with universal law as such. That is, it bids us to act on a principle valid for all rational beings as such and not merely on one that is valid, if we happen to want some further end.

This autonomy of the will, and the categorical imperative enjoining action in accordance with autonomy, is a necessary condition for the validity of moral judgements. Kant makes it clear that all heteronomous principles must be rejected. That the will is good only if it acts purely for the sake of duty, that its maxims cannot be material but must be universal and objective. Here, he classifies heteronomous principles as empirical or rational. When they are empirical, their principle is always the pursuit of happiness, although some of them may be based on natural feelings of pleasure and pain, while others may be based on a supposed moral feeling or moral sense. When they are rational, their principle is always the pursuit of perfection, either a perfection to be attained by our own will or one supposed to be already existent in the will of God which imposes certain tasks on our will.

Empirical principles are always unfitted to serve as a ground for moral laws. The universality with which these laws should hold for all rational beings without exception—the unconditional practical necessity which they thus impose—falls away if their basis is taken from the special constitution of human nature or from the accidental circumstances in which it is placed. The principle of personal happiness is, however, the most objectionable, not merely because it is false and because its pretence that well-being always adjusts to well-doing is contradicted by experience; nor merely because it contributes nothing whatever towards establishing morality, since making a man happy is quite different from making him good and making him prudent or astute in seeking his advantage, quite different from making him virtuous; but because it bases morality on sensuous motives which rather undermine it and totally destroy its sublimity, inasmuch as the motives of virtue are put in the same class as those of vice and we are instructed only to become better at calculation, the specific difference between virtue and vice being completely wiped out.[1]

It is therefore surprising that intelligent men could have thought of calling the desire of happiness a universal practical law on the ground that the desire is universal, and, therefore also the maxim by which everyone makes his desire determine his will. For whereas in other cases a universal law of nature makes everything harmonious; here, on the contrary, if we attribute to the maxim the universality of a law, the extreme opposite of harmony will follow, the greatest opposition and the complete destruction of the maxim itself and its purpose. ...Because the occasional exceptions which one is permitted to make are endless, and cannot be embraced in one universal rule. In this manner, then, results a harmony like that which a satirical poem depicts as existing between a married couple bent on going to ruin, "O'Marvellous harmony what he wishes, she wishes also"; or like what is said of the pledge of Francis1 to the emperor Charles V, "What my brother Charles wishes that I wish also" (viz., Milan). Empirical principles of determination are not fit for any universal external legislation, but just as little for internal: for each man makes his own subject the foundation of his inclination, and in the same subject sometimes one inclination, sometimes another, has the preponderance. To discover a law which would govern them all under this condition, namely, bringing them all into harmony, is quite impossible.[2]

That happiness cannot be any part of a moral maxim seems clear:

1) Very importantly because, happiness and goodness, are separate. To make happiness a part of goodwill would be to place that will under sensuous motives which would be destructive of the distinction between virtue and vice. For Kant then, happiness as part of the goodwill is suspect as it would result in morality becoming calculative of personal ends under sensuous impulses and inclinations. This would mean that in principle vice and virtue would be the result of a similar kind of willing, willing under empirical natural impulses and desires. What makes morality cognitively safe and non-vulnerable to emotion and impulse, and therefore to mistakes, is the fact

that the will when it is moral, is under the maxims of reason and not of inclination.

2) Happiness cannot even be universalized as men will all desire their personal ends. Even the same person will be torn asunder under different impulses if he governs himself or herself by personal happiness. For Kant, happiness would be incapable of bringing different impulses in different people and in the same person into any sort of harmony. This would make the moral life fragmented and disparate, unruly and located in unique particularity of actions and situations, rather than in universal guidelines.

Consequently, then, for Kant happiness is not goodness. As a matter of fact, we do not have a direct duty to seek our happiness. Given his analysis of duty, it makes no sense to say that we can be under an imperative to do what is already subjectively necessary for us to do. However we have an indirect duty to promote our own happiness. This kind of duty may arise in one or more of four ways. Firstly as Kant says, '*Some natural qualities are even helpful to this goodwill itself and can make its task very much easier*'.[3] Secondly because adversity, pain and want are great temptations to transgress one's duty, we have an indirect duty to ward off poverty as a great temptation to vice and therefore to promote our happiness. Third, if we are convinced that we lack the happiness that we deserve, we have the right and indirect duty to try to seek our happiness accordingly. Finally if the concept of happiness becomes so indefinite and incoherent that the principle of self-love loses its power to motivate us, for example, to tend to our health by eating properly and exercising then an action that otherwise would only be prudentially good may be morally obligatory as an indirect duty. However in all such cases, ' it is not my happiness but the preservation of my moral integrity that is my end and also my duty' so that the end 'is not the agent's happiness but his morality'.[4] We have a direct obligation to do our duty, but to fulfil a positive duty to strive for moral perfection we may have to indirectly promote something that would be considered only prudential, either a means or a part of our notion of happiness.

In the *Metaphysics* of *Morals*, Kant clarifies, 'To secure one's happiness is a duty, at least indirectly; for discontent with one's condition, under a pressure of many anxieties and amidst unsatisfied wants, might easily become a great temptation to transgression of duty...'[5]

For Kant then we have an indirect duty to promote our happiness out of duty. So that we are not ever tempted to transgress the moral law. However, if one does the same out of an inclination and desire to be happy then the action loses all moral worth. Again if we promote, our happiness against all inclination, we act morally and if we do the same out of desire and a sense of anticipated pleasure the action would no longer have any moral worth. Kant's main problem seems to be that if moral worth of actions is entrusted to something as capricious and as vulnerably fragile as happiness must necessarily be, morality will also become cognitively unsafe, open to errors and based on particulars of sensuous perception, which necessarily throw surprises. Reason is a much better basis for morality as it saves the will from any vulnerability and all disasters of judgement and remorse. So happiness of others can be a direct duty, as it will not make the agent vulnerable to loss, as he is when he follows his own inclinations and his own happiness. Again if happiness of the other becomes a part of the agent's own happiness as in love and friendship, any action done from that kind of powerful feeling and desire would no longer be a duty at all or even, at the very least, morally uplifting. And yet, is not a human being at his very best morally, when he is able to so internalize the other that his happiness becomes essential to the agent's own happiness. In love, in friendship, in service proceeding from sympathy and wide universal love, the agent acts from inclination to promote the happiness of the other not as a duty but as a part of his own happiness. It is indeed as if his sum total of happiness begins to depend crucially on the happiness of the other. For Kant, this would make the action devoid of moral worth, as it is pathological love—a love from inclination and not from reason for the sake of duty. And yet, human beings seem to learn so much morally from this kind of love and these inclinations seem to further the moral life by actualizing it internally so that goodness flows out from the depth of one's being without any coercion or imperative at all.

Kant builds up his moral theory on reason and autonomy, which finds expression in moral law. Moral law necessarily appears as an imperative to men due to the struggle with unruly desires and inclinations. There is, in reason, a foundation for the moral life, which is universal, devoid of reference to unique particulars and therefore has no need to introduce the perception of the individual agent as a factor in making moral judgements. Reason makes morality cognitively secure in Kant. Reason also is expressive of self-rule by man of himself and his inclinations. It then becomes a powerful argument for the self-sufficiency of the moral agent. Autonomy means that the agent is free not only of the other but more importantly of himself. For frequently in moral matters, the greatest obstacles come from oneself. Reason makes man free of inclination, desire, and happiness as determining factors. It also thereby makes morality free of dependence on external factors upon which the agent's inner feelings would necessarily depend—factors like love, friendship, and approval of others. These factors are destructive of the universality required by morality but they also make morality dependent on factors beyond the agent's own control. In a word, they destroy self-sufficiency in the moral life. Reason, autonomy, and self-determination build up for Kant a conception of the moral life, which gives it a certain invulnerability. Note that the existence in life of circumstances that make for happiness, of fulfilling friendships, of mutual sharing, are also at some level a matter of great moral luck and good fortune. In Kant, morality is completely free of such essentially undependable matters.

Aristotle and Eudaimonia

In Aristotle, on the other hand, there is a moral theory grounded in the heteronomous principle of happiness. First of all, Aristotle is clear that when he talks about human good, the goal of the ethical discourse is practical and not theoretical. The good human life must be a possible human life, that is, one possible in terms of human capabilities. Again it should be possible in the sense of being a life that human beings can actually choose. In other words, it must contain things, which are important to a characteristically human life. Aristotle speaks of eudaimonia as the highest human good. In Books One and Two of *Nichomachean Ethics*, Aristotle gives an argument for eudaimonia.

Every art and every enquiry, and similarly every action and pursuit, is thought to aim at some good; and for this reason the good has been rightly declared to be that at which all things aim.[6]

These words mark the start of Aristotle's investigation, with the human function argument using an analogy from the crafts. The point is that just as good shoemaking requires an understanding of making shoes, it must be within the boundaries of what the nature of making shoes essentially is, so too, a good human life must contain essential features of what human life properly is. Aristotle affirms, *Happiness then is the best, noblest and most pleasant thing in the world'.*[7] However there is dispute regarding the exact nature of happiness. Pleasure, wealth, honour and health are mentioned as well as Plato's conception that these things are somehow caused by the idea of the good. Aristotle carries forward his argument seeking to establish happiness as a complete and final goal, as something, which is always pursued for its own sake and not for the sake of something else. He then comes to a preliminary account of happiness as the ultimate good, which he wants to identify:

If this is the case then human good turns out to be the activity of the soul in accordance with virtue and if there is more than one virtue, in accordance with the best and most complete. But we must add "in a complete life". For one swallow does not make a summer, nor does one day; and so too, one day, or a short time does not make a man blessed and happy.[8]

Aristotle then did not see happiness as a feeling even if that feeling was deep and permanent and purified of gross pleasures. Neither did he see it as a disposition or temperament. To him, happiness was an activity through which a man developed his capacities by living and faring well and being on the path to reach well-being in mind and body. Happiness was for Aristotle:

1) an activity and not simply a condition or static state of the soul;
2) something final, 'for the sake of which anything else is done'; and
3) taken to be a complete end in the sense, that it alone standing by itself made life desirable and lacking in nothing.

Aristotle's view that happiness or eudaimonia was an activity of the soul and not simply a good condition or state, made his theory vulnerable to the necessity of external goods from the start. For Aristotle, the good condition of a virtuous character like good athletic conditioning is a preparation for activity; it finds its natural fulfilment in activity.

No activity is complete if it is impeded; but eudemonia is something complete. So the eudaimon person needs the goods of the body and external goods and goods of luck in addition, so that his activities should not be impeded.[9]

For Aristotle, moral worth involves those features of human life, which make it truly human. So it involves living and faring well in accordance with virtue. Faring well is a part of human happiness and human goodness. Which is why external goods of different sorts are for Aristotle, constituents of moral worth, happiness and faring well.

Nonetheless, eudaimonia evidently needs the external goods as well, as we said. For many things are done through philoi and wealth and political capability; as through tools. And deprivation of some things defile the condition of being makarion; for example good birth, good children, good looks. For nobody will entirely be eudaimonikos if he is entirely disgusting to look at, or basely born, or both solitary and childless; still less perhaps, if he has terribly bad children or philoi, or has good ones who die. As we said, then it seems to require this sort of fortunate climate in addition.[10]

Friendship and Inclination

As a consequence of differences regarding the relationship between happiness and the moral life, there are very fundamental differences between Kant and Aristotle on friendship. Aristotle looks for the best human life in a life, which is possible for human beings and therefore one, which includes faring well and living well. Faring well makes Aristotelian happiness and thereby the good human life vulnerable and fragile. For external goods cannot make a good life self-sufficient. Friendship is one such good and source of tremendous vulnerability and yet, for Aristotle, friendship is an important part of the fortunate climate required for a man to be eudaimonikos. Further, given that happiness is an activity of the soul in accordance with virtue, for Aristotle friendship actually becomes a part of human goodness as it has direct influence on virtuous activity and moral worth. As I will demonstrate later in this section, friendship and love are powerful sources of moral education and training, and friendship can be seen as leading to self-knowledge, which is a part of moral life and growth. Kant, however, cannot allow friendship to intrude into the agent's living of a good life though it is, and can be, a part of moral life of individuals by making *them* more worthy. For Kant, happiness is not goodness and further the good life is invulnerable to feelings, emotions, happiness or to faring well. As a matter of fact, the best worth of character is shown not from doing good from a sense of love and friendship but in doing good where these are absent. For Kant, it is happiness, which can be augmented or diminished by faring well and by fortune and not what is deserving of praise or blame, that is moral worth. The efore for Kant, friendship can only be a part of human sociability and not human goodness.

We must conduct ourselves towards a friend in such a way that it would do us no harm if he became our enemy, we must not put anything in his hands... If I rely completely on my friend, and confide to him all the secrets that could threaten my happiness if he became my enemy and blabbed them around, then that would be extremely careless of me.[11]

There is a debate as to whether the eudaimon person needs philoi or not. For they say that makarioi and self-sufficient people have no need of philoi, since they have all good things already. If then they are self-sufficient, they need nothing further; but the philos, being another oneself, provides what he cannot provide by himself. Whence the saying, 'When the daimon gives well, what need is there of philoi?' But it seems peculiar to give all good things to the eudaimon and to leave out philoi, which seem to be the greatest of the external goods...And surely it is peculiar to make the makarios person a solitary; for nobody would choose to have all the things in the world all by himself.... therefore the eudaimon needs philoi.[12]

Kant defines three kinds of friendship, regarding only one of them as true or complete friendship and the other two as imperfect likenesses or incomplete forms of friendship. He distinguishes between friendship of need, friendship of taste, and the friendship of disposition or sentiment. He regards friendship of need as the original foundation of all friendship, but the friendship of taste (pleasure in the company of the other) as only an analogue of friendship. Friendship of disposition is the true or complete form of friendship as it involves a disposition that makes us worthy of happiness. It does this in a complicated sort of way. In Aristotle friendship between virtuous friends proceeds because they perceive the good character in each other. In Kant, friendship of disposition and sentiment does not proceed because of the morally good will one finds in the friend. It proceeds because of a need to overcome a natural constraint and mistrust of others by communicating and disclosing our dispositions and judgements to another. Yet, the friendship of disposition and sentiment exhibits mutual revelation and understanding in a manner that friendship of need or mutual advantage or friendship of taste cannot do. For mutual advantage friendship would be based on the reciprocity of need and therefore not able to share mutuality and sentiment through an easy intimacy. Need- and advantage-based relationships, perhaps, have a way of becoming very single-minded and target-oriented and do not seem to further intimacy of exchange on matters unrelated to the specific needs that brought the two together in the first place. Friendship of taste for Kant is only one of seeking pleasure in the company of the other and therefore is only an analogue of friendship and not true friendship at all.

Though its natural end is not a moral end, yet both moral virtue and action on moral principles are required for friendship to reach its natural end. The natural end of friendship is the relation of intimacy it provides to human beings who have a fundamental need to reveal themselves to others despite the dangers this involves to social beings as such. Moral virtue first enters into Kant's account of friendship not through the fact that a person must be virtuous for the other to wish her or him well. It enters instead through the perception that the agent himself must seek to be virtuous and to act virtuously towards the other in order to be worthy of the trust and benevolence he hopes the other will show him as a friend: as, 'everyone seeks to deserve friendship'. Further, people are not selected to be our friends on account of being virtuous or having virtues like our own but virtuous people make better friends because they are more likely to follow the principles that preserve the intimacy and mutual trust that we need in friendship.[13]

For Kant the basis of all friendship, which has as its natural end mutual intimacy and trust, is mutual benevolence. That mutual benevolence is ultimately grounded not in inclination or desire for a particular person as a friend but in a rational philanthrophy we feel towards others. It lies in a general love of humanity that arises through appreciating the absolute worth of the other's person, irrespective of the goodness of the other's will. The reason why I make friends with a particular person is not that he is virtuous or has a goodness of will or I desire him in particular, but to fulfil the need of sociability, through a general love of humanity, I have somehow succeeded in developing a relation of intimacy with that one person rather than any other. Kant believes that it is the 'savage'who prefers to have special friendships according to his taste and dispositions. The more civilized a man becomes, the broader and less specific his outlook.

But as a rule, men are inclined to form particular friendships because this is a natural impulse and also because we all start with the particular and then proceed to the general.[14]

In *Lectures on Ethics*, Kant formulates the nature of true friendship in this way: 'Friendship is an idea, because it is not derived from experience. Empirical examples of friendship are extremely defective. It has its seat in the understanding. In ethics, however, it is a very necessary idea.' And it is an idea which essentially involves reciprocity: 'The maximum reciprocity of love is friendship, and friendship is an Idea because it is the measure by which we can determine reciprocal love.'[15] There are two important points about Kant's argument here. One, it rigorously demands reciprocity as the condition of friendship. Kant states that the greatest love one can have for another is to love him as much as one loves one's own self. But in case I enter into any such love, I must be sure that the other loves me as much as his own self: '...in which case he restores to me that with which I part and I come back to myself again.'[16] Two, for him such true friendship is an idea, which enables us to measure actual empirical experiences of friendship and see to what extent they are defective. Kant is very clear that actual friendships are only approximations to this idea of mutual love and 'in practical life such things do not occur'[17] and yet in ethics, friendship is a very necessary idea. It seems difficult to understand Kant here as he seems clear that '..this idea is valuable only for reflection'.[18] The tension in Kant seems to be that while there are no true friends and all friendships are only approximations and defective yet the idea of true friendship is valuable for reflection. The other interesting point in Kant's argument is about equality. The reciprocal benevolence is always in true friendship, among equals. Any inequality among friends puts one in a position of superiority and hence undermines the trust required for mutual sharing and communication. In the context of the discussion on the friendship of need, in *Lectures on Ethics*, Kant clarifies, 'The relation of friendship is a relation of equality'.[19] Again, Kant says in the same text, that 'The name of friendship should inspire respect'.[20] This seems to be a problem as there is, seemingly, in Kant, a tension between love and respect. For Kant love always involves superiority over the one who is loved, while respect involves pain as our self-conceit is somewhere hurt by respecting the other. So, in love, love of well-pleasedness, pathological love, there is even an indirect expression of self-conceit because objects of love, are selected on the grounds of self-love.

'We love everything over which we have a decisive superiority, so that we can toy with it, while it has a pleasant cheerfulness about it... Love, like water, always flows downwards more easily than upwards'.[21]

It then seems that as friendship, for Kant, involves equal love and respect it carries this tension of love involving superiority, and, respect involving pain to self-conceit, within it. One may wonder how this inner tension between equals in a mutual balance of superiority and self-love on the one hand and respect on the other, sustains an intimate dialogue and sharing of one another. It then seems to have become a rationally ruled fulfilment of a natural need for sociability between people on the ground of a universal benevolence for all rational creatures. Always in a precarious balance of love and respect, self-conceit and pain. Accordingly the fact that Kant sets limits on the sharing and on the intimacy seems to be rather appropriate given this kind of conception of it:

The trust and confidence goes as far as disposition and sentiment, but decency must still be observed; for we all have certain natural frailties and must be reserved regarding them lest humanity be outraged. Even to one's best friend one must not reveal oneself as one naturally one is and knows oneself, for that would be loathsome.[22]

This last point takes me directly to Aristotle's conception of friendship and discussion in *Magna Moralia*, where friendship is actually seen as an aid to moral life in terms of the increase in self-knowledge and self-perception that comes of seeing and responding to the person about whom you care. However a little preliminary discussion about the Aristotelian conception will be required at this point. The comparison between the two is important as the two treatments can be seen as symptomatic of two different conceptions of the moral life; the one trying to save morality from the capriciousness of happiness, inclination, love and friendship and the other making all these elements part of that life itself. The moral life in the second conception becomes by its very nature fragile and vulnerable. The issue then becomes one of understanding the role of moral philosophy itself. Of trying to appreciate that given the moral life and our participation in it, what role should moral philosophy play? More importantly, should it be a rarefied cerebral activity removed from the tempestuousness of human relationships, or should it find its starting points right in the very midst of them? Again answers to such questions are not only of academic and intellectual interest but influence ideas of motivation and most important, moral education and training which, in a strife-torn, amoral and immoral world, are of tremendous significance.

Philoi 'are the greatest of external goods'.[23] *Philos* is usually translated as friend and *philia* as friendship. However, under *philia*, Aristotle includes many relationships that may not be ordinarily classified as friendships, for instance, all close family relationships, including that between a husband and wife, a mother and child. It includes the very strongest relationships that humans form including those that have a high sexual component though the emphasis is not on mad passionate longing but on benefit, sharing and mutuality. Mutuality is a very important part of Aristotelian philia and philos. In fact it is one of the two essential features of love and friendship which constitute Aristotelian philia; therefore, Aristotle clarifies that the lover of wine may love wine but its not philia, for,

there is no return of love, and there is no wishing the good for the other's own sake. For it is surely ridiculous to wish the good for the wine-or if one does, what one wants is for it to be preserved so that one can have it. But they say that the philos must wish the good for the other's own sake.[24]

Two requirements for philia emerge: mutuality and independence. The other must be seen as a separate good, not simply as an extension of the philos. Further, Aristotle makes it clear that the best love between persons will be love based on character and conception of the good. Here each partner loves the other for what that other is most deeply in him or herself, for those dispositions of thought and feeling that are definitive of his or her self and identity. And such a relationship will be all the more strong if the characteristics that are its basis are themselves good. As against the Kantian conception, for Aristotle, love and friendship is based not on an appreciation of the friend in his rational nature as an end, but on the appreciation of his particular character and nature, the unique sum of habits, inclinations and virtues that make him the person he is. The best of friends seeks in his philos, repeatable traits of character, virtues like generosity and justice, as well as the aspirations and desires that make up his person. However, he also cares about features like sharing the friends company and the specialness of their shared history of mutual pleasure and mutual activity. To these requirements for friendship, Aristotle adds something more, namely that the philoi must 'live together' sharing activities and enjoyment. 'For love is sharing...and whatever each of them takes to be living or that for the sake of which they choose living, in this they wish to live with their philos.'[25]

Aristotle gives certain arguments in support of why such friendship should be taken to be a part of eudaimonia or a good human life. I would like to look here at some of these arguments for they demonstrate powerful ways in which friendship is important to moral motivation, moral psychology and moral life. Relationships that develop from inclinations and desires may, through a complex process of sharing, feeling and nurturing, become powerful motivations to the development of good habits of character. They may, through nurturing feelings of love and care, and not besides such feelings, teach people involved about themselves as they do about the object of love. Such self-knowledge being a very central part of what we take to be a good moral life. Inclinations, desires, love and happiness, which are able to produce the all too human, experience of friendship with all its fragility, may yet be very valuable to human goodness. For, it is such feelings that are at their best, in the mutuality of human relationships that can construct human goodness just as they can destroy that goodness by their tempestuousness. It might then be the case that trying to understand moral life and moral goodness without these human elements of fragility might actually detract from the worth of human goodness. It might also be that it is precisely when inclinations and desires no longer flower into human relationships like love and friendship that they become destructive of humanity itself. This happens as men then lose something very important to their sense of themselves.

Aristotle in Book 2 of the *Politics*, in criticism of Plato, says that the two strongest sources of human motivation are the ideas that something is your own and that it is the only one that you have. Again,

Just as in cities customs and ways have force so too in households do parental arguments and habits, and even more so because of relatedness and beneficence. For there is present beforehand a context of grateful love and a natural openness to persuasion.[26]

A platonic community cannot replace the concern and mutuality that binds children and parents in the enterprise of moral education. It is this concern and the thought that both are unique and irreplaceable to each other that facilitates the teaching and learning in the earliest moral lessons. Love, between them, eases the whole process of education. The *Nichomachean Ethics* adds to these considerations a further argument. Parental training has superior ability to respond to the particularity and individuality of the child. So for Aristotle human love and friendship plays a very important role in the development of good character and appropriate aspirations. This is so even in relationships between adults as he says,

The love of base people is harmful; for being unstable they share in base activities and they become bad through assimilation to one another. But the love of good people is good and increases with their association. And they seem to become better by their activity and correction of one another. For they model their tastes and values on one another's—from which we get the proverbial expression, 'excellence from excellence'[27].

The point regarding correction of one another is important when we remember how arduous and, at the same time, how important this process is to our moral life. Human goodness is in constant need of a mechanism to recognize the need for correction and then have sufficient motivation to correct. Think of how moral criticism hurts self-esteem even when it comes from a dear one. And yet it is perhaps the mutuality of love that has the strongest power to correct and transform. For love makes the lover and the friend want to sustain the mutuality of concern, care, and well-pleasedness.

Another important argument in Aristotle for friendship is one that is important from the standpoint of moral psychology.

Now if someone looking to his philos, should see what he is and of what sort of character, the philos—if we imagine a philos of the most intense sort—would seem to him to be like a second himself, as in saying, "this is my second Heracles". Since, then, it is both a most difficult thing, as some of the sages have also said, to know oneself, and also a most pleasant thing (for to know oneself is pleasant)—moreover, we cannot ourselves study ourselves from ourselves, as is clear from the reproaches we bring against others without being aware that we do the same things ourselves—and this happens because of bias or passion, which in many of us obscure the accuracy of judgements; as, then, when we ourselves wish to see our own face we see it by looking into a mirror, similarly too, when we ourselves wish to know ourselves, we would know ourselves by looking to the philos. For the philos, as we say, is another oneself. If, then, it is pleasant to know oneself, and it is not possible to know this without having someone else as a philos, the self sufficient person would need philia in order to know himself.[28]

Aristotle's argument begins by stating that self-knowledge is obstructed by biases and passions, which blind a person to his own faults. They make a person see himself as better than he really is, often obscuring access effectively to the person he actually is. It is easier for us to look at someone other than ourselves.

This reflective look at models of goodness enhances our understanding of our own character and aspirations, improving self-criticism and sharpening judgement. For this to be so, the model in question must be a person similar to us in character and aspiration, someone whom we can identify to ourselves as 'another oneself' for the purposes of this scrutiny.[29]

Nussbaum, in Aristotle's *The Fragility of the Good Human Life*, examines this argument in some detail and concludes that Aristotle's conception of ethical knowledge involves the perception of complex particulars. Perception is both 'cognitive and affective' and consists in the ability to single out the ethically salient features of the particular matter at hand. 'Frequently this recognition is accomplished by appropriate emotional response as much as through intellectual judgement.'[30] Nussbaum explains that to know a person's character in the Aristotelian way requires intellectual as well as responsive interactions over a period and across mutuality and sharing.

Philia's knowledge is guided by the pleasure discovered in that person's company, by the feelings of care and tenderness built up through the association and its shared history. Frequently feeling guides attention and discloses to vision what would otherwise have remained concealed. Only with this ability to perceive and to respond to the nuances of the other person's character and ways will the seeing of character, which is at the heart of this knowledge come about.[31]

Nussbaum terminates the discussion on the argument here. However it has become clear, from the above, that *philia* aids in understanding and seeing the character of the other or the *philos*. What needs to be further elaborated is how this friendship actualizes self-knowledge in the Aristotelian framework. For Aristotle is clearly saying that to be in an intimate love and friendship is also to begin to understand oneself just as one would stand in front of a mirror to see oneself. This argument is particularly fascinating vis-à-vis Kant's view regarding the limits of friendship and the idea that, in friendship, revelation of oneself should never be total as that would actually be *loathsome*. Ethical knowledge involves more than cognition. It involves a response in terms of feeling and emotion to the features in the other. This seems appropriate given the fact that moral knowledge is different from the knowledge of say a physical object like a table or even a concept like that of a triangle. For in both these knowledge situations the knower is cognitively approaching the object as a person who comes to know. He is not at any level part of the cognitive act in any emotional sense. However in moral knowledge situations the knower is involved, his perception cannot be cognitive alone but is always emotive as well. To know kindness is to respond to the trait in some manner or other in terms of feeling and inclination. When the situation involves the philos, it must all the more be so, given the shared history of care and concern, every increase in knowledge is to be accompanied by an emotive response, which will be part of the knowledge itself. To know my friend as unkind, will be an intellectual act but at the same time the knowledge will be a good deal more complicated than, simply, he is an unkind person. It will at some level reflect on me, my interactions with him, my own insecurities and weaknesses that kept me perhaps deluded for a time, a matter of grave concern to myself and my state of self-knowledge, perhaps. Then it is possible to understand how knowing the friend the loved one, helps to know oneself, in Aristotelian terms. Witness how, in friendship and love, as intimacy grows over time, there is a sharing of concern; knowledge of the character of the other deepens, but at the same time knowing that other as just, as generous, as humorous, teaches the agent through his own responses to these features a lot about himself. I admire my beloved's sense of justice, but I am not so strongly ingrained in the life of justice myself. My interactions with him teach me that I am frequently selfish and often angry. I could learn this about myself in other contexts but do not as I am not an emotive participant in those contexts to be able to see my characteristics or myself in an Aristotelian sense. At some level then, knowing another with love and friendship makes inclination and desire a part of knowledge acts wherein response to myself leads to self-knowledge. This certainly is a most important part of moral life.

And yet, in Kant there is the idea that too much revelation will most certainly be an undesirable thing and so my need for intimate exchange would have to be a reason-governed activity. Kant is suspicious of leaving friendship under the control of desire and inclinations. Perhaps Kant stresses the purity of the moral life, of friendship as a love of mutual benevolence, of happiness as no part of the categorical imperative, for he sees that to make goodness depend on a universal law of reason, on the autonomy of the rational will is to give it a less vulnerable foundation. Happiness as Kant says himself, will lead to a harmony like that between a married couple bent on ruin, of which one might well say, 'What he desires that she desires also.' In other words to admit happiness, emotion, love, and inclination, in matters moral would be to admit a whole host of factors completely beyond the agent's control. There would then be the possibility of making mistakes in fundamental moral matters, one would have to say that a man who was blessed with good friends, love and happiness and thereby lived a good life had moral luck. Yet, is human morality not necessarily fragile and vulnerable? In fact, is not being vulnerable and fragile a part of human goodness itself and therefore a belief internal to morality? For instance is not the belief that my moral judgement might be wrong, a part of my being a good person? Will I not lose something of human goodness if I believe that I have in my understanding a set of beliefs that make me morally invulnerable? Either I am a God, or every one of my moral beliefs could be a mistake—this seems to be a part of the make-up of moral humility. And without such humility men, even potentially good men can commit the very worst atrocities in the name of invulnerable rules and principles.

Again, a problem with Kant's treatment of emotion seems to me to be, that to exclude inclinations and desires from their most beatific culminations in human relationships could as a matter of fact make man in a sense free of all positive feelings which alone make him human and restrict him without really seeming to do so. Such men then become capable of the very worst tyranny as they lose all the learning and moral self-knowledge, which only such intimate relations grounded in desire and inclinations can teach them. Witness how terrorists can kill very small children. There must be so much displaced emotion and complex distorted self-perceptions that make them able to do this. A man who has been in very intimate relations in the family and learnt to care and share and thereby learnt about his own frailties, the man who is conscious about the fragility of his own happiness, perhaps about losing his loved friend, cannot really commit atrocities of such kinds. Therefore, in important ways emotion, desire, love and happiness are, or can be, a part of human goodness.

The question seems to be one about whether moral matters are capable of being understood without having to be a participant in those matters. For participants will necessarily have a different view. Hume thought that reason drove us to reject the views on which ordinary life depended, so that,

Since reason is incapable of dispelling these clouds, nature herself suffices to that purpose, and cures me of this philosophical melancholy and delirium... I dine, I play a game of backgammon, I converse and am merry with my friends: and when after three or four hours amusement, I would return to these speculations, they appear so cold, and strained and ridiculous that I cannot find it in my heart to enter into them.[32]

There is certainly some reason for thinking that as far as human relationships, friendships, and emotions are concerned we are participants and therefore need to take perspectives that are a part of the participation and take that participation into account. So, Paul Gilbert argues in *Human Relationships*,

In offering an account of social relationships, therefore, we seek the reasonable agreement of people who are already participants within them. And so we need to ask whether the account makes sense of the way we as participants think. Our interest, then, is not purely academic; it is an interest we have in becoming clearer about what we are doing, and cannot but do, in the course of our social lives.[33]

As participants, it becomes a matter of concern to realize that human goodness though it should not, as Kant says, be confused with individual happiness, cannot also be completely devoid of such happiness. Further, desire, inclination, love, and friendship need not only be disruptive of human goodness and make man a slave to passions and unruly impulses. They can be a part of goodness. For in them lies the strength to make man commit himself and exert himself far beyond what he ordinarily can do. Moral theory, which takes sympathetic note of them, can harness these forces and make them a part of moral motivation, through moral education and training, to build a world where moral atrocities instead of being generated through unruly impulses, are actually rendered impossible because of the same feelings and emotions. Further, the extent of moral depravity in modernity may, as a matter of fact, be proportionate to the fact that human desire and inclination is no longer part of human goodness through love and intimate mutuality. Enlightenment morality, with Kant and after Kant, then suffers from this serious lacuna in understanding human goodness without incorporating elements, which make humans truly good.

Notes

1. Immanuel Kant, *Groundwork of the Metaphysics of Morals*, (H.J. Paton trans.), Hutchison,1958.
2. Immanuel Kant, *Critique of Practical Reason*, (T.K. Abbott trans.), London, 1909.
3. Kant, *Groundwork of the Metaphysics of Morals*.
4. Ibid.
5. Ibid.
6. Aristotle, *Nichomachean Ethics* (trans. J.A.K. Thomson), Penguin, Harmondsworth, 1953.
7. Ibid.
8. Ibid.
9. Aristotle, *Eudemian Ethics*, in *The Complete Works of Aristotle: The Revised Oxford Translation*, J. Barnes (ed.), 2 volumes, Princeton, New Jersey, 1984.
10. Aristotle, *Nichomachean Ethics*.
11. Immanuel Kant, *Lectures on Ethics*, (Louis Infield trans.), Harper & Row Inc., New York, 1963.
12. Aristotle, *Nichomachean Ethics*.
13. Immanuel Kant, *Lectures on Ethics*.
14. Ibid.
15. Ibid.
16. Ibid.
17. Ibid.
18. Ibid.
19. Ibid.
20. Ibid.
21. Ibid.
22. Aristotle, *Nichomachean Ethics*.
23. Ibid.
24. Ibid.
25. Ibid.
26. Ibid.
27. Ibid.
28. Aristotle, *Magna Moralia*, as quoted in, Martha C. Nussbaum, *The Fragility of Goodness: Luck and Ethics in Greek Tragedy and Philosophy*, Cambridge University Press, 1986.
29. Nussbaum, *The Fragility Of Goodness*.
30. Ibid.
31. Ibid.
32. D. Hume, *A Treatise of Human Nature*, Volume1, J.M. Dent & Sons Ltd, London, 1956.
33. Paul Gilbert, *Human Relationships*, Basil Blackwell Ltd, London, 1991.

From Kant's Methodology of Pure Practical Reason to a Novel Ethical Education

Hülya Yetişken

Kant's Doctrine of Method on Ethical Education

According to Kant, the primary goal of practical philosophy is to search for the 'grounds determining the will'.[1] He states that the reason for this search should be the following question: 'Is pure reason sufficient of itself to determine the will, or is it only as empirically conditioned that it can do so?'[2] In terms of the derivation of concepts and principles of morality, when the grounds determining the will are concerned, he argues that

...every empirical element is not only quite incapable of being an aid to the principle of morality, but is even highly prejudicial to the purity of morals, for the proper and inestimable worth of an absolutely good will consists just in this, that the principle of action is free from all influence of contingent grounds, which alone experience can furnish.[3]

The reason why all the doctrines of virtue have been misleading until now is the derivation of these principles and concepts from empirically conditioned reason and not from pure practical reason. These doctrines make us embrace a cloud instead of Juno, in Kant's words. He illustrates the impasse of the views on morality and doctrines of virtue in his time in the following way:

We need only look at the attempts of moralists in that favourite fashion, and we shall find at one time the special constitution of human nature (including, however, the idea of a rational nature generally), at one time perfection, at another happiness, here moral sense, there fear of God, a little of this, and a little of that, in marvelous mixture...[4]

Then he emphasizes the importance and necessity of deducing morality and virtue as an idea from pure practical reason, since

to behold virtue in her proper form is nothing else but to contemplate morality stripped of all admixture of sensible things and of every spurious ornament of reward or self-love. How much she then eclipses everything else that appears charming to the affections, every one may readily perceive with the least exertion of this reason, if it be not wholly spoiled for abstraction.[5]

At this point, the significance of the critique of practical reason could be better understood. Kant emphasizes: '(T)he critique... of practical reason as such has the obligation to prevent the empirically conditioned reason from presuming to be the only ground of determination of the will'.[6] Furthermore, he adds that it is the objective of philosophy 'to examine the idea and the principles of a possible *pure* will...'.[7] This examination aims at showing the reality of the concept of 'freedom' that constitutes the keystone of Kantian philosophy. As it is known, according to Kant 'freedom' is a problematic concept, whose objective reality is denied by theoretical reason, which is led to an antinomy while trying to demonstrate its existence as well as its non-existence. It is the purpose of moral philosophy to demonstrate the reality of freedom in its practical use—in ethics—which is a different use of pure reason. This amounts to deriving 'moral law' from pure practical reason, independently from all experience, and to showing that 'free will', that is, a will necessarily determined by 'moral law', is possible.[8] According to Kant, neither moral law nor the concept of freedom in its purity and genuineness could be found outside of pure philosophy.[9]

Hence, according to Kant, a moral philosophy that deserves to be called philosophy should consist of pure knowledge, because

...it is clear that all moral conceptions have their seat and origin completely *a priori* in the reason, ...that they cannot be obtained by abstraction from any empirical, and therefore merely contingent knowledge, ...but it is also of the greatest practical importance to derive these notions and laws from pure reason, to present them pure and unmixed, and even to determine the compass of this practical or pure rational knowledge...[10]

At this point, we can ask: What was the ultimate goal of Kant's moral philosophy? Was it limited to the derivation of moral principles from pure practical reason? In other words, wasn't he interested in the possibilities of application in practice of these principles and concepts that he derived from his moral philosophy, that is, in the life of individuals? No doubt, he carefully thought about and examined these issues as well. Yet according to him, a pure philosophy that is totally independent from experience is a *sine qua non* condition, both for judgement and for a firmly grounded ethical education:

...For its application to man, morality has need of anthropology, yet, in the first instance, we must treat it independently as pure philosophy...knowing well that unless we are in possession of this, it would not only be vain to determine the moral element of duty in right actions for purposes of speculative criticism, but it would be impossible to base morals on their genuine principles, even for common practical purposes, especially of moral instruction...[11]

It could be claimed that Kant was never interested in deriving pure principles that could not determine the will of individuals in action. As a matter of fact, after his formulation of the 'practical imperative', he remarks: 'We will now inquire whether this can be practically carried out'.[12] He tried to show what kind of possible conflictual situations could emerge when viewed from the perspective of this pure principle by using examples of free will in the context of specific situations in real-life conditions.

Kant mentions the following on the place and the function of experience in the area of morality:

...Not only moral laws with their principles essentially distinguished from every other kind of practical knowledge in which there is anything empirical, but all moral philosophy rests wholly on its pure part. ...No doubt these laws require a judgement sharpened by experience, in order, on the one hand, to distinguish in what cases they are applicable, and on the other, to procure for them access to the will of the man, and effectual influence on conduct; since man is acted on by so many inclinations that, though capable of the idea of a practical pure reason, he is not so easily able to make it effective *in concreto* in his life.[13]

At this point, the place and significance of Kant's 'Methodology of Pure Practical Reason' in his moral philosophy becomes obvious. Yet the reason why he gave such an importance to the application of this method in ethical education and training could not be understood independently from his anthropology. Because, a pure will can be assumed for the human being, who is a finite rational being; in other words, because the possibility of determination of the will by rational grounds of pure reason can be accepted. However, due to the nature of the human being, who is stimulated by needs and the senses, these pure practical grounds do not necessarily determine the will of the human being. Kant says the following in connection with this issue.

...If the will does not *in itself* completely accord with reason (which is actually the case with men), then the actions, which objectively are recognized as necessary, are subjectively contingent and the determination of such a will according to objective laws is obligation...[14]

Hence, the function of the 'Methodology of Pure Practical Reason' is related to how objectively practical reason could be subjectively practical. Kant articulates what he means by this methodology as follows.

...We understand by methodology of pure practical reason the way in which we can secure to the laws of pure practical reason access to the human mind and an influence on its maxims. That is to say, it is the way we can make objectively practical reason also subjectively practical.[15]

Kant's doctrine of the method of pure practical reason is connected to the method of education. This education aims at sharpening the judgement of individuals, and especially of young ones, through experience, and to develop 'the method of founding and cultivating moral dispositions,'[16] as well as directing their attention to 'the respect for ourselves in the consciousness of our freedom'.[17] It also aims at providing a will that is in accord with the pure moral law and 'to make sure of the unending process of its maxims towards this model and of the constancy of the finite rational being in making continuous progress'.[18]

In the general framework of his methodology, Kant summarizes the way to be followed in order to become aware of the principles of various possibilities of action, as follows.

The method therefore takes the following course. The first step is to make judging according to moral laws a natural occupation which accompanies our own free actions as well as our observations of those of others, and to make it, as it were, a habit. We must sharpen these judgements by first asking whether the action is objectively in accordance with moral law, and if so, with which one; by this, heed to the law that gives only a *principle* of obligation is distinguished from one which is in fact obligatory... This teaches how to distinguish between the different duties which come together in an action.

The second point to which attention must be directed is the question as to whether the action is done (subjectively) for the sake of moral law, and thus not only is morally correct as a deed, but also has moral worth as a disposition because of the maxim from which it was done.[19]

In the course of this education, Kant refers to the importance of using examples which, by providing the opportunity to compare the content and the value of various actions, show the 'feasibility of what the law commands'[20] and 'the distinctive mark of pure virtue'.[21] As a preliminary preparation, he supplies examples from a poem and from a biographical narrative that he selects deliberately from a philosophical perspective. On this point, he says:

I do not know why the educators of youth have not long since made use of this propensity of reason to enter with pleasure upon the most subtle examination of practical questions put to the young, and why, after laying the foundation in a purely moral catechism, they have not searched through biographies of ancient and modern times with the purpose of having examples at hand of the duties they lay down, so that, by comparing similar actions under various circumstances, they could begin to exercise the moral judgement of their pupils in marking the greater or lesser moral significance of the actions. They would find that even very young people, who are not ready for speculation of other kinds, would soon become very acute and not a little interested, since they would feel the progress of their power of judgement.[22]

In connection with the function of such an education and training, he mentions the following:

Now there is no doubt that this exercise and the consciousness of cultivation of our reason which judges concerning the practical must gradually produce a certain interest in its own law and thus in morally good actions. For we ultimately take a liking to the observation, which makes us feel that our powers of knowledge are extended...[23]

Kant's doctrine of method could be considered as an initial sketch of an original ethical education. He himself remarks that he was contended with a preliminary delineation of this method. As far as the application and the results of this method are concerned, he states: '(F)or since this method has never yet been widely used, experience can tell us nothing of its results...'[24]

Kuçuradi's Method of Philosophical–Ethical Education

It could be argued that Ioanna Kuçuradi in her *Ethics,* 200 years after Kant, not only developed this method of ethical education sketched out by Kant, but also put this developed method into practice through her ethics and what she calls 'the philosophical-ethical education of human rights'. So far as I know and I was able to inquire, Kuçuradi's view is the first, and perhaps the only one, which puts in connection philosophical knowledge related to ethical value problems with concrete examples of the same problems that we find in works of art. In this way, she integrates philosophical knowledge with the knowledge of possibilities of experience and action, which works of art show us together with their ethical background.

As far as the sources of the knowledge of ethically right evaluation, ethical action and the possibilities of experience and action are concerned, Kuçuradi states:

The source from which we acquire this knowledge is certain persons in their interpersonal relations—persons who either in real life or in works of art carry out valuable actions. Their actions, though unique, make us see the ethical potentialities of the human being, which appear as ethical characteristics of those persons and thus provide us with the knowledge of the ethical human potentialities actualized by individuals, i.e., the knowledge of possibilities of experience and action from an ethical perspective.[25]

The curriculum of the Philosophy Department at the Hacettepe University, founded by Ioanna Kuçuradi in 1969, encompasses courses such as 'Philosophy of Value', 'Ethics', and 'Philosophical Problems in Works of Art', which are taught in the light of the above-mentioned philosophical approach. Particularly in the course entitled 'Philosophical Problems in Works of Art', anthropological, axiological and ethical problems we are faced with in everyday life, are studied on the basis of examples selected from works of art.

This educational method, which Kuçuradi applies also to the education of students in areas other than philosophy, including human rights education, is also a pioneering method of ethical education in various professions, such as medicine, public administration, and others. The ultimate goal of this education is 'to help the students... to reflect on problems of their profession or job, from a philosophical-ethical viewpoint'.[26]

One of the objectives of this education is to provide a comprehensive philosophical knowledge on the problems of ethics. Another objective is to equip students with the knowledge of possibilities of ethical experience and action, by shedding strong light on ethical value problems, which they could encounter in their relations with other persons in their private and professional lives.

The acquisition of this theoretical/philosophical knowledge also enables the students to make distinctions among concepts usually confused in daily life—among their content, extension and boundaries—that were not perceived before.

The method of transmitting this theoretical knowledge is the Socratic method. It consists in answering questions by questions, so that the student himself or herself can grasp the differences between concepts and conceive their objective correlatives.

What is novel and original in this type of ethical education is the way that it links theoretical philosophical knowledge to real-life practices, thanks to which the students are equipped with knowledge of possibilities of experience and action. Yet, theoretical knowledge, though indispensable for accomplishing the aims of this type of education, is not sufficient. Knowledge of the possibilities of *ethical* experience and action is also necessary so that the students can acquire the consciousness of being *human* beings and become able to find out what they should do in most of the situations in which they have to act—that is, to be able to find out the implications of this consciousness in each real situation in life or while performing their professions.

How could the student, according to this novel method of ethical education, acquire knowledge of the possibilities of experience and action? This could be achieved by reflection and discussion on the basis of philosophical value knowledge, of cases selected from daily life and of experiences and actions exposed in literary and other works; and by comparing and evaluating different possibilities of action in a given situation, on the basis of Kuçuradi's view on 'right evaluation,' that is, by exercising students in evaluation. As Kuçuradi states, the main aim of such exercises is 'to help students see the difference among modes of evaluations—those which can lead to the knowledge of the value of the evaluated object and those which cannot'.[27]

This method of education, which I tried to summarize here, aims at developing the ethical sensitivity and ethical value consciousness of the students and their capacity to make ethically right evaluations. It makes it possible for the students to realize the consequences of looking at the others only as a means and of evaluating by using prevailing value judgements, that is, to realize how they cause damage to human dignity and to ethical values. This is why this method of education has proved particularly fruitful in the education of human rights. Furthermore, it makes it possible for the students to become aware of the fact that despite our good intentions we can cause damage to values by evaluating and acting only in accordance with norms, that is, without taking into account the specificity of the concrete situation—sometimes even by acting according to norms deduced from the knowledge of the value of the human being. As Kuçuradi puts it, this method also intends to help the students to become aware '...of the fact that we can force people to act according to norms, but we cannot force them to look at the other as an end (and not as a means) and act accordingly. For the latter each of us has to settle accounts with himself or herself as early as possible'.[28]

To conclude, it could be claimed that this particular method of ethical education initiated by Kuçuradi and applied under her leadership, is an originally developed form of the ethical education that was initially sketched by Kant 200 years ago.

Notes

1. Immanuel Kant, *Critique of Practical Reason*, (Lewis White Beck trans.), Macmillan Publishing Company, New York, 1993, p. 15.
2. Ibid.
3. Immanuel Kant, *Fundamental Principles of the Metaphysics of Morals*, (T. K. Abbot trans.), Prometheus Books, New York, 1998, p. 54.
4. Ibid., p. 37.
5. Ibid., p. 55.
6. Kant, *Critique of Practical Reason*, p. 16.
7. Kant, *Fundamental Principles*, p. 13.
8. Hulya Yetişken, 'Kuçuradi's Ethical View in Relation to Kant's Philosophy', *Frankofoni/Revue d'études et recherches francophones* 17, Ankara, 2005, p. 205.
9. Kant, *Fundamental Principles*, p. 12.
10. Ibid., pp. 38–9.
11. Ibid., p. 39.
12. Ibid., p. 58.
13. Ibid., p. 12.
14. Ibid., p. 40.
15. Kant, *Critique of Practical Reason*, p. 157.
16. Ibid., p. 159.
17. Ibid., p. 167.
18. Ibid., p. 33.
19. Ibid., p. 166.
20. Kant, *Fundamental Principles*, p. 36.
21. Kant, *Critique of Practical Reason*, p. 161.
22. Ibid., p. 160.
23. Ibid., p. 166.
24. Ibid., p. 159.
25. Ioanna Kuçuradi, *Ethics*, 3rd edn, Ankara, 1999, p. 539.
26. Ioanna Kuçuradi, 'Teaching Philosophy to Students of Other Disciplines', *Socrates for Everybody: Teaching Philosophy to Non Philosophers*, J. Ferrari, P. Kemp, D. Evans, and N. Robinet-Bruyére (eds), Paris, 2003, p. 10.
27. Ibid., p. 11.
28. Ibid., p. 12.

Respect for Morality and Value Judgement

From Kant to Neo-Kantianism

Xie Dikun

'Two things fill my heart with constantly renewed and gripping wonder and awe, the more often and more intently my thought focuses on them: the starry heaven overhead and the moral principle within.'[1]

This is a sentence from Kant's *Critique of Practical Reason* and also the inscription on his tombstone. As we commemorate the 200th anniversary of the death of Kant and the influence of his ethics on the modern world, it is all the more important to interpret this sentence anew and reconsider a thinker who 'looks back upon the great ancients and leads the way to the coming century.'

I

What is philosophy? This is indeed a question very difficult to answer. Most philosophers nevertheless share the opinion that philosophy is a form of knowledge that inquires into the secrets of the cosmos and the meaning of life. It is no small thing to explore the cosmos. Many conjectures and hypotheses concerning the invisible heavens originated with the ancient philosophers. As knowledge and the classification of disciplines progressed, this task was gradually assigned to the natural sciences. Although the young Kant made an important contribution to natural science with his charming musings on the nature of the cosmos, the Kant of the

Critiques made the human being the cornerstone of his inquiries. Reduced to a summary formula, in his three great *Critiques* Kant sought to answer three questions: first, what can I know; second, what should I do and third, what should I hope for. These three questions, in turn, can be summarized in one key question, namely, 'What is a human being?' In this way, the sense and meaning of Kant's philosophy is very clear, namely, to bring the human being to rule himself, to have a clear conscience, and to be his own master. For this reason, 'the human being will only recognize his full potential if he philosophizes'.[2]

'To bring the human being to recognize his own full potential' is easy to say, but difficult to do. In the first place human relationships must be considered, and these are the subject matter of ethics. In Kant, moral philosophy involves practical reason, and practical reason is placed above pure reason because for him problems that pure reason cannot solve are open to solution through practical reason. This process is based on the three postulates of practical reason, namely, *the freedom of the will*, *the existence of God* and *the immortality of the soul*. In this way reasonable beings can set up laws for themselves and transform the norms of their good will into general legal principles.

The ethics of Kant is built precisely on *the freedom of the will*. According to Kant, moral philosophy has as its goal *the highest good*. By *the highest good* it is meant that the human being freely follows moral law on the basis of free will, out of duty or responsibility. Such actions are *the highest good*, because they are absolute and without conditions, differing from the instinct for self-preservation or sensual pleasures, and having nothing to do with inclinations, wishes, necessities, interests or results; they serve only the fulfilment of moral law. Such a moral law Kant summarizes thus: 'Always act in such a way that the principle of your action can serve as a universal law.'[3] This is Kant's *categorical imperative* or *absolute imperative*. But without freedom of the will this imperative can be neither 'categorical' nor 'absolute', because only the subject can set up laws for himself, fulfil his silent commands, and practise genuine self-discipline, not yielding to any outside coercion or interests; in this way *the highest good* can be realized. In Kant's view such a moral self-discipline is clearly majestic. Precisely because the living, sensitive human being possesses such a pure moral law can he awaken his reverence towards moral duties as well as perceive our human worth and elevation that transcends the material. The *immortality of the soul* and *the existence of God* are essential conditions for the realization of moral law, or more exactly stated, they are conditions for the practical application of moral concepts. To be sure Kant repeatedly stresses that the moral law 'itself needs no justifying grounds'[4] and 'it (morality) in no way requires (so far as either the will, as objective, or ability is concerned) religion but is by virtue of pure practical reason self-sufficient'.[5] Nevertheless, Kant perceives clearly that, first of all, complete agreement between will and moral law is a kind of holiness. A limited rational being can never achieve such holiness in this life, but only when he enters on an ever-lasting existence is it possible for him to fulfil this eternal, unattainable task; hence the *immortality of the soul* has to be postulated. Second, a human being living in this world always has an inclination to seek happiness, whereas complete conformity between the quest for happiness and non-self-interested virtue makes it necessary to find the foundation of the inevitable connection between the two. 'Therefore the highest good in the world is possible only so far as we assume the highest good of nature: a causality commensurate with moral sensibility.'[6] It is obvious that we must assume the omnipotent, supreme and most beneficent God. Exactly therein lies the paradox of Kant's philosophy. On one hand, he emphasizes the simplicity of moral law and, on the other, he must nevertheless postulate the *immortality of the soul* and the *existence of God* in order to realize moral law in practice. On the one hand, moral law does not here serve 'immortality' and 'God;' rather, 'immortality' and 'God' are there in order to make moral law possible. On the other hand, religion and morality also achieve a new connection precisely here; as Kant puts it, that 'morality necessarily leads to religion'.

Here we should note that the concept of so-called practical reason in Kant is the symptom of an object, which can appear through freedom. This signifies nothing other than that practice means everything which can come to pass through freedom. Not everything which can happen is good, however; it can also be evil. In this light the question arises: where does the consciousness of moral law originate? To this Kant answers: 'Because we attend to the necessity which reason prescribes and to the abstraction from all empirical conditions to which it directs us.'[7] Here Kant shows us clearly not only that reason entrusts us with its concept of good before the practical law, but he also shows us that moral law is for him a moral form without any empirical factors.

In fact, in this inborn moral form is implied the respect of the practising subject for morality. This is the main reason why freedom can have positive value in the domain of practice and, indeed, why moral law can be realized. Kant is opposed to moral fanaticism, and he is also opposed to unnecessary religious rituals. Nevertheless he clearly recognizes in practical reason the necessity of moral respect. In Kant moral respect means not general moral feelings in the normal sense, but a moral motif introduced into the field of practice through reason, indeed morality itself, which is seen subjectively as an incentive. This type of moral respect indeed does not establish a foundation for moral law, neither can one pronounce moral Judgements with it. Nevertheless it constitutes the incentive to make this moral law into a general norm. The 'respect for moral law is thus the sole and at the same time indubitable moral motive, inasmuch as this feeling is not directed to any other object, and on this basis alone'.[8] Moral law is an unavoidable duty for the will of a reasonable being precisely because of this moral respect, an elevated, holy mission and a maxim that defines the actions of a reasonable being. It is precisely because of this moral respect that free will is able to bring about positive results in the field of the practical, and not the contrary. Precisely because of this moral respect, moral philosophy and religion are joined and ultimately transformed into moral religion.

II

Kant's formalistic moral philosophy has had important influences on Western philosophy in early modern and modern times. It also has roused serious debate among philosophers of recent times. Summarizing and analysing their disputes is not only indispensable for a correct understanding and evaluation of Kant's moral philosophy, but also valuable in understanding the evolution of Western moral philosophy.

Within classical German philosophy, it was Fichte, the direct follower of Kant, who further developed Kant's ethical thought. As he clearly says in his 1798 article written during his time in Jena, 'Concerning the Foundation of our Belief in a Divine World Governance,' a direct and intrinsic connection exists between moral decisions of the will and religious belief, and belief stems from moral decisions. If a person is aware of his moral duty, in his heart he will surely make his own a belief in a moral order. For this reason 'the living and functioning moral order is itself God'.[9] Thus, for Fichte, morality and religion are the same thing; the former is shown as action, while the latter finds its expression in belief. Actually this moral-religious concept of Fichte is not only the most fundamental development of Kant's ethics, but is even more radical than Kant. It was precisely for this reason that apostles of moral feudalism drove Fichte out of the academic community of Jena in 1799.

In contrast, Schelling, another representative of German classical philosophy, does not agree with Kant's ethics. Instead, he attempts to solve moral-ethical questions through discussion of the question of freedom. In 'Philosophical Inquiries into the Nature of Human Freedom and Its Associated Circumstances', Schelling points out that Kant's moral theory severs the connections between theoretical and practical philosophy. To be sure, Kant has established the concept of the highest moral goods being based on formal freedom. In Kant, however, there is only formal, not actual, freedom. Although living, real freedom is the highest good in Kant, it is taken fundamentally as formal and not real.

Schelling represents the view that the human being is a free and consciously acting being who can make decisions himself.

Since both good and evil deeds find the source of their actions in human beings themselves, these are exactly the possibilities and necessities of the realization of good and evil in reality. It would not only be unrealistic, but would also hinder the solution of problems to only recognize good and not consider evil. In Schelling's view, evil is not only desire and animalistic. He points out that evil is both the condition for negation and the condition for the revelation of God. Through victory over evil, God reveals his omnipotence and his highest good, while the human being, as God's creation, will ultimately turn his back on evil and move towards good. This insight of Schelling is clearly religiously coloured. What he actually wishes to show us is that although evil stems from human beings themselves, it can certainly be overcome through rational resolution. From this we can conclude that it is our moral orientation to distinguish between good and evil, to unmask the nature of evil and to self-consciously heighten our moral awareness; in this way, each of us is answerable for his actions. Hegel is inspired by this concept of Schelling's and fully recognizes the positive meaning of evil in the process of humanity's development.[10]

Among the classical German philosophers, it is Hegel who makes the most serious and keenest criticism of Kant's moral philosophy. Like Schelling, Hegel maintains that the greatest deficiency in Kant's moral philosophy lies in its excessive formalism as well as in the lack of concrete, understandable content. Practical reason should be concrete and not provide solely abstract norms. No concrete content or postulates can be acquired from Kant's moral law except for the formal identity of individual will. Concerning this Hegel says ironically: 'This is the deficiency of the Kantian-Fichtian principle: it is formal. Cold duty remains the last undigested morsel in the stomach, the revelation given to reason.'[11] Hegel's solution is different from that of Schelling. He opts for a strict distinction between morality and ethics. For him, morality is the reversion of the will to itself and something purely spiritual. For this reason morality is simply subjective and assumes no binding duty towards family, society and state. Ethics, by contrast, is social, and social ethics is the union of the subject with the object in the objective spiritual sphere and the objective development of moral concepts. In Hegel, morality takes on actual existence, only when it develops beyond itself into social ethics. For this reason good is more than conscience; the good should also be an object of will and that with which the subject—relying on its own actions—makes and erects the objective world. With this Hegel goes from subjective morality to objective ethics and realizes his ethical system in three parts: family, civic society and state. It is notable that although Hegel's ethics seems to go beyond Kant, in fact his critique confounds the differences between general moral law and concrete, realistic claims. Hegel makes the kingdom of Prussia into a paradigm for the moral ethics of the whole world precisely because he draws excessively on empirical and real factors. Exactly this proves that Hegel's ideology not only lacks the pure and critical aspects of Kant, but also more easily yields to real, existing authorities.

In the second half of the nineteenth century, the moral philosophy of Kant received an even greater challenge. The chief representatives of this challenge are Schopenhauer and Nietzsche. The analysis and critique of the moral philosophy of Kant by Schopenhauer are pregnant and incisive. First, like Hegel, Schopenhauer also makes the claim that concrete contents are lacking in Kant's moral philosophy, but his critique is even sharper. For Schopenhauer, morality is made up of human beings' practical actions. If one wishes to put moral law into practice, there must be preliminary catalyzing factors; human beings must be brought to perceive and recognize these factors automatically under all circumstances so that a positive result will be obtained. Kant's moral law is nevertheless completely based on a non-circumstantial and entirely abstract concept; it lacks understandability, offers no support and leaves one untouched. 'Of the substance of this law, therefore, nothing remains for him except its own form.'[12] Second, Schopenhauer sees keenly that one of the main flaws in Kant's moral philosophy is that the moral law which is to be represented is seen as an actually occurring event, and then Kant's philosophy comes to the position that this assumption possesses complete and absolute necessity. Thus this assumption becomes a basis and even the foundation of his whole system, so that Kant's moral philosophy is false from the very beginning. Schopenhauer speaks ironically of Kant's law of practical reason and describes it as the Delphic temple: all divine instructions are supposed to come from its dark hall, but cannot be obeyed! Third, through the observation of the history of moral philosophy Schopenhauer comes to the view that the origin of moral Judgements, prohibitions, and prescriptions has its roots in the realm of practical reason and, above all, cannot be separated from religion. Kant's postulation of the moral law as pure reason and his disconnection of concepts such as duty and responsibility from their history and their theological contents therefore neither correspond with historical facts nor have realistic meaning.

In turn, it was left to Schopenhauer's follower Nietzsche to overturn the entire tradition of western culture. Kant's moral philosophy is already negated in the very formula of the *re-evaluation of all values*. Nietzsche's critique is ironic. He holds that Kant with his postulates of the existence of God and the immortality of the soul is trying to substantiate his own moral law. This is like a parson saying to a farmwoman who has left potatoes on a field: 'You may not leave any potatoes on a stranger's field, otherwise you will be punished by God and will never enter the kingdom of heaven.' From this it is obvious that Kant's *categorical imperative* is not absolute, and also his freedom of the will is not fully free; there is no essential difference between Kant's moral law and the hypocrisy of moral theology. Nietzsche's critique is biting, and crucial for correctly understanding Kant's moral philosophy. Nevertheless there is more destruction in Nietzsche than construction. He expounds *the death of God*, but can only fantasize about a 'Titan' like Napoleon, and is unable to express a correct moral concept in rational language. He elevates the individual's will to live and ignores the social meaning of the existence of human beings; he has no sense of the rational good. For this reason, Nietzsche's theory is destructive for all society.[13]

III

As the nineteenth century came to an end, no more criticism of Kant was heard, but rather the rallying cry 'back to Kant'. This cry came from the school of Neo-Kantianism, which was most influential among Western philosophers at the end of the nineteenth and beginning of the twentieth century, and was the expression of the new insight of people of that time into the philosophy of Kant. In contrast to Nietzsche who rejected the Western cultural tradition, Neo-Kantianism, under the banner of 'back to Kant', critically advanced and further developed Kant's thought. The Southwest German school (also called the 'Freiburg School' or the 'Baden School'), represented by W. Windelband (1846–1915), recognizes not only the universal and eternal meaning of Kant's moral philosophy but also connects Kant's moral ideal with the human perception of truth, draws absolute claims of value from morality, and attempts to guide humans' moral judgement.

Windelband, the leader of the Southwest German School, accepts Kant's theoretical structure of the three critiques. He is of the view that with the three categories of thought, will and perception, Kant lends expression to knowledge of and prescriptions for humanity, which is precisely the most important subject of philosophy—the true, the good, and the beautiful form the embodiment of the world-orientation of humanity. Generally acceptable standards of value, nevertheless, stem from human history, and exactly here is the doubtful point for people of the nineteenth century. When Nietzsche claimed the *revaluation of all values*, he made the question of value the core of philosophy. Windelband recognizes that 'philosophy is never derived from value claims, but is often strongly influenced by them only in consciousness'.[14] However, if value claims often influence people, they necessarily stand in close relationship to human life. Philosophy is by no means a concrete science, which limits its knowledge to a certain area; on the contrary, its foundational principles touch all facets of human life. Philosophy may and must inquire into and know all categories and fields connected to human life. Exactly in this sense Windelband says: 'Philosophy always holds that it has the right and the means to investigate this world, going beyond all not yet fully understood phenomena to penetrate their innermost regions. At the same time value Judgement is also the living reality of human intelligence.'[15] The pre-eminence of value means not merely that value Judgement must be regarded as the recognition of the deepest level of human intelligence, but on the contrary, that intellectual values must be granted special importance and are natural in the sense that everyone has these values and that they are valid for all humanity, whence the moral principle, to which the aesthetic principle and formal logic belong. Here is an extract from Windelband: 'Philosophy has its own sphere and its own task with regard to those eternal and inherently worthy values which form the ground plan of all functions of culture and the backbone of all particular experiences of value. But philosophy will describe and explain these only in order to account for their validity: it does not treat them as facts but as norms. For this reason philosophy will have to develop its task as a kind of legislation, not as arbitrary, dictatorial law but as the law of reason, which philosophy finds and understands.'[16] Obviously Windelband has adopted the idea that *the validity of value is pre-eminent* put forward by his teacher Lotze (1817–1881). That is, close connections exist between values and human beings, and for this reason values and validity must be brought into relationship. Windelband further developed and emphasized this idea: *The meaning of value consists in validity.* In particular we must concentrate on the validity of value in the area of moral philosophy and give attention to the moral meaning of the validity of values. The core of Windelband's philosophy of value is the emphasis on the moral-normative meaning of value. In his analysis of different claims of value in the nineteenth century, he says: 'All of these perspectives on life, whose typical extremes are here compared with one another, indeed vary in many ways with regard to the recognition and gradation of individual values and objects of the will, but they nevertheless generally agree in recognizing the dominant moral code and especially its altruistic keystone.'[17] However different our understandings and views of value—formal and substantial, subjective and objective, reasonable and emotional for Windelband values have primarily a moral meaning; ethically, they are ultimately related to humanity and the positive moral formation of humanity. The fact that in explaining ideas of value the relationships between individuals and between individuals and society are emphasized still more consciously and clearly than before, constitutes the foundation and the criterion for all valuations. Concerning the normative role of values, Windelband emphasizes its psychic and ideal nature. That is, only if values are understood as reasonable legislation can values be effective as norms. Here Windelband explains categorically that norms fulfil a double function. First, they form the criterion for the evaluation of the condition of consciousness (first and foremost as regards the truthfulness of the conditions of consciousness); second, they are norms that must be observed in order to attain this or that object. Insofar as the consciousness of norms is the criterion for human empirical thought and an unattainable object of ordinary powers of thought, consciousness of norms is elevated over the accidental process of human empirical thought. In order to avoid falling into the swamp of radical psychologism and subjectivism, Windelband emphasizes that ideas continually appear and disappear in human consciousness, and that in examining the psyche philosophy already has to make a 'generally valid' evaluation. Agreeing or disagreeing with many ideas, considering them true or false, ought not to be grounded in personal satisfaction or dissatisfaction, but rather in 'norms' with general validity. Finally Windelband still holds to homogeneous, generally valid representations of value and fully agrees in this regard with Kant's previously developed generally valid moral law.

Windelband's thought deeply influenced the entire Southwest German School. His follower B. Bauch (1827–1942) is of the opinion that Windelband's idea that *the meaning of value comes from validity* should be developed into the idea that *validity is the presupposition of existence*, since human existence and validity stand in such close relationship. Furthermore, Bauch makes the analysis that this maxim can be extended to 'truth is the condition of being', since 'values touch the category of truth'.[18] Bauch accepted Cohen's ideology of the close connection between logic and value and, based on that, made the concept of value into one of the three great factors alongside truth and reality. Bauch's argument is: all valid Judgements made on the basis of facts rest on the validity connected with logical Judgement; in other words, logical Judgement is the basis of the validity of values. From this we can conclude that the worth of knowledge has validity as its a priori foundation. At this level, it presents itself as pure value. Since all thought that has value is connected with this a priori basis, it possesses value as truth. Nevertheless, since this pure value does not exist in reality but rather in validity, these values as objective validity are dissolved in the system of validity. On this basis we should recognize the objective validity of values throughout the fields of ethics, religion, art and so forth, even though these fields at first sight seem to be subjective. With this formulation Bauch gave a special truth value to cultural phenomena and, unlike the positivists of his era, did not solely consider the role of science and technology. Bauch's ideology would later be interpreted as 'the objectification of the spirit' and has similarities to the objective spirit of Hegel.

Following the discussion of the general validity of values, Bauch concentrates on the moral meaning of values. For him, if the nature of the validity of values is truly treasured, a fact must be recognized: 'Value presents itself in a relationship with reality as a problem which, in order to be an actual problem, must have a super-subjective value-content, but it can only have this content because value is simply objectively valid, because ethical value encompasses the whole world.'[19] Earlier it was already noted that Bauch closely connected values with truth. Now, however, he claims that ethical values contain all the contents of value. So it appears that Bauch actually has equated the moral-ethical meaning of values with the truth-value of values, and thereby has brought the moral-ethical meaning of values to a new high point. In addition Bauch explains that he means only a single value-whole and is simply emphasizing the moral or truth-value of values on different planes. In the emphasis on ethical values, moral duties which are absolutely to be performed are pre-eminently stressed, while the emphasis on truth chiefly concerns possibilities and the reality of knowledge. It is obvious that both Windelband and Bauch stress the absolute value of morality on the basis of an extension of Kant's moral-philosophical thought, and attempt to reject relativism in morals and values. But their theories seem in a certain sense to be empty, and so within Neo-Kantianism different ideas about their theories are heard. H. Richert (1863–1936) was the first to claim that for a nation moral ethics is not to be undervalued, that the positive or negative status of a nation is dependent upon its moral level, and that the investigation of the moral-ethical constitution of a nation is a pre-eminent task of value Judgement. The value claims of H. Richert must consequently place the state in the centre and be strongly coloured politically, so that ultimately his moral ideology is degraded to nationalistic theory. The critique of L. Nelson (1882–1927) differs in turn from Richert's. Concerning value Judgement in the practical field in Kant's sense, he argues that attention needs to be given to the interpersonal relationships of real life and especially to people's actual interests. The foundation of our moral Judgement therefore lies in the observation of whether the motives of human action are morally derived, while moral law in his eyes is a *rule which limits our positive purpose*. In Nelson, it is permissible to speak of moral ethics and therefore concrete, empirical claims, which touch on political economy, law, history, education and politics. At first sight, Nelson's understanding of moral philosophy seems to return to Kant, but would rather more accurately be said to be closer to the ethical ideology of Hegel.

In turn, another representative of Neo-Kantianism, E. Tröltsch (1865–1923), analyses and criticizes value judgement from the perspective of historicism. He maintains that one can detect the problem of the anarchy of values by observing historical questions. Here, a fundamental problem is that value claims are different for each person, while an absolutely valid value system must be unified. Thus there is a tension between different individual values and absolute values; likewise, at the same time a tension exists between absolute values and their concrete, historical manifestations. Here Tröltsch does not follow Cohen in seeing history as an unending process of near rational ideals. For Tröltsch, Cohen's is ultimately only an absolutely rational moral theory, while he himself believes that an absolutely rational moral theory can give rise to no results in historical practice. For him, existence and value, action and sensation, as well as facts and ideal things, belong to strictly divided categories, and express themselves in the process of history. History cannot develop as we might hope in the direction of generally valid values, rather it is a factual process and has its own intrinsic movement. But history is also a reality, and each person will intuitively share in the realistic as well as historical movement. Therefore the foundational elements of history are individual persons and groups of individuals, like tribes, classes, nationalities and states. Through every meaningful activity these foundational elements demonstrate on the one hand their essential character and on the other their own values.[20] In this way, Tröltsch gives history the meaning of world realization; for him the value assessment of the causal sequences developing in the historical process and the historical results that arise therein rests on a value system based on rational norms. With the help of this system one recognizes not only the development of history but also deeply inscribed moral norms. Precisely in this sense Tröltsch says: 'Ethics becomes, as in Schleiermacher, a rule and category book for history.'[21] Clearly Tröltsch wishes to move beyond 'the fixed concept of the thinking substance or the norm-establishing consciousness' in order to realize 'an identity of the ephemeral and eternal spirit while maintaining

finitude and individuality,'[22] in order to thus connect historical reality
with moral ideals. To be sure there are many open questions in
Tröltsch's philosophy of history, for example, how the limitlessness
of history and the limited nature of individuality are connected and
how the explanation of moral ideals can occur without rational
precepts. Nevertheless he has ultimately raised the important
question of how values are connected with historical facts.

The raising of questions such as values, validity, and truth by Neo-
Kantianism against a far-reaching historical background. At the end
of the nineteenth and beginning of the twentieth century, Western
society found itself in the midst of an era of upheavals; traditional
culture, norms and beliefs were called into doubt, social development
lost direction and could not determine the individual. It was precisely
under these conditions that adherents of Neo-Kantianism raised
anew the questions discussed above. To be sure, their views did not
completely coincide. Nevertheless in a certain sense their discussions
clarified the conceptual content of morality, value and truth,
emphasized the absolute worth of the moral concept, and thus
satisfied certain needs and longings of the society of that time. An
important development in Neo-Kantianism is its overcoming, so
far as possible, the connection between economic value as the *original
reification* and value as moral law, in order to realize the *absolute
apotheosis of value* and thus establish the absolutely supreme status of
moral value..[23]

In moving from Kant's moral *categorical imperative* through
Hegel's and Schopenhauer's critique of the 'formalism' of Kant's
conception of morality to the elaborations made by Neo-Kantianism
with respect to self-conscious duty and the development of Kant's
moral philosophy, as well as the emphasis on the absolute value of
morality, history seems to have taken a detour. But when we carefully
observe this period of history and draw experience as well as doctrines
from it, we not only recognize the purity and elevation of Kant's
moral philosophy, but also come to the following conclusion: in
matters of morality and ethics there can be no place for relativism;
instead, people must be brought to respect morality. Only when
such a conception of values becomes part of the self-consciousness
of the majority of people and is connected with our existential order

can we advance spiritual civilization and moral development at the same time as the economic prosperity of our nation.

Notes

1. Immanuel Kant, *Critique of Practical Philosophy*, (Han Shifa trans.), Commercial Press, Beijing, 2000, p. 177.
2. Zheng Xin, *On Kant's Theory*, Commercial Press, Beijing, p. 8.
3. Immanuel Kant, *Critique of Practical Reason*, p. 31.
4. Ibid., p. 50.
5. Immanuel Kant, *Religion Within the Bounds of Pure Reason*, (trans. Li Qiuling), People's University of China Press, Beijing, 2003, p. 1.
6. Kant, *Critique of Practical Reason*, p. 137.
7. Ibid., p. 30.
8. Ibid., p. 85.
9. *Selected Works of Fichte*, Volume III, Commercial Press, Beijing, 1997, p. 391.
10. For elucidations of Schelling and commentary, see Xie Dikun, 'The Absolute and Human Freedom', in *Modern Philosophy*, no. 1, 2004.
11. Hegel, *Lectures on the History of Philosophy*, Volume IV, Commercial Press, Beijing, 1996, p. 291.
12. Schopenhauer, *The Two Fundamental Problems of Ethics*, Commercial Press, Beijing, 1999, p. 163.
13. Adorno, *Problems of Moral Philosophy*, Suhrkamp Verlag, Frankfurt, 1997, p. 178.
14. Windelband, 'Introduction to Philosophy' in *Classic Philosophical Texts of the Twentieth Century*, Fudan University Press, p. 649.
15. Ibid., p. 650.
16. Windelband, *Course in the Philosophy of History*, (Luo Daren trans.), Commercial Press, Beijing, 1993, p. 927.
17. Ibid., p. 919.
18. B. Bauch, *Truth, Value, and Reality*, Felix Meinex, Leipzig, 1923, p. 372.
19. Ibid., p. 472.
20. E. Tröltsch, *Historicism and its Problems*, Tübingen, 1922, p. 665.
21. Ibid., p. 156.
22. Ibid., p. 675.
23. Adorno, *Essays on Social Theory and Methodology*, Suhrkamp, Frankfurt, 1970, p. 239.

SECTION 2

SELF AND AUTONOMY:
ISSUES OF FREEDOM AND SELF-LEGISLATION

The Difficulty of the Subject

Goenawan Mohamad

To commemorate someone's death is to adjourn it graciously. In the case of Immanuel Kant, it means to invite him as our contemporary. This will inevitably engage him in a setting quite different from his time and his Europe. But while a universal Kant can be problematic, one has to assume that truth or untruth cannot choose its own detour.

Today, in a time of murders and repression, Kant is the one who, through long, restless, and complicated search, provided us with a theoretical support for the idea of freedom, and yet he insists that freedom is basically a necessary presupposition of reason. And he adds: there is no way to know it in the realm of phenomena.

So freedom is possible—and yet as precarious as it is simple. Implied in Kant's presupposition of freedom is the idea of a being that is not wholly empirical: a subject that elevates man above himself as a part of the world of sense both in the act of knowing and in the act of following the imperative of the moral law. It is a transcendental subject, *a subject of ends*, which is the origin of rights.

This essay, therefore, is not exactly about Kant. I cannot claim I know his ideas well enough. This essay is about what I see as an interesting shift in philosophical conversations in the last ten years: the subject, a notion pregnant with the issues of freedom and rights, is, as it were, being reinvented.

Invoking Kant's legacy is not unwarranted. With Etienne Balibar we can justly locate the invention of the modern subject in the three *Critiques*. What is also true is that the Kantian *Copernican revolution* was by no means an isolated event.

The word 'subject', as Balibar points out—a play between *subjectum* ('an individual substance or a material substratum for properties') and *subjectus*, which refers to 'subjection' or 'submission'—implies a transformation.[1] The name which meant 'suppression of freedom' became the very name which modern philosophy adopts to think and designate the originary freedom of the human being. And it was not a mere lexical evolution.

As Balibar's thesis describes it, the change took place in the wake of *two historical breaks*. The first is the decline of the ancient world in Europe. The hierarchical social structure of the past, the setting of Aristotlelian model of the *polis* and man, faded away, and 'the figure of *inner* subject' emerged. This subject, as in St Augustine, saw obedience as a business of our inner self. Furthermore, obedience did not signify an inferior stage of humanity; on the contrary, it was 'a superior destination, whether terrestrial or celestial, real or fictitious'. In other words, the outside, the genesis of heteronomy, was no longer crucial.

The second 'break' is the revolutions at the end of the eighteenth century and the beginning of the nineteenth in North America, France, Latin America, and elsewhere: when man (woman would come later) ceased to be *subjectus* and became the subject that is a 'legislator', accountable for the consequences, the implementation and the absence of it, of the Law he had himself made.[2]

This is precisely the setting of Kant's idea of the Enlightenment, typified by the moment when individuals free themselves from a self-incurred dependence or tutelage or *Unmündigkeit*. Since the eighteenth century, the subject as emancipation is both an appeal and a hope.

But as usual, the hope of an era is darkly mirrored on the next. The twentieth was remarkably a self-conscious century, particularly of its own failures. We remember the grim verdict of Adorno's and Horkheimer's *Dialectics of Enlightenment,* written with the traces of pain in the shadow of Auschwitz.[3]

Since then, or parallel to it, in the 'post-existentialist' Europe, the subject has been dissolved into an effect of something else (structure, discourse, history, writing or the semiotic). Otherwise, it has been put under endless scrutiny by *the hermeneutics of suspicion*—or decentred. We know that Foucault has pronounced its imminent demise. Althusser has dismissed it, describing history as a process without a subject. Habermas offers an alternative approach, focusing on discursive *intersubjectivity*.

In short, it was a trend so powerful that it generated diverse resonances in different parts of the world, prompting Joan Copjec, a lamenting Lacanian, to write just before the end of the twentieth century: 'We have, in fact, for a long time now...been dwelling in the graveyard of the subject.'[4]

But no death is a joy forever. Now Copjec herself has come to declare that, from her psychoanalytical perspective, 'the subject discovers itself *in* its very effacement, *in* its own graveyard.'[5] Her words lend support to Žižek's lonely announcemert that 'the specter of the Cartesian subject' is 'haunting Western Academia'.[6] Soon, the beginning of the twenty-first century sees a noticeable *Lacanian shift*—from Kristeva's notion of 'subject-in-process' (with an emphasis on the 'process', that in French, also means 'trial'), to Zuzpancik's reappraisal of Kant's idea of 'subject of freedom'.[7]

It seems that the dismissal of the subject does not have much appeal in this part of the world, especially by theoreticians of the Lacanian persuasion with Eastern European background. A similar reservation is pronounced by theoreticians of *radical democracy*, primarily by Laclau, who started his career as a labour activist in Argentina.[8]

There is also a different resistance to the Western European disillusion with vigorous subjectivity—among Muslim religious revivalists. As I will argue in the later part of this essay, strangely the Muslim revivalist's challenge to the Enlightenment project, like the one proclaimed by Sayyed Qutb, ends up creating a problem just like the *Kantian* Enlightenment did.

At any rate, today there is a sense of uneasiness at 'the end of history,' as philosophers of the status quo name our era. As emancipatory politics is staged as *procedural democracy*, the passion wanes, and to redeem it, a strategic subjecthood is summoned. Meanwhile, the force of a borderless market spreads fears of a sense of meaninglessness, *sans frontieres*. No wonder that the twenty-first century began with a jolt: a body destroyed is a signature of the subject. The suicide bombers, like the people who killed themselves and thousands others in 9/11, believe that self-destruction is a statement of a subject enhanced by faith, of identity exploded by ideology, and of the power of purposeful reason. Or perhaps it is the victim's mimicry of domination.

Another kind of urgency is also noticeable. Tangled in an overpowering social tutelage, one is pressed to construct a vigorous subject to break it through, while at the same time there are legitimate reasons to be wary of the subject's predominance.

This is obviously a perspective coloured by an Indonesian setting. But this is also a perspective that allows us to appreciate the anxiety of subjectivity.

II

The anxiety finds its paradigmatic expression in a poem by Chairil Anwar, a short piece so famous that almost every Indonesian high school kid remembers it. Actually, the poem is about a rejection of *Unmündigkeit*. It is a subject coming out of total social tutelage. Its title is *Aku*:

Kalau sampai waktuku
'Ku mau tak seorang pun 'kan merayu
Tidak juga kau.
Tak perlu sedu sedan itu.
Aku ini binatang jalang, dari kumpulannya terbuang
Biar peluru menembus kulitku
Aku 'kan tetap meradang, menerjang
Luka dan bisa kubawa berlari
Berlari
Hingga hilang pedih peri
Dan aku 'kan lebih tidak perduli
Aku mau hidup seribu tahun lagi

(When my time comes
I want no one to sway me away from it
Not even you.
Lament and weep are pointless
I am a wild beast, after all, cast out from the pack
Bullets sliced my skin

But I will stay furious, ferocious
With venom and wounds
Rushing, rushing on
Until the pain wanes
And I will even be more unperturbed

I want to live another thousand years).

Doubtless, the poem is a defiance against Death and *the pack*, or, in the Lacanian lexicon, *the Big Other*. But the defiance, a gesture of autonomy, has also a trace of melancholy in it, something probably indiscernible in my English rendition of the poem. *Aku* is basically a 'story' of the birth of the subject as an anxiety-ridden event: the 'I' is also an injured self, a body in agony, and yet it desires the infinite to grip and transform its finitude: 'I want to live for another thousand years'.

You can read Chairil's *Aku* as a manifesto of autonomy, or emancipation, with ambivalence. In other words, you can read it as the determination of the subject to resist the other—his body included—and master it.

But another reading is possible: *Aku* speaks of an acute awareness of the irreducible, but destructible, phenomenal self: 'With venom and wounds, rushing...'. On this second reading we can quote Adorno: 'Suffering is objectivity that weighs upon the subject'.[9]

III

I believe it is necessary to refer to Adorno on this matter. He is the one who criticizes what he sees as the Kantian subject, and does so by claiming the need for a *new categorical imperative*, that is, an imperative to arrange thoughts and actions 'so that Auschwitz will not repeat itself'. This implies a look into 'the unbearable physical agony to which individuals are exposed even with individuality about to vanish'.[10]

With such a trajectory, Adorno, I imagine, would appreciate Chairil's *Aku*. The poem is a violent self-portrait of a battered subject who speaks from his autonomous position in pain. The fury, the pierced skin, the wound, and the rushing towards no definite end, constitutes a metaphor of a subject in the 'last epistemological quiver of the somatic element, before that element is totally expelled'.[11]

That somatic element is totally expelled in the prevailing tendency in epistemological reflection—a tendency to reduce objectivity more and more to the subject. Hence the need to reverse it. Adorno's strategy is to put the subject back to the pulses of the earth, to regain the throb of the body, its body. From this perspective, Chairil's *Aku* celebrates 'the dignity of physicality'.

Insisting on *physicality*, Adorno sets himself against Kant. Or, to be more precise, against *Kantian rigorism*. It is, of course, a further resonance of the interpretation of the Odysseus myth in *The Dialectics of Enlightenment*: the hero and his self-imposed ropes tightly binding his body are an allegory of bourgeois ambivalence to the promise of happiness (a promise to be held back and subsumed at the end by 'the ethics of labour').

On this matter, *Negative Dialectics* is more insistent: Adorno devotes almost hundred pages to expose what he sees as the antinomical character of Kantian doctrine of freedom, complete with an un-flattering caricature of Kant and his philosophy: 'His timid bourgeois detestation of anarchy matches his proud bourgeois antipathy against tutelage'.[12]

In short, Adorno's rejection of the Kantian ethics is due to its implied repressive tenor. Kant's practical freedom is perceived as *utterly tightened freedom*, and the empirical subject can only achieve if there is *a restriction of its own impulses*. We remember that in a rather outrageous way, *The Dialectics of Enlightenment* draws a parallel between Kant and Marquis de Sade, whose *Juliette*, despite its violently erotic content, speaks for the self-overcoming of pleasure, and the subjugation of somatic moment.[13]

'Impulses', 'physicality', 'somatic moment'—Adorno's words mark his 'unvarnished materialistic motive', and with good reason. Like I said earlier, the normative aspect of it is critical: the physical side of our knowledge can tell us 'that suffering ought not to be, that things should be different.' This goes hand in hand with the call to 'remove the illusion of the autarky of thought'. A passage to materialism serves as a *skandalon* of the haughty march of rationality, or, to be more precise, 'the falsehood of an unleashed rationality running away from itself.'

The problem with such a materialistic motive is that it may not be able to recognize the possibility of freedom. How can materialism explain the human choice to exit from the self-incurred *Unmündigkeit?* Adorno is certainly aware of the intricacy of the complex of freedom and determinism. He criticizes Kant for negating the possibility of discovering *the dawning sense of freedom* beneath the doctrine of the noumena. But he knows that in the realm of the phenomena, modern positivists rule. For him, the positivist ethos is part of the principle of dominion. The positivists rely entirely on the equality of their quantifying method that allows no *evolving otherness.* Worse, they presuppose the subject's passive dependence on each given situation: 'The interaction of subject and object is spirited away, a priori, while spontaneity is excluded by the very method.'[14]

Yet between both extremes, Adorno does not make his position exactly clear. He seems to see freedom as the outcome of what self-preservation demands in its history, which is not merely conditioned reflexes, but something more, something crucial for it to eventually transcend the reflexes. 'Freedom opens as the difference that has evolved between the self and the reflexes', he says. But he also speaks—in half-mystical and half-materialistic language—of 'pre-temporal freedom', of 'the archaic impulse not yet steered by any solid "I"', or of freedom 'that which is not tamed by the I as the principle of any determination'.[15]

It is not clear how Adorno would put such impulse for freedom in words. His metaphors, often lyrical, may well be his insistence that things like 'archaic impulse', or 'pre-temporal' freedom, are outside the subject-shaped language. Regretfully, Kant, Adorno charges, makes the whole moment of freedom 'rationalistically narrowed'.[16]

Choosing to be openly polemical, Adorno tends to ignore other possibilities to view Kant's idea of reason. But he is not the only one to see Kant's tendency to be closer to the traditional and rationalistic epistemology. Heidegger, for example, in his controversial *Kantbuch,* which, if I follow Weatherston's critique, tries to pull Kant back to 'Kant-the-empirical-realist', by putting a 'non-rationalist' stamp on his predecessor.[17]

He starts from the beginning: in the flowchart he draws of the cognitive process, he prioritizes the 'transcendental imagination' as the 'common root' of the capacity of understanding (the faculty of concepts) and the capacity of sensibility (the faculty of intuitions). Hence his interpretation of Kant is coloured by a surprisingly non-cognitive and pragmatic persuasion. By emphasizing the role of imagination (something Kant later reportedly ejected from his epistemology), and not the more active and constitutive side of human cognitive faculty—which is reason—Heidegger suggests the importance of passive receptivity of knowing. A trace of Husserl's phenomenological approach is unmistakably hiding: *lets the phenomena show themselves*. The subject is not the Author. Here we can detect a sparkle of Heidegger's wish to see humankind as the shepherd of Being.

Probably for this reason Heidegger is blamed for the disappearance of the subject. His concept of *Dasein*, says Balibar, 'destroys the concept of the Subject'.[18] It is true there is in Heidegger a trace of what Adorno would see and dismiss as 'romantic'—a yearning for the harmony between subject and object, between human and the other: the neighbour, the sky, the earth, the divinity.

Balibar, however, stops short at questioning Heidegger's presupposition that remains of value: that the subject is part of its practices and not external to them, that *Dasein*'s primordial existence is one of engagement with its surroundings, that conscious acts of reflection are not something privileged.

That is the start of Heidegger's critique of purposive (technical) rationality, and also his warning of the menace of a vigorous subject that objectifies and enframes the world, a subject that acts like the conquering Lord of Being. In other words: a timely call for the ethical. After all, it is a time marked by a fresh American imperial ambition and a new religious passion that, curiously, mimes the force of secular humanistic premises.

IV

Two centuries after Kant wrote his famous phrase that 'for its own sake, morality does not need religion', religion remains a great supplier of maxims. For two hundred years, the legacy of the Enlightenment did push religion into the recesses of our memory. Today, however, the faithful return with a promise, force, and haste, both in the United States and some Muslim parts of the World.

A closer look at the twentieth-century revivalist movement, the Muslim one, that is, will indicate that its disagreement with secular modernity, filled with twists and turns, prompts all kinds of mimicry. In the recent past, it was the secularists, epitomized by Marxists and later by Maoists, who mimed the grand narrative of religion, with all its belief in The Truth and its promise. Today, it is the believers who often unwittingly, yet coherently, develop voices resembling those of the secularists: the revivalist's ferocious will to heal the world has made them even closer to the modern temper.

Emerging from the damaged life of the colonial past, revivalism often looks like a parody of modernity—'parody' being a mimetic act of contempt and of wonder, inexact yet perceptive, inadequate yet effectual.

To be sure, revivalism, in its various avatars, can be interpreted as a denial of the impulses of the Enlightenment. Nonetheless, the revivalist undertaking—to return to the putative 'origin' of the faith—is necessarily reliant on a well-grounded human subject. The 'origin' is presumably preserved by the 'purity' of the Text. To make people stick to the 'purity' of the Text, one has to presume their ability to attain a clear and distinct representation of it.

As I see it, this is the underlying thesis of Sayyd Qutb (1906–1966). He is arguably the most articulate ideologue of Muslim revivalism in the twentieth century. To put him on the Enlightenment line-up would be odd. There is no *Copernican revolution* in his thinking. And yet, not unlike Kant, Qutb's thesis depends on the constitutive role of consciousness.

Therefore he has emphatic words for the sovereignty of the human subject. He uses the famous Qur'anic message that humankind is God's *vicegerent* (*khalifah*) on earth. He associates human 'vicegerency' with the task and the capacity to pursue 'material inventions'. His critique of 'apologist' stance vis-à-vis 'Western' rationalism notwithstanding, his bias is for a certain feature of modernity. Encouraging Muslims to 'preserve and develop the material fruits of the creative genius of Europe', his agenda is, unwittingly, to replay the European

humanist legacy. His '*khalifah* on earth' has its shadow in the
Heideggerian metaphor of the human subject: God's vicegerent is
'the lord of Being', who 'enframes' Nature and sees it mainly as
'standing reserve'.

With a large dosage of Weberian 'purposive rational action' in his
version of rationality, Qutb warns Muslims against pursuing
thoughts that relate to 'faith, religion, morals and values'. He seems
to insist that there should be a block. His persistent appeal is to
acknowledge the limits of human inquiry.

In his best-known work, *Ma'alim fi'l Tariq* ('Milestones'), he warns
the faithful not to bestow human thought 'the status of a god so that
its truth or falsity is not to be judged according to God's guidance'.[19]
In effect he bars thinking from approaching the 'life-world', avoiding
the world of human experiences science fails to grasp. His Islamic
project, to bring Muslims to triumph over the dark *Jahiliyyah*, only
allows the kind of thinking used in the area of 'abstract sciences'
and 'their practical applications'; in fact, he puts them into a category
beyond good ('Islamic') and evil (*jahili*).

The primacy of the cognitively alert subject is underlined in his
idea of *vanguard*: a highly qualified person analogous to the Leninist
class-conscious revolutionary who is not merely, to use Lenin's words,
a *wretched amateur*. His or her job is, as Qutb puts it, to 'know the
landmarks and the milestones of the road'[20] toward the goal. In so
doing, he or she 'may recognize the starting place, the nature, the
responsibilities and the ultimate purpose of this long journey.'[21]

'To know', 'to recognize': the words betray a premise that 'theory'
(or 'doctrine', to adopt Qutb's vocabulary) is supreme and praxis
plays only a secondary role; in fact, it is a mere replica. Experience is
viewed as something so ephemeral, particular, and unsettled that
it has to be put under the subject's jurisdiction. The revivalist view
maintains the 'prejudice of the Enlightenment', to borrow Gadamer's
words: a presumption that truth is in principle obtainable by those
endowed with the ability to command meanings. Qutb's *vanguard* is
an icon in the preponderance of the subject.

Hence the revivalists' paradox: while emphasizing human flaws and
transience, they repress irony, the unpredictable and the playful; they,
in effect, refute to assume the vulnerability of truth in the life-world.

While tirelessly speaking on behalf of the divine, they relegate God to a concept accessible even to the sciences (Qutb mentions 'astronomy, biology, physics, chemistry and geology'). While speaking persistently of human finitude, the revivalists beget their assurance from a presumed consciousness completely identical with the clarity of the Text.

Someone says that there is an ancient clandestine friendship between light and power, and this is also pertinent to Qutb's Islam. His doctrine is not only a straight path into the light, as it were, but also a resolve to curb the recalcitrant Other. Clarity is a form of discipline. Putting praxis completely under the directives of 'theory', it forces 'theory', or the Text, out and beyond the precarious life of words.

It is a mark of revivalism (or 'fundamentalism', if you will) to deny that words have turbulent histories. The words' historicity produces a limit, even violence, whenever they try to represent the infinitely undefined being, divine or otherwise. This problem besets philosophers like Lévinas, but the revivalists take no notice of it. Any one prioritizing the purity of the Text, as if it were eternally untouched by the world's din and dust, does not think of the inevitable failure of language. The fetishism of the text mirrors the reification of the subject.

Ultimately, Qutb's revivalist's promise is everything but emancipation.[22] Freedom finds no place in the house of God's 'vicegerent on earth', precisely because it is not a house, but a site where the khalifah is deified in what Adorno calls 'peephole metaphysics'. This metaphysics locks up the subject in its own self, 'imprisoned for all eternity to punish it for its deification', sur-rounded by 'the shadow of reification' that casts on whatever the subject conjures.

V

Out of imprisonment, emancipation is fluidity. Its allegory can be a different reading of Chairil's *Aku* as an 'I' that keeps 'rushing, rushing on...'

Doubtless Chairil's poetry is part of our modernist temper. Modernism is modernity's eroticized dream. It cherishes the memory of a wild, physical 'I'. Chairil's *Aku* does not say when, or if, s/he will stop. Maybe s/he never will. But the allegory can lead us to a subject unfrozen by self-worship. It gives a story that freedom has no metaphorical house. It comprises of moments. The subject as emancipation has no presence, has no substance.

Actually even Kant should have no problem with this. The Kantian subject is not an enigma; it is a stammering. But instability can be indicative of fecundity. There is always the possibility to see the philosopher in different trajectories.

In a rare lyrical passage in *Critique of Practical Reason*[23] (the introductory part of the chapter called 'The Ground of the Distinction of All Objects in General into Phenomena and Noumena'), Kant projects himself as a cartographer in the geography of human cognition. We know that a cartographer is both an explorer and a marker of boundaries. Adorno, for one, noticing his *topological zeal*, tends to underline the latter. Yet maybe there is something to recognize in the first: an explorer's position is perpetually in imagined borderlands, even when s/he stands still.

The first Critique may portray Kant as someone following the unexpectedly difficult map he himself draws, in a journey to find the boundary of the noumena. We will listen to his stammering along the way. Sometimes Kant speaks about the noumenon in a positive sense, as 'an object of a non-sensible intuition'. Other times he tries to grasp and define it negatively. 'It is there of only negative employment', he says.

In the first case, as we see, he uses the word 'object', or to be more precise, 'non-sensible object'. As follows, some people think of the noumena as being 'something' our transcendental knowledge can register, suggesting that 'appearances' are grounded on things-in-themselves outside us. In this position, there is a trace of an ontological allusion of 'presence'.

The second sense implies a radical unknowability. To put it differently, about this one cannot use the word 'knowledge' in the Kantian term, since it implies a synthesis involving intuition, and the noumenon is by definition 'non-intuitable'. The word 'noumenon' denotes a merely limiting concept, as Kant puts it. He describes it as 'domain' that is empty, but the metaphor can be misleading. The thing-in-itself is pure negativity. It is a constructed point in our thinking.

So is the notion of cognitive subject, which Kant refers to in his notion of 'consciousness as such', 'the spontaneity of thought', 'the unity of synthesis in the act of thought', or 'transcendental apperception'.[24]

The classical problem is how the *personalitas transcendentalis* is possible without a link to the empirical subject. When Adorno, in his Marxist temper, defines the transcendental subject as 'a society unaware of itself', his emphasis—analogous with communitarian voices against 'deontological liberalism'—is on the limit of abstraction.

Kant would want to argue, of course, that some sort of transcendent self must be postulated in thought in order to help bring 'systematic unity' into the structure of one's overall philosophy. To him, a self is never a real object, a synthetic a priori condition for the possibility of empirical knowledge. Its existence is neither empirically nor transcendentally knowable. It is a non-intuitable concept.

For this reason, we will have to reach the subject hidden on the other side of Kant. I think Žižek is the first one to attempt to put it in such a crucial site, and yet in the very essence of emancipation—in fluidity, not in any hypostasized form.[25]

This subject, a manifestation of transcendental freedom, according to Žižek, takes place only in the phenomenal domain: I am free because I am there, in the world. In the presence of God, in the realm outside of the phenomenal, there is no freedom. Žižek quotes a passage from *Critique of Practical Reason:*

God and eternity in their awful majesty would stand unceasingly before our eyes... Thus most actions conforming to the law would be done from fear, few would be done from hope, none from duty. The moral worth of actions... would not exist at all.

So the subject, a manifestation of transcendental freedom, is 'in-between', neither phenomenal nor noumenal, but 'the gap which separates the two'.

Žižek's interpretation is, of course, deeply rooted in the Lacanian notion of 'the subject as lack'. Actually, it may remind us of what Kant thinks, when he conceptualizes the subject as a constructed point in our thinking: the subject is not a substance. And yet the Lacanian subject is not consciousness as such, but a 'deficit' that endlessly needs to be eliminated. Žižek's 'Cartesian subject' is therefore not 'the self-transparent thinking subject'. It seems to me what is crucial is the continuous act of generating 'subjecthood', of identification, analogous to desire that is never fulfilled. The subject will act without solidifying itself into an idol to be worshipped and its act will recognize its very contingency.

Perhaps this is the virtue of 'vertiginousness', to use Adorno's word, and the power of truth that can 'plunge into the abyss'. Today's madness of fast changes and uncertain dispersal of all centers may need the insight from such a story of fluidity.

Notes

1. Etienne Balibar 'Subjection and Subjectivation', in Joan Copjec (ed.), *Supposing the Subject*, Verso, London, New York, 1994.
2. Ibid., pp. 9–11
3. Max Horkheimer and Theodore Adorno, *The Dialectics of Enlightenment*, (John Cumming trans.), Herder and Herder, New York, 1972.
4. Joan Copjec, *Supposing the Subject*.
5. Ibid.
6. Slavoj Žižek', *The Ticklish Subject: The Absent Centre of Political Ontology*, Verso, London, 1999.
7. Alenka Zuzpancik, *Ethics of the Real: Kant, Lacan*, Verso, New York, 2000.
8. Simone Critchley and Oliver Marchant, eds, *The Critical Laclau Reader*, Routledge, London, 2004.
9. Theodore Adorno, *Negative Dialectics*, (E.B. Aston trans.), Routledge Kegan and Paul, London, 1973, p. 18.
10. Ibid., p. 365.
11. Ibid., p. 203.
12. Ibid.
13. Horkheimer and Adorno, *The Dialectics of Enlightenment*.
14. Adorno, *Negative Dialectics*.
15. Ibid.
16. Ibid.
17. Martin Weatherston, *Heidegger's Interpretation of Kant: Categories, Imagination and Temporality*, Palgrave Macmillan, 2002.

18. Balibar 'Subjection and Subjectivation'.
19. Sayyd Qutb, *Milestones*, online version, http://www.sinc.sungsb.edu/stu/mwaali/milestone/mi.
20. Ibid.
21. Ibid.
22. See also, Sayyd Qutb, *Keadilan Sosial Dalam Islam*, Penerbit Pustaka, Bandung, 1994.
23. Immanuel Kant, *Critique of Practical Reason* in *Practical Philosophy*, Mary J. Gregor (trans. and ed.), Cambridge University Press, 1996.
24. Immanuel Kant, *Critique of Pure Reason* (Paul Guyer and Allen W. Wood ed. and trans.), Cambridge University Press, Cambridge, New York, Melbourne, Madrid. See also, Wood Allen, *Kant*, Oxford, 2000; Blackwell, 2005.
25. Žižek, *The Ticklish Subject*.

Autonomy and the Virtue of Self-Legislation

Bijoy H. Boruah

The Outer and the Inner

An epitaph that has the rare force and significance of immortalizing, not just the person buried in the graveyard but also the works and ideas that are the person's lifetime achievements, is the one inscribed on the tombstone of Immanuel Kant (1724–1804). The text of the epitaph is authored by Kant himself. It is the opening sentence of the passage—what may be the single most famous passage of the entire corpus of Kant's works—with which he concludes his *Critique of Practical Reason* (5: 162), Kant writes: 'Two things fill the mind with ever new and increasing admiration and reverence, the more often and more steadily one reflects upon them: *the starry heavens above me and the moral law within me*'.[1]

Apart from being remarkably profound and noble, this autobiographical expression is expressive of an intriguing complexity of human consciousness—that is the complex synthesis of the *outer* and the *inner*, the *physical* and the *spiritual*, dimensions of existence in the inscrutable unity of a human personal being. These two aspects of human consciousness, highlighted in the above remark as objects of the attitudes of admiration and awe respectively, are, in essence, representative of an apparently irreconcilable duality of the human condition. It is the duality of the inexorably deterministic *natural* order of the Newtonian universe on the one hand, and the inwardly free *rational* order that defines the space of morality on the other. The crux of this duality is that the human person leads, or at least is capable of leading, a life that steers through these two heterogeneous orders of reality without succumbing to the irrationality of split personality.

It is not the central purpose of this essay to dwell on the relation between science and morality, nor on the tension between determinism and freedom, even though both these issues are relevant to what I have to say in the course of this essay. I am particularly concerned here with the idea of human consciousness, or the human self, in all its complexity and efficacy, that underlies Kant's conception of autonomous human agency. It seems to me that this conception of human autonomy is unique and extraordinary, not just in showing the ideal human person's self-image, but also in providing an illustration of philosophy's self-image at its best.

Autonomy as Auto-nomous

Human autonomy, in the Kantian sense, is to be explicated by reference to the concept of freedom defined in two senses, one negative, and the other positive. Freedom, negatively construed, is the rational person's independence from determination by the causality of nature. When connected to the will of the person, it would mean the will's capacity 'to work independently of *determination* by alien causes'. In this sense the rational person's will is said to be 'spontaneous', and freedom in this sense is freedom as *spontaneity*.

However, the negative sense of freedom as spontaneity does not quite capture the essence of freedom. But it leads to a positive conception which does specify the essence. Freedom, in essence, is autonomy, which is defined in the *Groundwork of the Metaphysics of Morals* (4: 440) as 'the property of the will by which it is a law to itself (independently of any property of the objects of volition)'.[2] Autonomy in turn is contrasted with heteronomy, according to which 'the will... does not give itself the law; instead the object, by means of its relation to the will, gives the law to it'.[3] In plainer language, freedom as autonomy means the rational person's capacity to act from principles of pure practical reason alone. Here I quote a succinct remark made by Karl Ameriks:

For Kant, our freedom involves a capacity to be not merely an occasional uncaused or self-directed force; above all, it is a power whose action is ever present in an internally generated and law-governed way. The Kantian self is literally 'auto-nomous,' that is, defined by a *self-legislation* that is carried out on itself as well as by itself.[4]

Kant pronounces autonomy to be the 'supreme principle of morality' in the sense of being the condition for the possibility of action on the basis of what he calls the *categorical imperative*. However, autonomy involves not simply the capacity of the will to determine itself to act on the basis of self-legislated principles. For, self-legislated principles may also include ones that are heteronomous. It is to eliminate this possibility that Kant specifies the particular way in which the capacity for self-determined and self-legislated acts is exercised, namely 'independently of every property belonging to the object of volition'. Exactly what this independent condition involves can best be shown by considering a mode of volition which lacks this condition, that is, one in which what gives the principle is not the will itself, but the object, in so far as it relates to the will. What would be the character of the agent whose action is governed by such a heteronomous principle?

Such an agent would act out of needs that arise from its sensuous nature, or needs that are attributed to the agent as a sensuous being. This of course is contrary to Kantian moral agency, which must not be subject to this limiting condition of being able to act only out of needs as a sensuous being. The Kantian moral agent would have to have the capacity to recognize sufficient reasons to act that do not stem from any desire and inclination. Such reasons would have to stem from pure practical reason, in which case, the will (as practical reason) would be self-legislative in the fullest sense. Morality requires not merely that our actions *conform to duty* or the categorical imperative. Our actions must be done *from duty*, that is, the duty-motive *of itself* must provide a sufficient reason to act.

Autonomy therefore involves more than the satisfaction of the negative condition of independence from determination by 'alien causes' or the 'causality of nature'. It also involves a positive capacity to be motivated by reasons that are totally independent of one's needs as a sensuous being. A divine will, for example, would possess motivational independence from sensuous inclination *ex hypothesi*, because such a will would not receive any sensuous input. Surely this is not true of the human will; and yet it is the case, according to Kant, that the human will does have the capacity for genuine motivational independence. For it is capable of disregarding all claims of inclination and acting solely from respect for the moral law. Thus the rational human agent is capable of framing and adopting ends on purely rational grounds, independent of any input from inclination.

The Moral-Practical Copernican Revolution

What has been said thus far, both on freedom as spontaneity and freedom as autonomy, can be roughly recapitulated and clarified in the following words. The idea of a rational agent presupposes that one is capable of projecting ends, acting on the basis of self-imposed general principles (maxims) and in the light of objectively valid norms. But if the rational agent has these capacities, it implies the agent's independence from determination by antecedent causes, including the agent's desires. Even if desires enter into what the agent chooses to do, these cannot constitute *sufficient* reason for the chosen act. And to attribute such independence to the agent is to conceive of the agent under the idea of spontaneity (or 'transcendental' freedom in Kant's terminology). Consequently, it is because the agent is (transcendentally) free from the causality of desire and inclination that he or she can actually generate maxims or principles or pure practical reason and legislate them upon himself or herself.

The epistemology of the *Critique of Pure Reason* elucidates the concept of freedom as spontaneity, that is, the faculty of initiating a new causal series in time. Here the human mind is revealed as a 'law giver' to nature as a condition for the possibility of cognitive experience. And it is the same epistemology that sets limits to cognitive (theoretical) reason by binding its application to what can be given in experience. The simultaneous epistemological revelation both of freedom of spontaneity (that is, reason's independence from nature) and of the limits of cognitive reason to phenomenal data, leads Kant towards the conclusion of the *primacy* of moral practical reason. From the notion of the spontaneity of cognitive faculty in its employment of theoretical reason, we are drawn towards an examination of the *practical* employment of reason in its freedom as autonomy. In other words, what started as a reflection on the idea of transcendental freedom in the theoretical domain of cognitive reason, eventually culminated in a reflection on the role of reason in the practical context of human life. In this context, pure reason constitutes the autonomous *moral self*, which is the embodiment of practical freedom, the freedom to be the author of maxims of conduct.

The autonomous moral self, the free will, is the faculty of pure reason in its practical role of creating laws or objectively valid rules of conduct, and also of legislating them upon itself. This unique combination at once of self-creation and self-legislation of moral laws by the rational human agent is a feature of Kant's moral philosophy that is as revolutionary as the 'Copernican turn' heralded in his theoretical philosophy. For it presents a picture of the human person in terms of moral possibility of a kind unprecedented in the history of western moral thought. On this I invoke the comment of Lewis White Beck: 'That the will of man both creates and executes obligations is one of the most dramatic theses in Kant's philosophy. It is as dramatic as, and comparable to, the "Copernican revolution" of his theoretical philosophy'.[5]

The peculiarity of the rational human person at once to be the *master of the self* (self-legislation) and to be *mastered by the self* (self-obligation) reflects another apparently paradoxical juxtaposition of two radically diverse aspects of the human condition. The human being, again in the words of Beck, is 'the only being in the world who is a citizen of two worlds, subject to both *psychological explanation* and *moral exhortation*, and the only being in the world who is torn between the roles of *spectator* and *actor*.'[6] The human person as spectator (the phenomenal self) and subject to deterministic psychological explanation is governed by the causality of nature. But the same human person, *qua* actor in general and moral agent in particular, is a self-determining agent in an 'intelligible' (non-natural) order of reality. Is this sort of life one of 'double standards' that cannot help betraying alleged human personal *unity* and *authenticity* of personal being? Otherwise, what kind of conceptual integration is conceivable of natural causality and moral freedom? Is there any indication in Kant's overall philosophy of a possible reconciliation between, on the one hand, the idea of freedom as the supreme principle of practical reason and, on the other, the concept of causality as the supreme principle of theoretical reason?

On Kant's own admission, the idea of freedom and of free agency presupposes an explicit acknowledgement of the causal constraints of nature. It is also admitted that, given human finitude, we cannot *know*, by virtue of the employment of theoretical reason, whether our will is *really* independent of the causality of nature. However, the impossibility, and hence non-availability, of theoretical knowledge about our rational autonomy creates a space for the idea of ourselves as autonomous agents in the sphere of practical reason. This is how Kant argues for the primacy of practical reason, which in turn constitutes a constructive response to the recognition and acknowledgement of the limits of theoretical rationality. Human cognitive finitude constitutes a valid reason for the opening up of a practical dimension of human rationality, within which emerges the human agent who can rationally frame an order of ideas of his/her own for his/her own life.

It is in the context of this argument for the primacy of practical reason and human autonomy that Kant makes the very famous and succinct remark in the *Critique of Pure Reason*: 'I must therefore suspend *knowledge*, in order to make room for *faith*'.[7] The suspension of theoretical knowledge allows for the possibility of practical faith, that is, faith in autonomous rational agency, or the free will, and the moral dignity of human beings. Thus, acting morally involves affirming faith in our freedom from natural causality. But the disturbing question that looms large is: is this no more than just a 'leap of faith', in the usual sense of the phrase?

Of course the above claim does not mean that knowledge must be limited in order to allow us some *non-rational* basis for belief in morally relevant free agency. Rather, what Kant means is that the limitation of the foundational principles of theoretical knowledge to the way things appear to our experience is *necessary* in order to allow us to conceive of ourselves as rational agents who are not constrained by the deterministic grip of nature, and who can govern themselves in accordance with the principles of practical reason. This way of interpreting the meaning of the above claim does make it look quite reasonable, and it does seem to reconcile our existence bound by the causality of nature with our simultaneous existence as autonomous moral selves. Nevertheless, the question persists as to whether the limitation of theoretical knowledge is used as a *pretext* for metaphysical indulgence in practical faith in human rational autonomy.

Construing the Kantian question in the above way poses a challenge to the justification of the *harmonization* of causality and freedom. It would of course be quite easy to dissolve the challenge, and deny any such harmony, simply by adopting the stance of incompatibilist determinism, and then accuse Kant of really engaging in unwarranted metaphysical indulgence. On the other hand, the Hobbesian-Humean compatibilist outlook is quite clearly contrary to Kant's position on freedom. The compatibilist reconciliation between freedom and causality is therefore also not an option. Is Kant then an incompatibilist libertarian wedded to the problematic conception of 'contra-causal' freedom?

The Intimation of Inner Infinity

The three theoretical alternatives mentioned above of dealing with the problem of human autonomy vis-à-vis human being's embeddedness in the natural world have been much discussed and are unendingly controversial. My own strategy here is not to join the bandwagon of this controversy, but to explore a different mode of making sense of the reconciliation in question. I intend to set the reconciliatory task against the background of the relation between *nature* and *morality*, and for me this background is adumbrated in the way Kant expresses his heightened self-perception in relation to the unimaginable vastness of the cosmos on the one hand, and the unfathomable depth of inwardness that the moral will represents on the other. In order to fulfil this intention, I wish to return once more to Kant's movingly suggestive remark on 'the starry heavens above' and 'the moral law within'. For I tend to believe that a closer reading of this remark is likely to reveal ideas that might shed new light on the character of the relation between nature and morality. Admiration and reverence are said to fill his mind when Kant compares 'the place I occupy in the external world of sense' with the immensity and grandeur of the starry heavens—that is, the natural universe in its entirety—of 'unbounded magnitude... and unbounded times'. The 'view of a countless multitude of worlds annihilates, as it were, my importance as an *animal creature*', adds Kant. This perspective of vision on himself as a part of nature makes him realize, in utmost humility, that he is 'a mere speck in the universe'.[8] His *natural* or sensuous identity is thus rendered utterly insignificant in his own eyes. And what accounts for this lofty realization of insignificance is his innate capacity for *rational* self-understanding in a cosmic scale of self-appraisal. A *non*-rational sensuous being is wholly incapable of such self-appraisal and self-understanding.

On the other hand, admiration and reverence are said to fill Kant's mind upon reflecting on 'my invisible self, my personality' in so far as that reflection 'presents me in a world which has true infinity'. His invisible inner self is held to have a 'universal and necessary' connection with that world of 'true infinity'. It is this spiritual self-understanding that 'infinitely raises my worth as an *intelligence* by my personality, in which the moral law reveals to me a life independent of animality and even of the whole sensible world'.[9] By any standard, this is *inner* or *spiritual* self-understanding *par excellence*, and I contend that this intimation of inner *infinitude* is owed to the same innate capacity for rational self-understanding which underlies the realization of utter *finitude* of sensuous self-identity. What is indicated here is the argument that the moral world is truly infinite in as much as the moral self, being purely 'intelligible' (or rational) in nature, encounters no invincible empirical limits of phenomenal existence.

A further indication of the intimation of inner infinity set against the finitude of sensuous or phenomenal self-identity is to be found in Kant's concern with the *feeling of the sublime* poignantly described in his *Critique of Judgement*. The sublime is a feeling awakened in us as we face the mightiest and most terrible exertions of nature. What explains the awakening of the feeling of the sublime even in the face of such a terrifying mightiness of nature—which would otherwise be experienced by us with sheer fear and make us recognize ourselves as specks of cosmic dust—is our capacity to judge the exertions of nature independently of our physical relation to it. There is this inner ability within us to resist the impending dominion of mighty nature over us. We are able to overcome our emotionally vulnerable sensuous or physical personality by making it subservient to the purely rational or intelligible personality of infinite moral spirit. It is this infinite inner spirit of the moral personality that constitutes our freedom as autonomy, that is, our freedom from phenomenal finitude or the capacity to make ourselves independent of our phenomenal nature.

Our finitude and the temporality of our existence go together. As temporal beings we are subject to the fetters of natural impulses, or the tendency to submit our exercise of choice to the guidance of objectives such as material prosperity and worldly happiness. In so far as our will is influenced by urges and inclinations of temporal existence, we inevitably come under the dominion of nature, and are fully governed by the universal causality of nature. But serious self-reflection and self-appraisal lead us to the recognition of the triviality of our finitude in the cosmic order of things.

However, given that the spirit of rational consciousness elevates us to conceive of our inner identity (our will) independently of our sensuous relation to the natural order, we experience rational autonomy over ourselves conceived as sensuous being subject to the vicissitudes of temporality. The life of the heteronomous will submitted to the causality of nature is subordinated to the life of the autonomous or self-legislating will, which is, in an important sense, *ahistorical* and *atemporal*. It is so because any choice truly made by the autonomous will is immune to the contingencies of history and ever-fluctuating conditions of sensuous existence. Even in the midst of fluctuations of temporal existence, the life of self-legislation is inviolably regulated by principles anchored in the timeless order of pure practical reason.

Between the Beast and the Angel

To the extent that the life of self-legislation is elevated to the timeless order of pure practical reason, the moral self of self-legislation can indeed be conceived as a *universal* self that admits of no individuation. Moral autonomy is predicated upon a self that is universal in this sense. However, the ahistorical and atemporal universal self of morality is not *as a matter of fact* seated in a noumenal reality beyond all history and contingency of phenomenal existence. For the actual moral life—-the *human* moral life, that is—has its unavoidable temporal matrix, marked by the vagaries of a sensuous personality. The moral course of life is in fact tied to the phenomenal field of life of an individuated self, even though the moral driving force has its source in an unindividuated or universal self. And the universality of the moral self is an integral part of the actual moral agent in as much as rationality is an integral aspect of the agent. Rationality, and not the metaphysics of noumenal reality, is the essence of the universal moral self.

Kant recognizes the reality of actual moral life to be one of relentless struggle of reason against inclination, of the rational self over the 'pathological' one in us. Indeed, the virtue of being a moral person is defined by him in terms of the moral struggle, the 'moral strength of will', on the part of an *imperfectly* rational agent, to overcome temptations to transgress the moral law. However, the moral condition that the struggle must satisfy is laid down in terms of the idea of a *perfectly* rational agent, whose will is completely determined by its own inner lawfulness. Kant allows no compromise on the rational strictures of human morality. No concession is made for human moral agency on the ground of human imperfection. Rather, Kant invokes the idea of rational perfection innate to divine agency, and adds that what such an agent with its *holy will* necessarily *would* do is what we imperfectly rational agents *ought* to do.

If the moral strength of will is the true measure of human morality, then it should be clear that the actual moral life of a human person embodies a continuous interplay of the temporal, contingent heteronomous self and the atemporal, universal autonomous self. Moral failure is a failure of the will to accord itself fully with the purely rational consciousness of the universal self, a failure of the will to disengage itself from the clutch of sensuous needs or motivations. Conversely, moral success is earned by the will when it succeeds in aligning itself with the universal self of pure reason.

Thus, the actual course of a human moral life always consists in the working together of the two diverse aspects—that is, the spontaneous forces of sensuous individuality and the legislative drive of rational universality. The former aspect provides the concrete setting of human finitude in which emerges the moral challenge, and the latter meets the challenge by virtue of the efficacy of its spirit of rational infinity.

A human person is neither an angel nor an animal, as Kant says. But a human *moral* life is what it is because of the possibility of instantiating the angelic virtue of unconditional freedom necessary for morality. However, the angelic independence from the impact of sensuous inclinations is only an ideal. And yet this ideal is a necessary postulate of morality. So the rational human agent is conceived as having a kind of kinship to angelic agency. On the other hand, the human person is akin to the beast in so far as its sensuous constitution is concerned. Hence the possibility of human morality poses as a problem for the human agent. Unlike the effortless exercise of freedom on the part of the angel, the human agent earns her success in that exercise by virtue of persistent struggle against the countervailing forces of animality. Indeed, being virtuous in Kantian morality consists in being able to persevere in this struggle without fail.

The fact that the human agent has the potentiality for angelic freedom even as the agent is constitutively propelled by beastly instinct tells something interesting about the relation between virtue and human morality. Kant does not view morality as springing from virtuous dispositions that make us altruistic or benevolent. Since the 'human beast' of natural inclination is a constant obstacle in the way of the 'human angel' of rational freedom, the moral life of the human person is always a life of *trying* to be moral. The obstacle is required to be overcome by the person through ceaseless struggle of reason over inclination. It is this necessity and importance of struggle in the moral life that leads Kant to his view that virtue cannot be defined as a settled habit or disposition. The rational angel, or God, would by nature, or effortlessly, act morally and for that reason cannot have virtue. No moral struggle, no moral virtue. This point is stated succinctly by J.B. Schneewind: 'Only beings who find morality difficult and who develop persistence in struggling against temptations can be virtuous. We finite beings will never get to the point at which we do not need the strength to resist desire. We are neither angels nor animals. Virtue is our proper station in the universe'.[10]

Moral Elbow Room in the Space of Causality

What I have tried to show in the above discussion is to depict the picture of a complex but unified human personality that accommodates, though in a problematic way, the co-existence of the sensuous life determined by natural causality and the moral life of rational autonomy. The sensuous and the rational are both genuine aspects of a single personal whole, and this is why it looks appropriate to conceive of the ontological location of the human person somewhere between the angel and the beast. Though in their own ways these two aspects represent contrary or incompatible char-acteristics, their co-presence in the complex constitution of human personality does not necessarily threaten the unity and integrity of a personal life. Rather, the personal unity and integrity of a human moral life gains unique momentum precisely in virtue of the remarkable *adjustment* between these two aspects. This is an adjustment between the rational life governed by the *regulative* principle of moral freedom and the sensuous life subject to the *constitutive* principle of natural causality. But what exactly is the crux of this splendid adjustment?

It would of course be pointless to ask, with regard to this 'adjust-ment', whether a human person is essentially sensuous or essentially rational. In a way the human person is essentially both, and I believe that such a *dual-aspect characterization* of the human person is true to Kant's own view on the matter. However, there is an important caveat that needs to be attested to this (as it may be called) *dual-aspect essentialism*. Granted that the human person is as much essentially a sensible being as she is essentially a rational being, the rational aspect in her has an *edge* over the sensible aspect. In virtue of pure practical reason, the human agent is capable of 'creating' an order of existence for her own life which is regulated by self-legislated moral laws. It is not that the moral order of existence is not superadded to the sensible order. It rather *overrides* the sensible order to the extent that, even though the morally led life inevitably has a sensible matrix, the constitutive law of causality that otherwise governs sensuous existence is not allowed to interfere with the course of that life. Natural inclinations are kept away from determining the guiding principles of ethical conduct.

Heteronomy is the necessary conceptual background against which the idea of moral autonomy has to be understood. Whereas the non-moral life of natural inclination is the space of causality, the moral life occurs within the 'space' of rationality and freedom. If the space of rationality were to eclipse, so to speak, under the unrestrained extension of the space of causality, that is, the full reign of natural inclination, the angelic person would descend to the level of a beast. If, on the other hand, natural inclinations were, *per impossibile*, to be fully sublimated and rendered volitionally inert under overwhelmingly austere rational self-control, the human person would transcend its humanity and ascend to the level of an angel. The person would then become a superhuman moral saint. These are the two diametrically opposite extremes in the spectrum of human personhood, the extremes of the utterly non-moral at one end, and the most perfectly moral at the other.

Understandably, an angelic moral life would draw its full sustenance from within the space of pure reason alone. Since there would be no countervailing space of causality (of inclinations), the angel would face no moral constraint whatsoever. By contrast, the human person has her space of rationality and freedom within the same overall *orbit of existence* with which the space of causality (of inclination) is connected. Unlike the angel's condition, the human condition is not that of an uncontested moral space or reason. However, the possibility of morality in the human condition does not depend on a prior nullification of the source of heteronomous choice altogether. The possibility of human morality does not really require a complete neutralization, and replacement, of the space of causality by the space of rationality.

What indeed is required is the creation of moral *elbow room* within the space of causality. The space of reason, which is always in competition with the space of causality within the total orbit of a human life, needs to neutralize *at least* some space of causality in order to realize a *minimally* moral life. What is meant by this is that the human moral life gets going as soon as the human self begins to make choices of action from within the space of reason. And so to begin to make choices of action is, correspondingly, to withdraw oneself from making choices from within the space of causality. A person who makes all her choices entirely under the influence of forces emanating from within the space of causality would have no 'elbow room' at all for moral freedom.

It is the creativity of pure practical reason that enables the human self partially to neutralize the stronghold of causality (that is, of inclination) and thereby to create some elbow room for the possibility of human morality. The true measure of a moral life is therefore determined by how much, or how less, of that life and its conducts is given over to forces in the space of causality. In an imaginably idealized case, a maximally moral person's choices would be exercised within the space of the largest possible elbow room.

The appropriateness of the metaphor of 'elbow room' needs to be articulated. The concept of elbow room means that there is a spatial enclosure within which one is so situated as to be able to move freely. It also means that the space of obstruction is reduced in proportion to the available space for free movement. Furthermore, it implies that elbow room can either increase or decrease depending on the prevailing condition of the situation. Hence it follows from all this that the spatial enclosure constitutes the frame within which the concept of elbow room makes sense. There can be no elbow room that has so much room that there is no proximity to an enclosure which would limit its extent.

Now, if the space of pure practical reason, or for that matter moral freedom, is nothing but the elbow room within the space of causality, then it follows, in accordance with the above line of reasoning, that the space of causality is the framing enclosure with reference to which the moral elbow room has to be conceived. Consequently, imagining the creation of moral elbow room outside the space of causality, and in a noumenal or transcendent space of reason, would be quite untrue to the actual nature of human freedom and morality. In this sense, the actual matrix of morality is phenomenal rather than noumenal, even though pure practical reason by itself is not phenomenal. And it would be a mistake to think that a human moral elbow room could ever turn into a cosmic elbow room having no limiting frame other than the limitless cosmos.

Concluding with a Note on Radical Evil

To end this essay I now wish to invoke an idea that Kant introduces and discusses in *Religion within the Limits of Reason Alone*. Kant defines a moral life in terms of a striving for moral perfection, which is a pursuit of virtue. The morally good person is idealized into a person of *perfect virtue*, a perfectly virtuous character. Kant maintains that the human pursuit of virtue always begins from a state of *moral imperfection*, which is, in his own words, a condition of 'radical evil'.[11] This propensity to evil is the all too human tendency to make self-excusing exceptions to oneself in the face of the daunting strictures of the Moral Law. It is a tendency to escape the command of the moral law and thereby to subordinate moral considerations to those stemming from *self-love*. Even though we humans do not always in fact do this, it is a propensity that even the best among us are not free from. Since this propensity is innate in us all, we must constantly struggle against the subordination of the moral incentive to self-interested motivation.

We can surely imagine the possibility of a transition from radical evil to perfect virtue. But we cannot imagine the actualization of that possibility within the mortal course of human life. For moral imperfection, or proneness to radical evil, would not be overcome until the moral agent attains the condition of a holy will, which a human person is unlikely ever to attain. The persistence of this propensity for radical evil, or subordination of the moral incentive to self-love, is part of our ineluctable confinement within the space of causality. Condemned to live with an unholy will, the human person is destined to live a life of continuous struggle for moral existence. However, the purported end of this struggle is nothing less than the unattainable perfect virtue, which is the condition of complete reversal of the 'order of incentive' from the tendency to evil to that of reverence for the Moral Law.

The reversal of the order of incentive referred to in the above is clearly indicative of the suggestion that Kant wants the human moral agent to recognize the inner infinity of the moral self. The inner world of the moral self presents a glimmer of the angel of virtue, and the human rational agent is expected to have glimpses of the glimmering angel. Finite and temporal though this agent is, its moral course of life is to be led in tune with the intimation of infinity.

Notes

1. Immanuel Kant, *Practical Philosophy* (ed. and trans. Mary J. Gregor) Cambridge University Press, Cambridge, 1996, p. 269, italics original.
2. Ibid., p. 89.
3. Ibid.
4. Karl Ameriks, *Kant and the Fate of Autonomy*, Cambridge University Press, Cambridge, 2000, p. 4.
5. Lewis White Beck, 'Kant's Two Conceptions of the Will in their Political Context' (1965), reprinted in Ronald Beiner and William James Booth (eds), *Kant and Political Philosophy*, Yale University Press, New Haven and London, pp. 38–49.
6. Ibid., p. 46, italics added.
7. Immanuel Kant, 'Preface to the Second Edition', *Critique of Pure Reason*, Second edition, (Norman Kemp Smith trans.), Macmillan and Co., London, 1933, p. 29.
   Immanuel Kant, *Critique of Judgement*, (James Creed Meredith trans.), Clarendon Press, Oxford, 1992.
8. Kant, *Practical Philosophy*, p. 269, italics original.
9. Ibid., pp. 269–70.
10. J. B. Schneewind, 'Autonomy, Obligation and Virtue: An Overview of Kant's Moral Philosophy', in Paul Guyer (ed.), *The Cambridge Companion to Kant*, Cambridge University Press, Cambridge, 1992, p. 318.
11. Immanuel Kant, *Religion Within the Limits of Reason Alone*, (Theodore M. Greene and Hoyt H. Hudson trans.), Harper and Row, New York, 1960, pp. 23–4.

Krishnachandra Bhattacharyya on the Unknowability of Self in Kant

Problematizing the Programme of Indian Remedies to Western Problems

A. Raghuramaraju

This is the story about Paramanandayya and his disciples. Ten disciples of the Guru Paramanandayya went to the forest to collect firewood. On their way back they lost their way and had to cross a river, which was flowing full. After crossing they wanted to make sure that all of them had crossed the river. One of them started counting out got only nine, finding one missing, which worried him. Subsequently, each started doing the counting but could find only nine and not ten. They were worried that one of them was missing. They ran to their Guru and reported to him that one of them was missing. The Guru asked all of them to stand in a row and counted and he found all ten disciples. And the disciples felt happy. (Folk tale from south India)

Kant and India

Kant is one of the pre-eminent bonesetters history has produced. If we accept that it is Descartes who, in formulating the project of modernity, removed everything of the pre-modern and retained only the skeleton in the form of a bare and brittle cogito, Hume broke the spine of this skeleton. However, it is Kant who bestowed a wonderful maze and set the broken bones together. So it is befitting that we remember him after two hundred years. Kant is important especially to India in two specific respects. He is an important enlightenment thinker. Remember postmodern philosophers like Foucault found it important to take on Kant seriously, especially in his essay 'Question concerning what is Enlightenment'. Or feminists like S.M. Okin, who trace the modern political philosophy's gender bias, particularly in the writings of John Rawls, to his participation in Kantian legacy.[1] That is, though Descartes is the founder of Enlightenment, it is in Kant that it becomes more responsible, at least in its social aspects. Let us recall the extent of radical postures in Descartes.

Declaring his normative scale, which consists of cogito, reason and certainty, he embarks on excluding the following: childhood (as it is the domain governed by appetite and teachers rather than reason),[2] language,[3] history (to him past is like travelling which takes us away from the present), oratory, poetry (poetry is the 'gift of mind rather than fruits of study'),[4] moral writings of pagans,[5] customs, and evolutionary growth of societies (he rejects gradual growth of societies).[6] He even rejects classical logic and mathematics as they are 'mixed up with' all sorts of things.[7] This exclusion and their subsequent inclusion (this time according to the standards of modern thematic), some by Descartes himself through modification such as logic, mathematics, language, and other aspects by subsequent thinkers, such as history by Hegel, evolution by Darwin, and the unconscious by Freud, constitute the major preoccupation of Western modernity.[8] While there is a total radical posture in Descartes' formulation of the project of enlightenment or modernity, this posture, however, turns out to be too abstract and thus tends to be diminutive. Alternatively, while the project of enlightenment is totally radical, mostly without compromises, except through the notion of the penal gland, in Kant, it becomes more responsible. For instance, the autonomous self of Kant does become responsible to other autonomous selves, thus paving the way for inter-subjectivity, or later developments in Hegel and other phenom-enological thinkers. Without Kant, Western philosophy taking off from Descartes would not have spread like it did later. It could have vanished like a whimper. It is this that makes Kant's contribution to the project of modernity very significant, whose spread has not been confined only to the place of its origin but spread like wild fire across the globe, which makes someone like Heidegger say that the earth is getting Europeanized. In this spread it has affected India too. Apart from this macro-level influence, Kant is also important to India in another respect. This time in a specific and academic sense. A contemporary Indian philosopher like Krishnachandra Bhattacharyya specifically bases his philosophical analysis by providing a critique of Kant. In this essay, I shall discuss Bhattacharya's critique of Kant, focusing on his work *The Concept of Philosophy*.[9]

Following a brief discussion of Bhattacharyya's critique of Kant the essay in turn presents a critique of Bhattacharyya's Indian solution to the Kantian problem. In this context it asserts that instead of travelling in space, which is fraught with many problems of cultural translatability, there is a need to travel in time and in the process the essay points out the disguised divinity in Kant and offers traditional Western solutions to modern Western problems.

Kantian Self

While classical philosophies both Western and Indian have accepted agentless consciousness or divine consciousness, this essay discusses the problems related to the relation between self as a knower and the unknowability of self or self-knowledge. It will focus on two aspects, namely self-knowledge and certainty, to understand the Kantian problematic. Kantian problematic, for Bhattacharyya, lies in the 'knowability of the self as a metaphysical entity'. While Kant makes self the source of knowledge, but for him, says Bhattacharyya, 'self is not in itself knowable'. Kant postulates the unknowability of the self in order to avoid a logical impasse. That is, if self is knowable then that self needs to be known, this in turn has to be known by something else, and this goes on towards an infinite regress.[10] Bhattacharya believes that, to avoid this, Kant justifies this choice by making self a 'necessity of thought' and an 'object of moral faith'.[11]

Taking off from Bhattacharyya's diagnoses we can show Kantian justification to be a weak justification to establish the existence of self, particularly, when self is the key and central concept in modern Western philosophy. Bhattacharyya traces the inevitability of this agnosticism to make 'thinking' equivalent to 'knowing'.[12]/[13] He alleges that it is this equating which underlies the Kantian problematic. The diagnosis of Kantian problematic in this manner by Bhattacharyya is novel. Other philosophers like Brentano, Menong and Husserl who largely toed the Hegelian track in understanding and overcoming the Kantian problematic have not seen this problem in Kant the way Bhattacharyya did. They tried to overcome this problem by naturalizing self or offering formulations such as being-in-the-world *a la* Heidegger. Apart from these developments within the phenomenological tradition, this solipsism of the modern self is also sought to be overcome in the analytical tradition by Wittgenstein's well-known ordinary language argument. Bhattacharyya approaches Kant away from these trajectories. His ingenuity lies in his ability to use Advaitic position or insights to understand the Kantian problematic, through critical comparison. In this way, he becomes a fine and fitting example of his own observation in his famous essay 'Swaraj in Ideas' where he talks of contributing to the culturally informed understanding of Indian thinkers in their reading of texts from other cultures. He says in a lecture delivered to students as Principal of a college:

One would have expected after a century of contact with the vivifying ideas of the West that there should be vigorous output of Indian contribution in a distinctive Indian style to the culture and thought of the modern world,—contribution specially to humane subjects like history, philosophy or literature, a contribution such as may be enjoyed by our countrymen who still happen to retain their vernacular mind and which might be recognized by others as reflecting the distinctive soul of India. Barring the contribution of a few men of genius,—and genius is largely independent of the times,—there is not much evidence of such creative work done by our educated men.[14]

In my assessment Bhattacharyya no doubt belongs to those few men in whose writings the 'distinctive soul of India' has been reflected. Now let us discuss his solution to overcome this problem in Kant. He offers Advaita solutions to overcome the Kantian problematic. Let me discuss Bhattacharyya's Advaitic, spatial (space) solution to the Kantian problematic. He suggests the need to break open the equivalence between 'knowing' and 'thinking' assumed by Kant and recommends that in addition to thinking there are ways of knowing outside the mode of thinking. To quote him:

My position is… that the self is unthinkable and on the other that while actually
it is not known and is only an object of faith, though not necessarily only of
moral faith, we have to admit the possibility of knowing it without *thinking*…[15]

At the outset let me point out that his position is closer to the Advaita
position if not Advaita *per se*. As part of elucidating this knowing
without thinking he distinguishes four grades of thought.

Four grades of thought

Empirical Thought (ET): Empirical thought is theoretic consciousness
of a content involving reference to an object that is perceived or
imagined to be perceived.

Pure Objective Thought (POT): Pure objective thought are contents
that are object but have no necessary reference to sense-perception.
He also calls it contemplative thought.

Spiritual Thought (ST): The contents of spiritual thought are not
objects, nothing that is contemplated here is in the objective attitude.
It being subjective in the sense of being appreciated in a subjective
or 'enjoying' attitude.

Transcendental Thought (TT): Transcendental thought is a consciousness
of a content that is neither objective nor subjective. In his reckoning
transcendental truth is that aspect of thought which is knowledge
which is not, strictly speaking, thinking but beyond thought. This
is also the domain of truth. He says of the absolute:

The absolute as transcending the enjoyed reality of religion is positive being
(truth) or positive non-being (freedom) or their positive indetermination
(value). The absolute is conceived rigorously as truth in (Advaita) Vedanta.
What is loosely called nihilist Buddhism apparently understands the absolute
as freedom. The Hegelian absolute may be taken to represent the
indetermination, miscalled *identity* of truth and freedom which is value. All
these views belong to what may be called the transcendental grades of
philosophy.[16]

Though he refers to nihilist Buddhism and Hegel, I will not discuss
them here as his focus is Advaita and these two schools are used

mostly to further illustrate his point about truth. Having distinguished four grades of thought, he also ET as fact, POT as self-subsistent, ST as reality and TT as truth. He further goes on to classify them under two broad categories, namely, the domain of science and the domain of philosophy. He places fact under science and the other three, namely, self-subsistence, reality and truth under philosophy. Specifying the major differences between these two broad domains which he sharply demarcates, he says that fact is spoken of as information and understood without reference to a spoken form. It need not be spoken to be believed because speakability is a contingent character of the content of ET. In sharp contrast, speakability is a 'necessary character of the content of pure philosophic thought.' Further, speaking is not merely speaking as information and all speech is not expressed in the form of judgements. Even in those cases where thoughts are expressed in the form of a judgement, it is only artificial and symbolic. And of the spoken which necessarily refers to the speaking of it, there are three forms accordingly as it is spoken in the objective, the subjective or the transcendental attitude. Correspondingly, there are four grades of speakables. Like different grades of thought Bhattacharyya makes a general distinction between science and philosophy with reference to speakability. He says that the contents of the fact are spoken as information and are intelligible without reference to the speaking of it. Whereas contents of philosophy are not spoken as information and they are necessarily dependent on the speaking. Elucidating different grades of speakability he says that in the factual domain, that is ET the statement, 'x is' 'x', 'is' and their combination are literal. In POT, 'x' is literal, 'is' is literal but not their combination, which is symbolic. In ST, 'x' is literal 'is' and their combination is symbolic. In TT, all 'x', 'is' and their combination are symbolic.

Thus, by distinguishing four grades of thought he shows how knowing consists of not only thinking but also non-thinking knowledge. That is, there is a non-cognitive source of knowledge by way of aesthetic and spiritual knowledge (or self-knowledge), which also constitutes the knowledge domain. And this eluded the attention of Kant, which forced him to relapse into agnosticism. This non-cognitive knowledge can save the Kantian self from agnosticism.

Two important aspects in Bhattacharyya's engagement are his critique of Kant and Advaitic solution to overcome Kantian problem. While admiring his critique of Kant, let me however add a caveat, namely, there is a problem associated with Bhattacharyya, particularly in his attempt at fashioning or participating in an already existing fashion where Indian solutions are offered for Western problems. This wittingly or unwittingly makes the West a reservoir of problems and correspondingly East or India a reservoir of solutions. More specifically, this merely inverts the view, which at a structural level was authored by the colonial discourse, where India is the reservoir of problems and the West, solutions. What is problematic to me is not so much who is the reservoir of what, but the very binary that underlies this formulation.

Here let me digress a bit and point out that there are great resemblances between Gandhi and Bhattacharyya, for instance, in their rejection of the positing of a continuity between matter and spirit or materialism and spiritualism. That is, unlike the maze where continuity is posited between science and spiritualism or matter and spirit, authored by Swami Vivekananda and Sri Aurobindo, Bhattacharyya is in the company of Gandhi in rejecting any such continuity project. Moreover, and more importantly, both have authored a text each bearing the name *Swaraj*, *Hind Swaraj* by Gandhi and 'Swaraj in Ideas' by Bhattacharyya. Incidentally the authors of both these texts are influenced by Jainism. Notwithstanding these entrenched resemblances, more specifically about offering Indian solutions to Western problems Bhattacharyya is in the company of Swami Vivekananda and Sri Aurobindo and not with Gandhi. The latter, unlike Bhattacharyya, mostly refrained from these civilizational remedies. For instance, he would see spiritual Christianity as a solution to the material West, not Advaita or yoga from India. Conversely, he would find out internal resources to overcome or eliminate the evils in Indian society like untouchability or caste problems and many others. At a more general level he would find in these remedies from across the culture a tendency which deflects the interiority and internal preoccupation of the individuals within the community.[17] Here I am not suggesting that Gandhi was a cultural puritan, but pleading for taking his metaphor of house with open windows seriously. For Gandhi, the remedies from across the cultures, if sought, are to be diligently deliberated. This should also be preceded by a thorough search for internal remedies. If they are not found, then one can go for outside remedies. They also need to be sensitive to the cultural differences, and be as cautious as in choosing the blood group for transfusion.

While noting these differences between Gandhi and Bhattacharyya, it is necessary to note that the latter in his eagerness to propose Advaitic solution to overcome Kant's problematic does not sufficiently point out interesting and important details available from his diagnosis of Kant. Thus, he traverses a spatially different philosophical school, namely, Advaita. In this essay, I want, instead, to reopen a route in temporal terrain, relate Kant to theology in the West, and similarly shift the ground from epistemology to metaphysics or ontology. For instance, the theological or meta-physical aspects in disguise surround the Kantian self. That is, Kant is trying to embellish self with the aspects associated with divinity of the classical thought which they at one level rejected, and installed the self in its place. That is, God is rejected and in His place self is installed. Like God, who is a creator but not created, self in Kant, is the knower but cannot be known. It is my contention that while Enlightenment claimed to be radical in rejecting tradition, some crucial aspects of the tradition have sneaked in, either surreptitiously or because of the somnolentness of modernity. Further, there seems to be specificity in this sneaking thus making us reconsider the claims of success of modernity in its onslaught on tradition.[18] In order to detect this aspect let me recall two important and profound cautions against the complacency regarding the disappearance of the tradition, by Althusser and Ronald Barthes.[19] In his well known piece entitled, 'Ideology and Ideological State Apparatuses,' Althusser says:

Even after a social revolution like that of 1917, a large part of the State apparatus survived after the seizure of State power by the alliance of the proletariat and the small peasantry: Lenin repeated the fact again and again.[20]

Similarly, we have Barthes who reminds us or we can elicit from his essay 'The Death of Author', that God as the creator of the world is replaced by author as the sole creator of the text. Taking a clue from these thinkers, I want to explore those aspects of tradition which seem to have survived the onslaught of modernity. Taking Althusser's caution against complacency seriously, I want to explore some similarity between traditional aspects and Kant. In this context let me state classical arguments for the existence of God. Offering the proof for the existence of God, St. Aquinas says:

It is therefore impossible that in the same respect and in the same way a thing should be both mover and moved, that is that it should move itself. Therefore, whatever is in motion must be put in motion by another. If that by which it is put in motion be itself put in motion, then this also must needs be put in motion by another, and that by another again. But this cannot go on to infinity, because then there would be no first mover, and, consequently, no other mover; seeing that subsequent movers move only inasmuch as they are put in motion by the first mover; as the staff moves only because it is put in motion by the hand. Therefore it is necessary to arrive at a first mover, put in motion by no other; and this everyone understands to be God.[21]

Like the Kantian self, which is the only repository of knowledge, knowing the reality outside, the God in theology is the mover and cannot be said to move. Just as the effort to know the Kantian self leads to infinite regress, so too the effort to move the divine being relapses into infinite regress. So similar to the necessity to 'arrive at a first mover, put in motion by no other; and this everyone understands to be God' there is in Kant too the self which is the knower but not known. In this respect the problems of theology are not significantly different from those that are faced by Kant.

Taking the clue from Bhattacharyya or to extrapolate from his insights we can elicit that the problem with the Kantian self is its unknowability, which is an epistemological problem but its autonomy, is a metaphysical problem. The Kantian self is unknowable because it is autonomous and not vice versa. That is, autonomy of the self is the constitutive aspect in Kant. Since it is autonomous and not dependent, it is the source of knowledge but cannot be known. There is an intricate continuity and discontinuity underlying here. The discontinuity lies in the fact that, unlike the classical notions of self that is dependent on either nature or on divinity, the modern self, beginning from Descartes, is autonomous. Hence it is a radical departure from the classical framework. However, there is a surreptitious continuity that haunts the modern self, namely, its autonomy has major shades of classical divinity. Like God is the source of knowledge in the classical theories and man only participates in the divine discourse, similarly in the modern theories God is dispensed with and in His place an autonomous self is installed with the same kind of omnipotence. It is this metaphysical move that creates the epistemological problem in Kant.

In order to understand this more clearly we can compare this with yet another earlier position. There is no autonomous self in the classical philosophy. More specifically in Aristotle, what we have are pairs and not individuals. To quote Aristotle:

First of all, there must necessarily be a union or pairing of those who cannot exist without one another. Male and female must unite for the reproduction of the species—not from deliberate intention, but from the natural impulse, which exists in animals generally as it also exists in plants, to leave behind them something of the same nature as themselves. Next, there must necessarily be a union of the naturally ruling element with the element, which is naturally ruled, for the preservation of both. The element which is able, by virtue of its intelligence, to exercise forethought, is naturally a ruling and master element; the element which is able, by virtue of its bodily power, to do what the other element plans, is a ruled element, which is naturally in a state of slavery...'[22]

So, for Aristotle, pair is prior to the individual. Moreover this gets further reinforced in his famous argument that whole is prior to part. So within the Greek philosophy there is no place for an autonomous self. The autonomous self comes to be constituted more prominently by Descartes. But this autonomous self is not to be equated with the empirical self. The autonomous self is endowed with more of the divine qualities and it is human only in name.

So we can understand Kant through this Cartesian legacy. The Cartesian self, though reductionistic, is, however, less vulnerable for inconsistencies. It is Kant who in the process of naturalizing the Cartesian self makes it vulnerable to criticism such as the one by Bhattacharyya. This move by Kant to naturalize the autonomous self haunts the later Western philosophy of Hegel, Minong, Husserl, Sartre, and others. For these the transcendental status of self becomes enigmatic but indispensable. Husserl and Sartre tried to dispense with it but finally had to accept it. Viewed from this perspective, the quest for certainty is more a theological and classical quest rather than scientific. Further, the achievement of modernity is confined, to use Althusser's insight, to the removal of agency, in this case, God, and installing in its place the human, without destroying the structures inhabited by the erstwhile agency, that is, God. Here one starts wondering whether what Krishnachandra Bhattacharyya is alluding to is the presence of the Guru in the story, an appeal that obviates a return to the classical theories. It is against this that today one has to re-examine the relation between modernity and tradition. It is like the self looking at the mirror to see its own reflection. So Kant faced these problems because he inhabited in an adventure which installs an autonomous self, attributes to it those divine characteristics which make it vulnerable.

Further, we can also detect in modern quest an obsession with fool proof certain knowledge.[23] That is, there seems to be an inconsistency between finite human subjects and certain knowledge. Like the aspects generally associated with god or divinity in the classical period like unknowability of god, quest for certainty, what Kant does is that he embellishes the self with these divine aspects. In this changed scenario, the modern self does not become a natural and empirical individual or his or her ally but threatens to show its proximity to the divine, which is at the root of modern anthropocentric threats to ordinary empirical human beings.[24]

That is, notwithstanding the radical posture of the project of modernity, some crucial aspects from the tradition which they claimed to have rejected, survived, at least in a disguised form. Recognizing these features that survived is not only important for those who inhabit modernity as that would make them non-complacent and cautious, but also those who critique modernity, as this would save them from offering distant and special remedies when temporal and ingenious ones are available.

To come back to the main point, the problem with Bhattacharyya's attempt is that he tries to solve an ontological problem at an epistemological level. That is, self in Kant is unknowable which is similar to that of unmover in theology. The unmover in theology is understandable even though we may not accept it, but the unknower in modernity is embarrassing, as it smacks of the smell of divinity which they discarded. Instead of divulging these divine aspects in Kant, Bhattacharyya embarks on negotiating the problem at an epistemological level where he proposes to broaden it by including non-thinking as part of knowing. That is, this broadened knowledge proposed by Bhattacharyya makes even the empirical self which passes through the four stages suggested by him culminates in this self becoming divine. Alternatively, the self at TT does not remain an empirical self but a transcendental self or over-personal self, which is a form of divinity. If this is granted then, instead of routing the Kantian problematic though Advaita thus traversing distant cultures, and all this to achieve or face divinity, I am suggesting this is already there in Western thought, in theology and classical Greek thought.

It is this disguised theology in Kant that eluded the attention of Bhattacharyya, which interests me enormously. Perhaps it is this counting self (in the story) or the knowing self, which is not counted or known that is needed. Moreover there is a need to bring back the divine self. That is, while Bhattacharyya is attempting to humanize the Kantian self I want to disclose the divine aspects in it thereby neutralizing the radical stance in Kant. This makes Bhattacharyya's critique of Kant redundant, robing the Kantian self with the traditional dress. That is, unlike Bhattacharyya's attempt that tries to Indianize the Kantian self, I want to classicalize it. While his attempt traverses space, mine traverses time. In other words, there is a need to broaden the terms of Kantian problematic to include theology. Without paying attention to these significant developments taking place within Western philosophy, to jump suddenly like Bhattacharyya does, I am afraid, is hasty. And as a result 'the jump' may not be informed of the complexities.

Self in Indian Philosophy

It is true that there are closer resemblances between Kant and theology, which eluded the attention of Bhattacharyya. However, there are some interesting insights from Indian philosophy. These, though not remedies, throw important light on the Kantian problematic, details about which are not elaborated in Bhattacharyya. According to Kumarila, says, Hiriyanna,

…we become aware of our own self. It is known directly through the aham-pratyaya or the 'I-notion' as we may render it. [*Sastra-dipita* by Parthasarathi Misra with Yukti-snehaprapurani (*Nirnaya Sag* Pr. P. 122)]

Explaining this point further Hiriyanna says:

...Kumarila understands 'self-consciousness' literally and holds that the self can at once be both subject and object—the knower as well as the known (*jada-bodhatmaka*) and adduces as evidence therefore the common saying: 'I know myself.' Ascribing such an apparently contradictory character to the self is quite in harmony with the ruling principle of his thought, which as we shall see, is that the nature of things cannot be rigidly determined as such and such (*bhedābheda-vāda*). [*Sastra-dipita* by Parthasarathi Misra with Yukti-snehaprapurani (*Nirnaya Sag* Pr. P. 101)] In a sample of knowledge like 'I know the jar' there are two elements—one comprehending the self (*aham-vrtti*) and the other comprehending the object in question (for example *ghata-vrtti*). That is, self-awareness is constant and accompanies all states of consciousness, being absent only in deep sleep where no object is known. When we say that the self is thus known in all experience, we must not take it to mean that it is known as the *subject* in the act of knowing. The fact of knowing is itself not known at the time and has, as already pointed out, to be inferred later. We cannot, therefore, know the self then as characterized by or as owning such knowledge, which is what is meant by the term 'subject'. But yet the self cannot be unknown, for that would go against the felt personal identity in all one's experience. It is therefore explained as being known then as the *object* of the 'I-notion'. If we take this along with the view that the self to be known at all must at the time become aware of some object or other, we see that self-consciousness, according to Kumarila, implies not only an internal difference—a self which is opposed to itself as its object, but also an external difference—a self which is distinguished from the not-self.[25]

Elucidating further the disagreement with this view of Kumarila by Prabhakara, Hiriyanna says:

Prabhakara disagrees with Kumarila in two important respects in his view of the self, and in both he sides with the Nyaya-Vaisesika. Not believing in *parinama* he does not admit that the self suffers change. Again he objects to the description of the self as 'knowable', and avers that agent and object can never be the same in any act. It is only objects that are knowable. The self, on the other hand, is a subject and is revealed *as such* in all *jnana*. If it were not so revealed simultaneously with the object, one's jnana would be indistinguishable from another's. From this, it should not be thought that the *atman* is self-luminous. It is wholly non-sentient (*jada*), and therefore requires for its revelation the presence of some knowledge to which the character of self-luminousness is assigned. Though thus dependent upon an aid self, to be realized, does not require a separate mental act, it being manifest equally whenever any object is known. The word which the Prabhakaras use for knowledge or experience is *samvit* which, being self-luminous (*svaprakash*) needs nothing else to make it manifest. Though ultimate in this sense, it is not eternal.

It appears and disappears; and, as it does so, reveals both the object and the self simultaneously with itself. This triple revelation is what is described as triputi-jnana.[26]

Similarly, *Sankhya Karika* of Isvara Krsna talks about the prime mover who only moves but is not moved, and the problem of infinite regress, echoing somewhat the thesis of the proof for the existence of God. It says in one *sloka*:

Mulaprakrtir avikrtir
      Mahadadyah prakrti-vikrtayah sapta
Sadasakas tu vikaro
      Na prakrtir na vikrtih purusah.

Primal Nature is not an evolute; the seven, beginning with the Great One (the intellect) are both evolvents and evolutes; the sixteen (the five organs of sense, the five of actions, the mind and the five gross elements) are only evolutes; the spirit is neither evolvent nor evolute. (1973: 8)[27]

So likewise we can look at these similar standpoints in Indian philosophy to understand better the philosophical positions in the West. But to take these similarities further and offer them as solutions to problems across cultures can become problematic. In other words, I am pointing out that comparative philosophy while throwing light across cultures might neglect internal aspects that are important.

Let me summarize my arguments. While accepting novelty in Bhattacharyya's critique of Kantian problematic, I, however, have pointed the problem in his solution, namely offering Advaitic solution. Instead, I have pointed out that there is a need to disclose the disguised divinity in Kant and take him back in time to the traditional discourses such as theology and divine frameworks, also point out in this process the shift from metaphysics to epistemology, which eluded Bhattacharya's analysis. In the end, I have discussed some similar instances from Indian philosophy on this theme, though not as remedies but insights across cultures.

My purpose in this essay is to read carefully the comparative axis, thereby avoiding both mere dismissal and uncritical celebration of these scholarly criticisms on Western philosophy by contemporary Indian philosophers. This is important because these writings carry either willingly or otherwise vital cultural shades. However, in discovering these shades and admiring their brilliance, one needs to be vigilant about the gaps and lapses that might have led many not to take these writings seriously. One way of making these contemporary Indian metaphysical writings philosophically available to the community of philosophers is to read them seriously.

Notes

1. Susan Moller Okin, 'Reason and Feeling in Thinking about Justice', *Ethics*, Vol. 99 (2), 1989, pp. 229–49.
2. R. Descartes, 'Discourse on Method', in *The Philosophical Writings of Descartes*, Vol. I, (John Cottingham, Robert Stoothoff and Dugald Murdoch trans.), Cambridge University Press, Cambridge, 1985, p. 117.
3. Ibid., pp. 113 and 117.
4. Ibid., p. 114.
5. Ibid.
6. Ibid., p. 116.
7. Ibid., pp. 119–20.
8. This process of exclusion and ensuing transformation is not a smooth affair, but consists of violence and oppression. Foucault's work bears testimony to how modern knowledge unleashed power on human subjects within the West.
9. The reason why I have focused on Krishnachandra Bhattacharyya's essay, 'The Concept of Philosophy', and not his book, *Subject as Freedom*, is, that Kalidas Bhattacharyya gives following reasons to show that K.C. Bhattacharya's essay represents his mature philosophy. Pointing out the differences between *Subject as Freedom* and 'The Concept of Philosophy', Kalidas Bhattacharyya says:

These are not difficult theses for those who are acquainted with Bhattacharyya's *The Subject as Freedom*. But there are some additional points—some of which bear even adversely on what he has said in that monograph—which ought to be noted immediately.

First, there is no significant reference, in that monograph, and certainly no elaboration of it, either to pure self-subsistent object or to pure objective thought or the exact status of metaphysics (and logic) and their relation, on the one hand, to empirical object and empirical thought and, on the other, to pure subjectivity and spiritual philosophy.... He has rather shown how directly from science we turn to this latter. Metaphysics, has not been paid even a fraction of attention he pays to it in his *The Concept of Philosophy*....

Secondly, what he writes, in this essay, on pure spiritual thinking and its content is not only an improvement, in certain fundamentals, on what he has said on (spiritual) introspection in his *The Subject as Freedom*, but also adds a few accompaniments which go a long way to clarify his idea of the passage from introspection to what he has called 'beyond introspection' in that monograph and 'transcendental thought' in the present essay....

Thirdly, while in *The Subject as Freedom* Bhattacharyya placed the stage 'beyond introspection' under the class *spiritual subjectivity*, here in his 'The Concept of Philosophy' he understands the *absolute* as the content of a grade of thought which is *no longer spiritual*, the reason being that the content here – the absolute – has primarily to be called truth rather than reality, and truth is as much qualitatively distinct from reality as reality from self-subsistent object: while reality is all subjective, truth is neither subjective nor objective. (Kalidas Bhattacharya, *The Fundamentals of K.C. Bhattacharyya's Philosophy*, Saraswat Library, Calcutta, 1975, pp. 187–92)

This is the reason why I discussed his essay apart from the other reason, namely, it clearly articulates the relation between science and philosophy.

10. Reminiscent of this situation there is an instance in Brihad-Âranyaka Upanishad when Gârgî asks:
'On what then, pray, are the worlds of Brahma woven, warp and woof?' Yâjñavalkya said: 'Gârgî, do not question too much, lest your head fall off. In truth, you are questioning too much about a divinity about which further questions cannot be asked. Gârgî, do not over-question.'" (*The Thirteen Principle Upanishads*, translated from the Sanskrit by Ernest Hume, second edition, Oxford University Press, New Delhi, 2003, p. 114.)

11. Krishnachandra Bhattacharyya, 'The Concept of Philosophy', in *Studies in Philosophy*, Gopinath Bhattacharya (ed.), Motilal Banarsidass, Delhi, p. 462.

12. It is possible that Kant has not committed the mistake that is pointed out by Krishnachandra Bhattacharyya.

13. Here it may be noted that Bhattacharyya points out yet another problem or lapse in Kant when he says:
In taking the self to be unthinkable, I understand Kant's idea of the Reason to be not only not knowledge, but to be not even thought in the literal sense. The so-called extension of thought beyond experience and the possibility of experience means to me only the use of the verbal form of thought as a symbol of an unthinkable reality, such symbolizing use not being thinking. (Ibid., p. 462)

14. Krishnachandra Bhattacharyya, 'Swaraj in Ideas', in *Indian Philosophical Quarterly*, Vol. XI, No. 4, October 1984, p. 385.

15. Ibid., p. 462.

16. Ibid., pp. 478–9.

17. See also A.L. Basham, 'Traditional Influences on the Thought of Mahatma Gandhi', in *Essays on Gandhian Politics: The Rowlett Satyagraha of 1919*, Ravindra Kumar (ed.), Clarendon Press, Oxford 1971, pp. 17–42.

18. Here I am deliberately using the word tradition and not pre-modern as the latter is a larger reality and difficult to combat than perhaps the former.

19. Roland Barthes, 'The Death of Author', in *Image-Music-Text*, (Stephen Heath trans.), Hill and Wang, New York, 1997.

20. Louis Althusser, *Essays on Ideology*, Verso, London, 1984, pp. 14–15.

21. St. Thomas Aquinas, *The Summa Theologica of St. Thomas Aquinas*, Second and Revised edition, 1920 (trans. Fathers of the English Dominican Province), Online edition copyright © 2003 by Kevin Knight.

22. Aristotle, *The Politics of Aristotle*, (Ernest Barker ed. and trans.), Oxford, University Press, Delhi, 1986, p. 3.

23. I, in my essay entitled 'Internal Project of Modernity and Postcolonialism', in *Economic and Political Weekly*, Vol. XL, no. 39, September 24–30, 2005, pp. 4214–18, have discussed the reason for certainty in Descartes.

24. However, it must be recognized that this garb is removed only in the liberals, who through the method of induction rejected the certainty of knowledge and naturalized the self and morality.

25. M. Hiriyanna, *Outlines of Indian Philosophy*, George Allen & Unwin Ltd., London, 1967, pp. 305–6.

26. Ibid., pp. 306–7.

27. Isvar Krsna, *The Sankhya Karika of Isvara Krsna*, (S.S. Suryanarayana Sastri ed. and trans.), University of Madras, Madras, 1973. Explaining this sloka Sastri says:

There are four classes of beings—those which, though themselves not produced, yet bring others into existence, those which produce and are themselves produced, those which are products alone and cannot produce anything different from themselves, and those beings which, neither producing nor produced, are totally different in nature from the first three. The first of these is called Prakrti or Primal Nature. The diversity of effects leads us to look for their explanation in the causes that produce them. The manifold causes eventually lead us to a single cause, which is called Prakriti. Prakrti is itself not caused; if the cause were assumed, further cause of that cause would also have to be postulated and we shall thus have an infinite regress, a process that is not consistent with a rational solution. Prakrti is thus the uncaused cause, the evolvent that is not an evolute. It is the seed from which creation springs, but it has not begun to sprout not even to swell prior to sprouting....

We cannot, in looking for a cause, go beyond prakrti, it was said, because of the regress ad infinitum. But in the classification of effects why should we stop with the gross elements and the *indriyas* (senses)? Various modifications of the elements are known and with reference to these they may well claim to be evolvents. Thus animal bodies and insentient objects are different modifications of each; in relation to them earth is the cause, and yet it is said to be a bare evolute. The reason is that to be an evolvent is not to be any kind of cause, but the cause of a different mode of being. A pitcher or a cow is not a mode of being different from the earth of which they are modifications. They are just as gross as their cause, they are perceptible by the same senses as their cause. What we have, in short, is not evolution but a modification. This may be contrasted with the production of gross elements from subtle elements. The two sets of elements are different in that the former are perceptible by the senses while the latter are not. Among themselves too, the gross elements represent different modes of being, in that each of them is known by a different organ of cognition, as ether by the ear, fire by the eye and so on. If, then, the process of the division of the categories stops with the gross elements and the organs, it is for sufficient reason. (pp. 8–11)

SECTION 3

RELIGION

'Religion and Public Reasoning'

Enlightenment and Critical Deliberation on Religion in Western and Islamic Societies Today

Matthias Lutz-Bachmann

To Goenawan Mohamad, Indonesian poet and world citizen

Kant on 'Religion and Public Reasoning'

The programme of a 'public reasoning' as it has been developed in the Western liberal tradition goes back to the philosophy of enlightenment in the eighteenth century. One of its famous authors was Immanuel Kant whose two-hundredth death anniversary was celebrated in 2004. Kant defined 'enlightenment' as the public use of one's reason with respect to all problems which have an influence on the life of men and women in a society.[1] In Kant's view, 'reason' is generically understood as a capacity of human mind to raise and to answer the big questions not only about 'reality' and 'causality' in the physical world—which is one of the tasks of the sciences—but also about the rightness of moral norms and the legitimacy of social and political institutions. 'Public reasoning' or 'critical deliberation' in the general public therefore has been the key concept for Kant in order to explain how the enlightenment and the intended reform of the political institutions towards a civil society and a constitution of a republican state might become successful in Europe of the eighteenth century. As an eminent source for the interpretation of the sense of human life and an important factor in the society it was also religion which was thought by Kant to become subject of a public reasoning and critique. In the preface to his famous *Critique of Pure Reason* of 1781 Kant already maintains that in the 'age of criticism' which he described the way he saw his century, both religion and politics could only claim a future validity in as much as they underwent an examination by a free and public debate.[2]

This remark of Kant is informative since it makes us aware of the historical place of his reflections. Kant's statements on religion belong to the period of early modern philosophy when the mainstream of the philosophers looked for something like an ahistoric, so-called 'natural religion' based on a philosophical concept of reason beyond the diverse historic religions which defined themselves either by revelation or by textual and oral tradition. The idea of a 'natural religion' was insofar linked to a programme of a 'critique of religion'[3] in the name of 'reason' and judged by a criteria of reasonable arguments.

This programme connected such different positions like the English movement of Deism,[4] John Locke,[5] David Hume[6] or Jean-Jacque Rousseau[7] with Immanuel Kant's philosophy. Their contribution to a philosophy of religion is determined not only by the philosophical ideas of a rational examination of the truth claims of religions but also by the intention to discover a normative but secular fundament for the modern state. The European enlightenment had learned its lessons from the experiences of civil wars in the name of conflicting religious confessions after the time of Reformation and the break of a united Latin Christianity into diverse denominations. Consequently the enlightenment looked for a legitimacy of the political order of the modern state which was not depending on a mutual consent of all its citizens to one specific formula of religious faith in the tradition of the conflicting Christian denominations. Unlike Locke, Hobbes or Rousseau, it was Kant who did not refer to a 'natural religion' or a 'civil religion' in order to explain the constitution and legitimacy of the modern state.

According to his political philosophy the state was to be established on the universal concept of human rights and the basic principle of freedom of men in their intersubjective interactions with each other, but not on any religious principle or statement at all.[8] Kant's reasons for the necessity of a non-religious, secular fundament of the state neither imply any contempt of religion nor an atheistic ideology. On the contrary, as we can see in his famous book *On Religion Within the Limits of Pure Reason Alone*, he highly esteemed religion, in particular in its critically reflected form, as an ideal for moral perfection in an ethical commonwealth[9] and qualified the basic sentences of Christian belief in God, in an eternal post-mortal life or in redemption as reasonable statements. But he insisted on his judgement that the validity neither of the normative assertions of moral philosophy nor of the legal order of the state should be rooted in religion. On the other side, Kant didn't support a liberalist or extreme secularist position, namely to banish religion out of the public sphere of the state and to declare religion, strictly spoken, a private matter. Since religion always represents a kind of shared sense or significance for communities of men and women, the idea of the privacy of religion is obviously misleading, and Kant didn't follow this path. He even recognized not only a normative or practical meaning of religious belief but also an epistemic core of its truth. Therefore Kant stated the possibility and the necessity to examine the truth claims of religion in an open and unlimited process of public reasoning by which alone the legitimate authority of religion—as he expected—could come to light.

Religion and 'Public Reasoning': The two 'intellectual revolutions' before Kant

Kant and the other enlightened philosophers of the seventeenth and eighteenth centuries have not been the first philosophers in the West who argued in favour of an examination of the truth claims of religion by a philosophical concept of reasoning. The reflections on the relationship between the religious virtues like faith, hope and love on the one hand and the search for philosophical insight by reason, intellect and wisdom on the other are present already in the Old and New Testaments. In the first millennium of Christianity we find important statements on the relationship between religious belief and philosophical reasoning in the works of thinkers who identified themselves as philosophers in the ancient Greek tradition of philosophy and as theologians at the same time: Justinos the Martyr in the second century after Christ, Clemens, head of the intellectual School of Alexandria in the third or Augustin in the fourth century. It was Augustin who on the one hand claimed literary 'a philosophical truth' and reasonable insight for the confession of the Christian faith. In consequence of this truth claim in the proper sense he taught, on the other hand, that not the ordinary believer but the educated theologian is committed to argue for the truth he claimed by means of rational methods like grammar, logic or philosophy—well accepted by believers and unbelievers. This obligation was the rational consequence of Augustin's claim of a universal truth for the Christian faith. This programme did influence not only the concept of a Christian theology but also the later development of the 'kalam' and its influence on Islamic and Jewish thinking in the Arabic speaking world.

Here we can identify an early culture of 'public reasoning' on religion within the world of the late antiquity. Early Christianity accepted—even if not without internal quarrels—in principle the idea for both the necessity and the possibility to justify the religious creed in front of the audience of the dominant pagan Roman-Hellenistic culture by virtue of its most reflected and rational arts and sciences in the tradition of the liberal arts. This helped to transform the former esoteric or closed character of ancient philosophy, often taught in elite circles for the well educated youth of the ruling class of aristocracy, into a much more public discourse, open to everybody. And in the same process of transformation, religion changed its character from a certain kind of collective and ritual praxis in observing the cults linked to the political sphere and obedient to the omnipotent state of antiquity to a new reflexive praxis of individual and free members of a covenant, if necessary even opposing the authority of the state. In his City of God, Augustin draws the conclusions for the identity of the Christian church vis-à-vis the cruel reality of the Roman state which were taken up later by modern thinkers like Locke or Kant who looked for a fundament of legitimacy with reference to the republic and found this fundament in the idea of the covenant or an original contract of the free individuals, accountable only for their personal consciousness and to God.

In the first millennium of Christianity we can therefore identify two revolutions referring to the understanding of religion and its relation to publicity and reason. The first one affected the relation between religion and rationality with the result that religion was being transformed into a reflexive praxis including a speculative doctrine which could reach justification of its assertions by secular arts and disciplines like grammar and logic, whereas philosophy was being transferred into a public reflection with universal validity claims on truth and insight by general methods of reasoning. The second intellectual revolution was interconnected with the first one by which the religious belief was seen as the result of an arbitrary and voluntary act of a free person in the light of justifiable reasons. It was one of its consequences that the covenant of believers had been distinguished from the community of people in the state and if necessary the covenant of believers could radically be thought of as opposing the political state which was governed by power and military force alone, but not by good reasons or by actions of peace. Both revolutions belong to the history of enlightenment in western civilization.

These new prospects of religion and philosophy did neither immediately nor totally determine the later concept of religion, of arts and sciences in the Latin-speaking Middle Ages. But it was always present even in these centuries. The second one for instance in the permanent conflict between the two powers church and state, and was therefore responsible for—what modern sociologists or historians call—the emerging inner-differentiation of the Western societies and finally for the concept of the independence of the church and the secular state. In the history of this conflict, the foundation for a modern theory of secular law was established.[10] The first one led to the 'intellectual revolution'[11] of the twelfth and thirteenth centuries, which laid the conceptual fundaments for the modern sciences and the ideas of the philosophy of enlightenment in the seventeenth and eighteenth centuries. The scientific revolution of the Middle Ages was linked to the rediscovery of the full concept of the ancient sciences after the time of the migration of peoples by the Schools of Higher Education in the twelfth century.[12] The programme of University was born in that time and the legal independence of the universities helped to develop an institution of free discourse as one of the driving forces for a public and free reasoning, widely independent from state governments, feudal hierarchies and church leaders. In these times the concept of theology as a science[13] among the other sciences at the University was developed by Latin-speaking scholastic authors like Abelard, Anselm of Canterbury, Albert the Great, Thomas Aquinas, John of Scotia or William of Ockham. Here we encounter for the first time some of the ideas to which Kant later tied his programme of an autonomy of reasoning towards religious belief. They are focused on the important insight that all religious statements should be reflected in the light of reasonable arguments. Otherwise they could not be correctly understood or even justified to the audience of the public which was represented by the professional intellectuals in the schools and universities of that time.

The reception of the Aristotelian theory of sciences was the most important source for the medieval scholars and their project of public reasoning on religion at their universities and schools of higher education.[14] In his epistemology, Aristotle made the difference between the so-called *topic arguments*, that means only probable arguments, and so-called *necessary arguments* which have been scientifically proved and could therefore claim truth in a proper sense. The medievalist authors like Thomas Aquinas did pick up this theory of a decisive logical difference between the states of arguments in Aristotle's theory and applied it to the sentences which are present in the statements of the religious doctrines. This method did allow to introduce three different types or categories of religious statements with different claims of truth or probability.[15] The first type is represented by those sentences which could be demonstrated by the reason of the secular sciences or by philosophy. These sentences could claim a general truth relevant for all: for believers as well as for non-believers. The second type of religious statements only could claim probability and they did represent those doctrines which only believers could admit by their voluntary decisions like acts of faith. The third type of religious statements is represented by those sentences whose wrongness or incredibility could be demonstrated by rational arguments. This third category of religious statements was seen as refutable since disproved, and consequently one should not hold on to defend those statements.

This concept of an epistemological proof and critique of religious statements was the contribution of authors like Aquinas to the medieval enlightenment in the higher faculties of the University. But we should not forget that the authors of this scholastic theory of sciences developed their contribution to the debate on public reasoning of religion too by means of their reception and lecture of Islamic philosophers like Al-Kindi, Al-Farabi, Ibn-Sina or Ibn-Rushd. These Islamic philosophers did apply themselves to the programme of the ancient philosophies of Plato, Aristotle and the Neoplatonists to the doctrine of Islam and this inspired the scholastic authors to develop their own theories. Here we can identify that the Western philosophy also learned from the Islamic thinkers even if authors like Thomas Aquinas realized the fundamental dissent among the Islamic philosophers themselves. For example, the open contradictions between the position of Ibn-Sina, Aquinas did agree with, and the statements of Ibn-Rushd, that he rejected.[16] Nevertheless philosophers like Al-Kindi, Al-Farabi, Ibn-Sina and Ibn-Rushd represent a movement of philosophical enlightenment within the Islamic world between the foundation of the School of Baghdad in the ninth and twelfth centuries. Unfortunately this movement of a philosophical enlightenment and transformation of religion was not continued for several reasons in the Arabic culture after the death of Ibn-Rushd (1198) who himself was a victim of continued prosecution by Islamic orthodoxy and Arabic political authorities of his time. We can therefore understand better why neither a continued dialogue among Christian and Islamic theologians nor a philosophically based public reasoning on religion within Islam took place in the centuries afterwards.

Reflections from a Standpoint in Western Philosophy Today

With regard to the new discussions in Western philosophy one can presume that today neither the sciences nor the humanities, including philosophy, are continuing the older programme of modern enlightenment towards religion, namely to prove its credibility or validity in the name of 'the reason' or 'rationality' at all. The self-esteem of the sciences and their insight into their fundamental falliability according to Popper's epistemology prevent the sciences today from criticizing the religious language as such. This is at least one result of the former epistemological debate on the limits of scientific and hermeneutical understanding. With regard to philosophy, I recently diagnosed a new discourse on religion beyond the former concept of a critique of religion.[17] The debate on how to understand and even to get access to the proper epistemic state of religious statements is seemingly unfinished and its results are obviously undecided.

A programmatic new view on religion was prepared by the Critical Theory in the *Dialectic of Enlightenment*. In their analysis of the fate of the project of enlightenment and reasoning, Theodor W. Adorno and Max Horkheimer identified a deep crisis in the history of Western enlightenment linked to capitalism fundamentally under-mining the validity claim of the traditional Western concept of reason and rationality.[18] Only a philosophical reflection on the reasonable aspects in both abstract 'modern arts' and 'negative theology' in a Jewish tradition could help according to Adorno and Horkheimer to overcome the deep ambiguity or 'dialectic' within the Western concept of enlightenment.[19] I recently called this statement of the founders of Critical Theory 'a paradigmatic turn' in modern philosophy on religion.[20] It consists of the statement of the founders of the Critical Theory that a new critically reflected philosophical concept of reason should integrate the epistemic core of the truth claims of religion and should not judge on religious language from an inappropriate point of view in the tradition either of the early rationalist or empiricist criticism of religion. In his latest writings, Jürgen Habermas is obviously going to incorporate this 'paradigmatic turn' into his own theory, and in doing so he is transforming his earlier statements on religions into a new approximation to the epistemic meaning of religion from a post-secular point of view.[21]

I argue in favour of a new epistemological approach to the specific logic of religions in philosophy. This debate has to be carried out not from outside and above religion but in a public debate with the representatives and interpreters of religious language from within. The rules for this critical deliberation on religion have to be set by the conditions for a reasonable exchange of arguments. This is the way a civil society is going, not to exclude any longer the contribution of religions to the public debate, but to recognize its relevance. This assessment has obviously to do with a changed recognition of the specific epistemic state and meaning of the religious language. Religious language is not seen any longer as a private statement on private affairs, as a matter of taste or, as Max Weber suggested, as a statement according to the logic of an aesthetic judgement, depending on a special talent. Religious statements, at least some types of religious assertions and practices, are in the light of an analysis of religious speech acts both 'personal' or 'subjective' as well as 'intersubjective'. That means, in a religious language the believer is performing an 'I'—and simultaneously a 'we'—perspective. Additionally religious statements are 'informative' as well as 'performative' since they are referring to the facticity of the world and contingent events in human life and in doing so they are dealing with fundamental normative problems like freedom, guilt or reconciliation beyond the moral and legal discourse. And they are raising 'speculative' and 'reflexive' questions about the 'first principles' of the world as a whole and the human consciousness and about the final goals, including the decisive question whether or not there is a final goal for the individuals as well as for humanity at all. In doing so, the religious language is able to give answers in the light of which new theoretical and practical perspectives emerge which are transcending, but not destroying or substituting the language games of scientific theories or the practical insights in ordinary language.

   On the one hand these statements of religion and its proper contributions should not, and as a matter of fact cannot, be excluded from the universe of discourse in a civil society. On the other hand, there are good philosophical reasons that a modern state civil is not established on religious confessions but on the concept of the human rights and a secular constitution which recognizes human dignity independent of a religious or a non-religious belief. Pluralistic polities should not ask for a religious fundament at all. But civil societies and the political debate in the democratic state should ask their religious people and citizens to contribute to the public debate on the goals of politics, on moral virtues and social habits, and above all on the questions about an ultimate sense of human life and about the meaning of the reality, the relevance of the world or the history of human mankind as a whole for us. Without the input of religious sources—along with and in addition to the insight of philosophies, arts and sciences—a civil society would suffer from an 'entropy' of public reason and sense—with dangerous consequences for both society and politics. But like all statements in the public arena the contributions of the religious traditions have to be translated into the language of public reasoning. The necessity of a translation of the inner evidence of religious belief into a public language of universal reasoning will obviously affect the inner conditions of the religious language game. However, it will not destroy this core of religious belief insofar as the religions themselves have to be seen as a reflexive practice including a discursive reasoning, called if methodologically performed 'theology'. That implies that the public statements of the religions vis-à-vis the audience of a liberal or civil society must follow the rules and logic of a public deliberation as a fair discussion among egalitarian participants in which the power of the powerless argument is permitted alone. This might be the modern, revised version of Kant's concept of 'religion within the limits of pure reason alone' under the philosophical conditions of today. Even if this programme of public reasoning on religions does not continue the former project of enlightenment in the name of an 'abstract reason' we can see how helpful these rational obligations of this programme might be: Christian and Islamic theologians (as well as Jewish) are able to contribute to this discourse in the civil and pluralistic society—for reasons I referred to already in the second paragraph of my paper. And they will and can meet each other for an instructive dialogue on the basis of this programme of 'public reasoning'.

Notes

1. Immanuel Kant, *An Answer to the Question: What is Enlightenment?*, Paul Natorp (ed.), the Prussian Academy of the Sciences, Vol. VIII, 1907 (1784) p. 33.

2. See Kant, *Critique of Pure Reason*, first edition (1781), Preface A, XI: 'Our age is, in especial degree, the age of criticism, and to criticism everything must submit. Religion through its sanctity, and law-giving through its majesty, may seek to exempt themselves from it. But they then awaken just suspicion, and cannot claim the sincere respect which reason accords only to that which has been able to sustain the test of free and open examination.'

3. See my entry 'Religionskritik', in the *Routledge Encyclopedia of Philosophy*, Vol. IX, London, 1998 and my article, 'The Critique of Reason in Modern Philosophy and the Cognitive Status of Religion' in *ACPhQ* 74, 2000, pp. 53–63.

4. See Herbert of Cherbury, *De religione gentilium*, (1645/63) or John Toland, *Christianity not Mysterious*, 1696.

5. See John Locke, *Essay Concerning Human Understanding*, 1689, esp. Book IV, 17–21 and *The Reasonableness of Christianity*, as delivered in the Scriptures, 1696.

6. See David Hume, *Dialogues Concerning Natural Religion*, 1779.

7. See Jean-Jacques Rousseau, *Du Contrat social*, 1762, esp. Book IV, 8.

8. See Kant, *The Metaphysics of Morals*, Paul Natorp (ed.), The Prussian Academy of the Sciences, Vol. VI, p. 307, 1907 (1997/98).

9. See Kant, *On Religion Within the Limits of Pure Reason Alone*, 1793/94, Theodore M. Green and Hoyt H. Hudson (ed.), New York, 1960, p. 91. 'Hence an ethical commonwealth can be thought of only as a people under divine command, i.e. as a people of God, and indeed under laws of virtue.'

10. See Harold J. Berman, *Law and Revolution: The Formation of the Western Legal Tradition*, Cambridge/Massachusetts, 1983.

11. See Richard W. Southern, *Scholastic Humanism and the Unification of Europe*, volume I and II, Oxford, 1975 and 2001, esp. Vol. I, p. 31.

12. See R. Berndt and M. Lutz-Bachmann (eds), *Scientia und Disciplina: Wissenstheorie und Wissenschaftspraxis im 12. und 13. Jahrhundert*, Berlin, 2002.

13. See M. Lutz-Bachmann, A. Fidora, and A. Niederberger (eds), *Metaphysics in the Twelfth Century: On the Relationship among Philosophy, Science and Theology*, Turnhout, 2004.

14. See M. Lutz-Bachmann, A. Fidora, and P. Antolic (eds), *Erkenntnis und Wissenschaft/Knowledge and Science: Probleme der Epistemologie in der Philosophie des Mittelalters/Problems of Epistemology in Medieval Philosophy*, Berlin, 2004.

15. See my article 'Rationalität und Religion. Der Beitrag des Thomas von Aquin zu einer rationalen Grundlegung des Religionsdialogs', in *der Summa contra gentiles*, in *Juden, Christen und Muslime. Religionsdialoge im Mittelalter*, M. Lutz-Bachmann and A. Fidora (eds), Darmstadt, 2004, pp. 96–118.

16. Ibn-Rushd rejected himself in his famous 'Kitab al-Kashf' the proposal of Al-Gazali to subordinate the free speculative thinking of philosophy to the rules of Islamic law and religion, but in doing so he was not able to develop a reflexive and theoretically enlightened concept of religion which allowed a mutual integration or at least speculative mediation between religion and philosophy like we can identify in Aquinas' epistemology. The sharp conflicts between philosophers and Islamic orthodoxy did prevent a new understanding of religion in its relation to a concept of public reasoning which destroyed the possibilities for a future developement of enlightenment in the Arabic world.

17. See M. Lutz-Bachmann, 'Religion nach der Religionskritik', in K. Dethloff, L. Nagl, F. Wolfram (eds), *Religion-Moderne-Postmoderne*, Berlin, 2002.
18. See Theodor W. Adorno and Max Horkheimer, *Dialectic of Enlightenment* (1944/47), (John Cumming trans.), Herder and Herder, New York, 1972.
19. Ibid., 'The Concept of Enlightenment', pp. 3–42.
20. See M. Lutz-Bachmann, 'Religion—nach der, Dialektik der Aufklärung', in *Jahrbuch für Religionsphilosophie 1*, (2002), pp. 138–47.
21. See the latest statements of Jürgen Habermas on religion in 2004: 'Zur Diskussion mit Kardinal Ratzinger', 'Die Grenze zwischen Glauben und Wissen. Zur Wirkungsgeschichte und aktuellen Bedeutung von Kants Religionsphilosophie', and 'Die Religion in der politischen Öffentlichkeit'.

SECTION 4

AESTHETICS

Kant, Adorno, and the Dynamics of Artistic Appearing

Martin Seel

With Alexander Gottlieb Baumgarten's *Aesthetica*, aesthetics in the modern sense emerged as a reflection about the range of knowledge. Aesthetic perception was conceived of as *cognitio sensiviva*, being specialized on the recognition of the particular. But is it really plausible to call this perception in every case, a *knowing*? Can aesthetics be therefore grasped correctly as a subspecies of epistemology? 'No' is the response that Immanuel Kant gives in the first part of his *Critique of Judgement*. Nevertheless, he attaches great importance to the fact that all the *powers* of knowledge are involved in aesthetic perception. But, he adds, what matters in aesthetic perception is not an acquisition of knowledge. The powers of knowledge are not required here for knowledge—that is the kernel of the numerous paradoxical claims with which Kant characterizes the aesthetic attitude at the beginning of his aesthetics.

Being capable of epistemic determination, the subject of aesthetic intuition suspends determining epistemically. It does not determine the object of its perception in terms of particular features. Instead, the subject perceives the object in the unrepresentable repleteness of its features. For instance, when intuiting a beautiful flower—at the beginning of his aesthetics Kant considers primarily objects of nature—it is a matter of keeping 'the cognitive powers engaged [in their occupation] without any further aim. We *linger* in our contemplation of the beautiful, because this contemplation reinforces and reproduces itself.[1] In contrast to *theoretical* contemplation, *aesthetic* contemplation is not concerned with certain insights that are to be gained by turning toward the object. The object is not to be conceptualized, no more than it is to be directed to a certain practical purpose. Without being reduced to this or that determination, the object is perceived solely in the presence of its appearing.

With this notion, we arrive at a plausible initial determination of aesthetics. More resolutely than Baumgarten, Kant ties the analysis of the aesthetic object to an analysis of the perception of this object (and the analysis of this perception to the analysis of the Judgements that give an account of the exercise of this perception). Aesthetic object and aesthetic perception are recognized as interdependent concepts. The aesthetic object is the object of a genuine form of perception that is concerned not with some of its objects' *appearances* [*Erscheinungen*] but with their process of *appearing* [*Erscheinen*].

This theory of aesthetic appearing developed by Kant generates, besides a minimal concept of aesthetic perception, a minimal concept of the aesthetic object. These are 'minimal' determinations because they highlight something that is characteristic for aesthetic objects and modes of comprehension—however radically different they may well be in other respects. The aesthetic object is an object in the process of its appearing, aesthetic perception is attentiveness to this appearing.

Although this is nothing more than a minimal starting point, it is nonetheless a point of intersection at which the domains of aesthetics, epistemology and ethics—separated initially by Kant—are internally connected. In exercizing aesthetic perception, as he shows, we are free in a special way—free from the constraints of conceptual knowing, free from the reckoning of instrumental action, free as well from the conflict between duty and inclination. In the aesthetic state, we are free from the compulsion to determine ourselves and the world. This negative freedom has however a positive side according to Kant. In the play of aesthetic perception we are free to experience the *determinacy* of ourselves and the world. Wherever the real presents itself in a repleteness and changeability that cannot be grasped but can nonetheless be affirmed, there we experience a scope for the possibilities of knowing and acting that is always already presupposed in theoretical and practical orientations. For that reason, Kant sees the experience of the beautiful (not to mention the sublime) as an acting out of the highest capabilities of the human being. The richness of the real that is available—indeed, released—in aesthetic contemplation is experienced as a pleasurable confirmation of the extensive determinacy of reality by us human beings.

II

A minimal concept of the aesthetic object such as we find it developed at the beginning of the *Critique of Judgement* can nevertheless be nothing more than the starting point for a plausible aesthetics. The basic concept of appearing does not yet say anything about the specific aesthetic constitution of the objects of *art*. Any aesthetics that deserves the name, however, has to prove itself ultimately in the most complex of all aesthetic phenomena. That is the reason why Hegel defined aesthetics in his lectures on this subject simply as a 'philosophy of art'.

However, in this context I will have to leave the long and winding history of modern aesthetics aside.[2] Instead I will focus my attention to Theodor W. Adorno, for he too distinguishes between the mere appearance of artworks and their artistic appearing. He understands the work of art not as an empirical appearance in the sense of a complex sensory datum but as an 'appearance' in the sense of a reality that remains ungraspable. 'Artworks become appearances, in the pregnant sense of the term—that is, as the appearance of an other—when the accent falls on the unreality of their own reality.'[3] They relate to the rest of reality as an 'apparition' in which something is suddenly present and then in the same instant is no longer there. In this way, the appearing of an artwork differs radically from all phenomena that can be apprehended in knowledge and action; it is unread in relation to what is otherwise known and acknowledged as real. Hence Adorno writes, 'In each genuine artwork something appears that does not exist.'[4]

Since this sounds somewhat mysterious, an example may be helpful. Barnett Newman's painting *Who's Afraid of Red, Yellow and Blue IV* (Nationalgalerie, Berlin) is 274 × 603 cm; the huge canvas does not have a frame. On the left we see a large red space, on the right a large yellow one; in the middle there is a much narrower blue strip that is approximately 60 cm wide. The paint has been applied homogeneously throughout. Pure colours, symmetrical arrangement—the whole painting rebels against such an apparently well-tempered and well-balanced composition. It is above all the vast colour zones that generate a distinct imbalance. Whereas the red stands out aggressively, the yellow recedes from the beholder. This arrangement, which appears askew to a lingering perception, is further shaped by the different demarcations of the two large colour spaces to the blue surface in the middle. The blue overlaps the neighbouring red just a little, whereas it itself is covered minimally by the yellow surface. The aggressive red is restrained by the blue; the soft yellow, on the other hand, remains unbound. What could act like a balance between the colours' various spatial effects serves only to intensify the boldness of the red and the restraint of the yellow field. Moreover, the large colour spaces expand more and more when viewing the painting; they cross the borders of the painting, just as they continually cross the borders to the other colours. The colours illuminate each other. In perception, they let an oscillating continuum evolve, a colour space not limited in depth either, a space that gradually enfolds the beholder. In this manner, the painting stages an onslaught of the colour fields of which it consists, an onslaught that goes beyond the actual surface of the painting. It is a piece of anti-compositional and anti-purist painting. It breaks the form in which the beholder encounters it at first glance. It celebrates the ability to go perceptively beyond the order of the visible world.

'In each genuine artwork something appears that does not exist.' In this work of art, there appears a rebellion of colour against the coercion of balanced design. This cannot be seen in the *natural* attitude. What this attitude sees is just a red, yellow and blue surface, a piece of technically good painting, nothing more. Nor can an art-remote, *aesthetic* perception—one directed at the *mere* appearing of this object—notice anything of the excesses of this painting; some beholders could for instance stick purely to the glow, interaction and iridescence of the colour surfaces. Other beholders, those concerned not just with the sensuous intensity but with the *decorative* value of the object, could be pleased by its symmetrical surface and regard it as a manifestation of 'positive thinking'. This apparency disappears only with a deliberate *art-oriented* contemplation of the painting that is in a position to perceive it as a revolt against any decorative, symmetric, balanced style of painting. It is only here that the 'spirit' of the painting becomes noticeable, a spirit that 'appears through the appearance'.[5] Or, as Adorno circumscribes the status of artworks using one of his pyrotechnic metaphors: 'They become eloquent by the force of the kindling of thing and appearance'.[6]

The work of art—this is Adorno's plausible contention, which refers back to Baumgarten and Kant no less than to Nietzsche and Heidegger—reveals to its beholder that reality is richer than all of the appearances we can fix in the language of conceptual knowledge. It unfolds the difference between determinable appearance and indeterminable appearing; it underscores the fact that reality is not just given to us as a collection of facts. But in contrast to natural beauty and to the sensual presence of objects in an everyday surrounding objects of art are not only a manifestation, but at the same time an articulation of individual presence. As long as they are treated as objects of *art*, they are given neither only as objects of mere appearing nor only as objects of atmospheric appearing. They are ascribed the status of constellational presentations—the status of objects that can bring complex human conditions to light in the medium of their appearing. They are in this respect 'constructs of spirit', to use Hegel's language. 'The spirit of artworks', Adorno writes in his *Aesthetic Theory*, is the spirit 'that appears through the appearance'.[7] This spirit, Adorno elaborates, which 'infiltrates' the sensuous appearance of a work, cannot be cognized independently of this appearance; but it must not be equated with it, just as it must not be equated with the intention of the artist. 'Not even the appearance of the artwork as a whole is its spirit, and least of all is it the appearance of the idea purportedly embodied or symbolized by the work; spirit cannot be fixated in immediate identity with its appearance. But neither does spirit constitute a level above or below appearance; such a supposition would be no less of a reification. The locus of spirit is the configuration of what appears.'[8] For any theory of the arts this is a crucial point. The human spirit has its locus in very different media—in the sounds and writing of language, in gestures and pictorial symbols, in sign systems of a different kind;

'spirit' or substantive intentionality exists in no way other than in the use of these various media of articulation. Art, Adorno argues, is *one* kind of articulation, expression, or presentation of spirit's content—the one that is executed in the medium of appearing and is tied here to 'configuration[s] of what appears'.

III

It is an assumption like this, however, that was continually disputed in the twentieth century. The days of artistic appearing are numbered, was a prevalent conjecture. Important currents in modern art, it seemed to many, reject any sensuous address or animation. For this reason, a departure of art philosophy from aesthetics is overdue. Above all Arthur Danto made himself the advocate of this view. He posed the question of the status of artworks with great clarity and vividness. But the conclusion he draws fails to do justice to the state of recent art in particular.[9]

Danto's starting point is the observation that since Duchamp and Warhol objects become artworks that do not distinguish themselves externally from banal objects of everyday life. Of two phenomenally indistinguishable objects—be they bottle dryers, chairs, umbrellas, sand heaps, telephone directories or cartons of saucepan cleaners—one can be a work of art, whereas the other one is simply just what it is. Thus, Danto's conclusion runs, it cannot be objects' external appearance that is responsible for their art status. After all, both counterparts appear identical. 'It meant that,' Danto sums up, 'as far as appearances were concerned, anything could be a work of art, and it meant that if you were going to find out what art was, you had to turn from sense experience to thought.'[10] This theoretic turn away from the sensuousness of art leads to a bold diagnosis of the state of the visual arts. 'Visuality drops away, as little relevant to the essence of art as beauty proved to have been. For art to exist there does not even have to be an object to look at, and if there are objects in a gallery, they can look like anything at all.'[11] For Danto, it follows from the history of art since Duchamp: 'The connection between art and aesthetics is a matter of historical contingency, and not part of the essence of art'.[12] On contemporary art he writes: 'Now there is one feature of contemporary art that distinguishes it from perhaps all art made since 1400, which is that its primary ambitions are not aesthetic'.[13] Many artists of the twentieth century managed 'to extrude the aesthetic from the artistic,' in plain words, to chase all sensuous temptation out of the temple of art.[14]

In Danto the term 'aesthetic' stands largely for that which is sensuously perceivable. For him the dignity of recent art—and, ultimately, of all preceding art too—consists in its always having already moved beyond its sensuous appearing. Accordingly, art objects are in principle different from how they appear to the senses. They embody ideas that cannot be seen in them, but are ascribed to them by artists and beholders. However art-hostile or—in the case of Danto—art-friendly this thesis is advanced, it is fundamentally wrong. What is more, it is not needed to answer Danto's insightfully raised question of the status of art in the aftermath of Duchamp.

The entire argument is subject to a grave fallacy. Objects that are phenomenally identical, Danto assumes, are aesthetically of equal value. This is not however the case. The same sensuous appearance of an object, as we saw in the example of Newman's painting, can have very different aesthetic effects. One and the same *manifestation* of the three-part area can *appear* aesthetically in a threefold manner. As soon as one attends, while considering the simultaneity of an object's sensuous aspects, more to the mere, or more to the atmospheric, or to the artistic presence of this play of appearances, there emerges a different aesthetic valency for the object. And what holds true especially for art is that its gestures and contents can be experienced only in the dimension of an interpretatively and imaginatively appropriated appearing.

Confronted with this objection, Danto plays the trump card that is always played in such situations: he refers to some of the readymades by Duchamp. Here, it seems, something becomes an object of art and therefore of interpretation without however becoming an object of the imagination tied to this object's appearing. There is a lot to think about here, but not really something to see— beyond what can be seen anyway in a thing of this kind. Under the title *In Advance of the Broken Arm*, Marcel Duchamp affixed such a thing to the ceiling of his atelier in New York in 1915. It was a snow shovel made of metal, as was in use everywhere at the time. However one interprets this object of art, it is a clear counterexample to the view that all artworks are objects of the imagination. For this artistic object denies the sensuous transformation and imaginative transcendence that can be expected of other art objects. As Danto correctly sees, it is by virtue of this denial that the snow shovel chosen by Duchamp is distinguished from all the other snow shovels in this world, which at most just won't do the job, but they cannot deny anything. How is this artistic denial to be understood, however? Where does it occur? At the level of appearing or in a sphere of reflection above it?

To accept this alternative would be tantamount to a self-disembodiment of the philosophy of art. No work of art can be understood in terms of this alternative, and certainly not the ingenious point of Duchamp's manoeuvre. For the denial that is performed by placing a snow shovel in the space of art is possible only at the *level* of artistic appearing. Only at this level can the fulfillment of the expectations of a 'different appearing' be disappointed. For without the *attempt* to see in this thing something other than an arbitrary practical or aesthetic object, it would not be possible to recognize its exhibition as an artistic operation. In its shining metal gloss, the snow shovel remains unresponsive to the expectations of an imaginative appearing; it remains dismissive of all the expectations of allurement into another state—the expectations whose fulfilment art promised before Duchamp and continues to promise after him. But it presents itself as an object of art—as an object that *entices* precisely the perception that it denies in the same move. It reveals itself solely as a banal object of use—but it *presents* itself as such in full view of those who may expect something different and can expect something different in the same exhibition space. *Its* point is also artistic appearing—one, of course, that never transpires. Like every other denial, this one also operates at the level of the 'accusations' directed at it.

Nonetheless, not all of Duchamp's readymades operate in this purely negative sense. Neither *Fountain*, proposed for an exhibition in 1917, nor *Bottle Dryer*, which had been functioning as a readymade since 1914—to mention two other legendary examples—deny every sculptural or gestural presence, as the superbly banal snow shovel does. They allow an imaginative presence to appear and disappear.

They are objects *alternating* between art and non-art—and are for
that very reason subversive objects of art. They look like banal objects
and are nonetheless staged in such a way that they acquire a different
appearing. So, when Danto says in one of his more cautious moments
'that artworks and real things cannot be told apart by visual inspection
alone,'[15] he is indeed right. The innocent eye cannot always
distinguish art objects from other (aesthetic) objects. It does not
however follow that the visual is without relevance in the visual arts
or the sensuous without relevance in any of the other arts. What
follows is just that the perception sufficient for seeing any extra-
artistic object is not sufficient for the perception of an *art* object. As
soon as we regard something as a work of visual art, we can discover
in it visual characteristics that are completely different from those
any child could ascribe to it—for who would want to say of an
everyday urinal that it *alternates* between being a useful thing and an
ironic gesture? In artistic operations, I would therefore like to
conclude, it is impossible to escape the dynamics of artistic appearing
because they are the very basis of artistic operations.

Notes

1. Immanuel Kant, *Critique of Judgement*, (Werner S. Pluhar trans.), Heckett,
   Indianapolis, 1987, 12, p. 68.
2. For a more detailed story, see my *Ästhetik des Erscheinens*, Hanser, München,
   Stanford University Press, 2004.
3. Theodor W. Adorno, *Aesthetic Theory*, G. Adorno and Rolf Tiedemann (eds),
   (Robert Hullot-Kentor trans.), University of Minnesota Press, Minneapolis,
   1997, p. 79.
4. Ibid., p. 82.
5. Ibid., p. 87.
6. Ibid., p. 80.
7. Ibid., p. 87.
8. Ibid.
9. Martin Seel, 'Art as Appearance: Two Comments on Arthur C. Danto's
   After the End of Art', in *History and Theory*, Theme Issue 37, 1998, pp. 102–14;
   and Danto's response to Seel's critique, Arthur C. Danto, 'The End of Art:
   A Philosophical Defense', in *History and Theory*, Theme Issue 37, 1998,
   pp. 27–43, pp. 132–4. The topic of an overdue separation of art theory and
   aesthetics can also be found in Luhmann, *Art as a Social System*, Stanford
   University Press, Stanford, California, 2000, p. 306.

10. Arthur C. Danto, *After the End of Art: Contemporary Art and the Pale of History*, Princeton University Press, Princeton, 1997, p. 13.
11. Ibid., p. 16.
12. Ibid., p. 25.
13. Ibid., p. 183.
14. Ibid., p. 84.
15. Ibid., p. 17 (italics added).

Symbolizing Permanent Desire

Kant's Aesthetic Judgement and Duchamp's 'Painting of Precision'

Andrea Esser

In the *Critique of Judgement*, Kant develops four aspects of the reference of aesthetic judgement. With these so-called 'moments', he demarcates aesthetic judgement against other kinds of judgement like those relating to knowledge or morality. But the moments—'to which this power of judgement attends in its reflection'[1] as Kant formulates it—as well as their demarcating effect are results of a theoretical investigation proving the claims of our everyday judgements. Although it may be possible to use these moments in defining what art is or should be, this is, however, not obvious at all. First these are answers to the question whether the claim that others should agree to our aesthetic judgements can be legitimated, second they prove if there are any common criteria for judging aesthetics and last, they try to show that art is an autonomous—while aesthetic— way of 'presenting' ideas. What we call expression can't be fully translated into language and is different from 'visual communication'. The demarcation done by Kant's critical theory comes about within a transcendental investigation and concerns only the reference of a certain kind of judgement. Therefore it does not necessarily 'disenfranchise' art, as Arthur Danto formulates it.[2] Nor does it coerce art into formalistic figurations. To be sure, Kant's *theory* of aesthetic judgement leads to merely formal constraints and may therefore be called 'formal' itself, but it is this very formality that enables art to be concerned with any subject matter whatever, even with the question regarding its own nature. Nevertheless, I think that from this formal structure several criteria may be derived at least indirectly, not only with respect to the process of judgement but also to the objects in question. The content of these aesthetic criteria is made up of the very conditions of aesthetic communication, that is, in so far as we claim for art to be a specific and therefore autonomous way of presenting and communicating ideas, we must proceed in an 'aesthetic' way, a way that recognizes the logical constraints of aesthetic communication. As an investigation into the logic of aesthetic judgement, first of all the method must be capable of being applied to judging any specific kind of art and impervious to having its structure transcended by any new style of art. And second as a logical structure it should not hinder art from engaging in political and social issues as long as this structure remains realized. Following from these two criteria, any Kantian aesthetics would be normative in the sense that it always reminds both the production as well as the reception of art of the constitutive logical border that lies beyond our intentional grasp. However, the validity of these statements depends, as I am going to argue in the following, on the interpretation of two concepts of Kant's theory: 'the concept of form' and that of 'the play of faculties'. My understanding of these concepts may not be Kantian in the strictest sense, but it follows Kant in so far as it accepts that art must find autonomous forms of presentation that nevertheless are forms of universal communicability. It means understanding 'art as a certain kind of sign'. This is Marcel Duchamp's wording whose work and whose concept of 'Painting of Precision', I shall explain in Kantian terms so as to give the latter a pragmatic dimension.[3]

I

My shift to Duchamp may come as a bit of a surprise to you because it is Duchamp who in many interviews and statements stresses that what is most importantly avoided in art is 'aesthetics and aesthetic pleasure'. His *Large Glass* is, 'not supposed to be seen only with the eyes',[4] he says, and he often expresses his aversion against 'Retinal painters',[5] concerned only with pure sense impressions. He refuses an art, 'pleasing only the eyes'[6] and therefore combines his work with a sort of poetic text. These literary attachments comprise some cryptic, absurd and pseudo-scientific notes collected in the various so-called 'boxes'. In the case of the Large Glass and the Green Box he particularly emphasizes that he wanted to give 'glass for the eyes and text for the ear and the mind'.[7] The two moments are meant to work together and are intended above all to 'keep his work of art from adopting an "aesthetic" quality in the sense of aesthetic sensuality'. While refusing aesthetics and aesthetic pleasure, Duchamp's work seems to produce evidence against Kant and demonstrate the limits rather than the validity of his aesthetics.

II

But the 'aesthetic' quality or 'form' Duchamp seeks to avoid is of the sort equally rejected by the Kantian aesthetics. The first moment of the analytic demands that one should judge 'without any interest'.[8] The aesthetic form is not meant to make us feel happy. Therefore it is not supposed to give rise to an immediate desire or lust. Rather it is accompanied, if we follow Kant, by a special kind of desire resulting from a process of reflection. This is precisely the standpoint of Duchamp when he states that 'taste' isn't important. He pleads for a certain 'beauty of indifference' and this means first of all that we shouldn't take any interest in the sensuous and pleasant qualities of the beautiful work of art. On the other hand he wants to save art from conceptualization—just as Kant does. Both of them dismiss the intellectual treatment of art and the interference of knowledge which leads to concepts of the object represented in the work of art. Duchamp complains about us constantly translating everything into words and criticizes that we integrate our concepts in our craving for meaning. So whatever we perceive, it 'unfortunately' gets a meaning—'unfortunately' because we handle our perception as a tool, as an instrument.[9] Thus the work of art boils down to a gateway to knowledge and recognition. Taking art in this intellectual way makes it a mere illustration of thought. So when Duchamp links his work with poetic text and plays with words, he uses language like colour and tries to produce 'a poetic effect' of a specific kind. The challenge to the artist as well as to the spectator consists in regarding the signs of art as 'special kinds of signs' which are closely related to a process of reflection. That's why it is 'the spectator who makes the pictures'[10] just as does the artist when taking the role of a spectator of his own works in the process of creating them. What Duchamp calls 'art' and Kant calls 'aesthetic form' is produced in a process.

III

Now Kant describes this process of construction as the interaction of two moments: first, the individual composition of colours and structures which ends in the object of perception. This is what Kant calls the 'given form'.[11] And second, the active process of interpretation—better, of aesthetic reflection on this given form. Only within this twofold process a form gains an aesthetic value or qualifies as a sign with an aesthetic meaning. Kant specifies this process as the 'free play of the faculties',[12] *imagination* and *understanding*. These two aspects of the process belong to two different theoretical levels: the perception of an individual appearance which is called 'given form' and the aesthetic reflection which produces the aesthetic dimension or meaning of this form. The 'given form' Kant is talking about is not the 'good form' in the sense of the functional or significant form. It is just the individual form of a perceived object in contrast to the universal form that serves for gaining knowledge. By the way the 'cognitive form' is the form most painters and artists try to overcome in their work of art as this form drives his individual form back into the 'cliché' or the sketch. So it is not a strange quirk of the isolated Koenigsberg philosopher to deny the predominance of 'cognitive form' in art. It is rather a necessary condition to get rid of the stereotypical ways of connecting visual images to intellectual meanings. That is what Klee talks about when he says, that the concept is a 'seducer' and has the 'disastrous' effect of leading away from the individual painting. And that is why Duchamp is suspicious of the talk of 'clear and obvious sense'. Kant has put it this way when he says: we must judge the beautiful 'without a concept'.[13]

IV

But the individual form is not yet the aesthetic form. It is only the empirical condition and the starting point for the aesthetic reflection. The process is to be continued by producing aesthetic meaning.

This second part of the constructive process, the 'play of the faculties' is not at all easy to understand. The key to an understanding lies in the third moment of the analytic, which states 'that the consciousness of the merely formal purposiveness (die 'Zweckmaessigkeit') in the play of the cognitive powers of the subject (...) is the pleasure itself'.[14] In this state the faculties of imagination and understanding (but not taken as faculty of concepts) can cooperate in a harmonious purposive interaction. Regarding a particular 'given'—we better say 'perceived' form imagination can act freely and in doing so it creates what one may call 'aesthetic effects'. This means we are aware of the perceived colours and individual shapes of that particular appearance, we regard them in their relations, we even form relations. The focus therefore is not only on the 'given form' we see nor is it on the conceptual meaning. Our consciousness refers to the process of perceiving. We register what happens in this process inside us.

With regard to this process of generating aesthetic effects one might suggest that the aesthetic judgement only refers to the perceived form called 'purposive'? But these aesthetic effects are not sufficient for ascribing the predicate aesthetic to a form . An aesthetic theory which limits aesthetic reflection to the combination of impressions reduces the aesthetic process to an 'insipid dot-spotting'. But Kant's analytic does not end at this point. He emphasizes not only the sensual side of the aesthetic process, but also an intellectual side: only with understanding coming into play the aesthetic form is completed in a certain sense. It is a harmony of imagination *and* understanding, of presentation *and* idea—or as Duchamp puts it: art ought to create signs that address both the eye *and* to our 'grey substance'.[15] Otherwise our pleasure of aesthetic objects and even of the constructive process of aesthetic reflection itself would be a merely private one. So which are the structures of reflection that guarantee communicability so that we can at least hope for sharing our feeling and our judgement with others? The crucial aspect is the individual character and the way of perceiving this individual character. This leads us to structures of sense.

V

Kant has characterized the connection of intellectual structures and the process of perceiving a form as a process of symbolizing. In order to recognize a form as a symbol we have to transform our experience of perceiving into the semantic medium. And I think it is the realization of this possibility that creates the 'aesthetic form' of an object. Kant's paradoxical formulation of a 'finality without an end' is to be interpreted as the subject's active perceiving of a certain presentation which can be understood as a realization of an idea. The perceived aesthetic object serves as a symbol of this idea and it is obvious, that only a special kind of idea can be symbolized that way, namely the so-called aesthetic ideas. Symbol in this sense isn't a conventional sign. Kant develops the structure of symbolical presentation in the context of morality, in order to be able to say that beauty is a 'symbol of morality'.[16] But I think the symbolical presentation covers a wider scope of application and we can characterize the process of creating and understanding signs of art on this basis. Works of art are presentations of complex ideas, of a 'realm of ideas', so that 'no expression designating a determinate concept can be found for it', as Kant says.[17] Thus they are intuitive presentations of ideas. Following this concept art has to generate new signs, signs with a special code that didn't exist before. Duchamp calls such signs 'prime words' and adds that 'they are divisible only by themselves and by unity'. In this sense signs of art are symbols and it is only aesthetic reflection that allows for communicating about these signs. They are 'a special kind of signs', like Duchamp says, making sense only within the process of reflection.

VI

The Large Glass is such a symbol in the Kantian sense. Duchamp called it a 'marriage' of 'intellectual and visual reactions' and a manifestation of both: 'presentation (Darstellung) and idea'. The spectator's first glance refers to the 'Appearance' of the Glass—that is, we see the various figures, forms and machines on the Glass; in parallel to this we read the title: 'The bride stripped bare by her bachelors even'. The figures on the Glass seem to point at a meaning. They are precisely drawn, painted or made—Duchamp used different techniques. Anyway the appearance seems to rule out any absence of intention. Moreover the high degree of precision suggests that the whole thing is ordered by an end to which these figures are formed. Therefore one is led to assume that the presentation (Darstellung) must be understandable—if only one knew this end. This kind of meticulous presentation appeals to our common striving for meaning. In a completely different way the title is inviting: at first sight the title talks about erotics and there seems to be a tension between this content and the presentation which shows a mechanism rather than a romantic scene. The erotic content of the Large Glass isn't presented directly, it is not materialized in a 'cognitive form'. So the spectator has to find out the code of this sign, has to trace the system of meaning to which the meaning of the Large Glass can be assigned. The most obvious way to do so is to identify the elements of the Glass, to clarify their functions by reading the cryptic notes of the Green Box and to put them together to tell a more or less coherent story. A very mechanical trial, which produces a mechanism in turn! 'The machine runs only on words', Suquet says, but when we conceptualize the appearances on the Glass like this we won't gain an erotic sense—it's an endless labyrinth of absurdity.[18] Everything to be seen on the Glass pretends to pursue an end but the spectator always keeps discovering just a 'finality without end'. Hence this mistaking will make him aware of the fact that it is *his desire* for a clear and well-formulated sense that produces the absurdity. The second approach to the Glass calls for analysing this effect. We need to look at this way of treating this work of art, maybe every work of art, and will probably get the idea that in the field of erotics, analogous problems may occur. The same way the Large Glass keeps escaping fixation to a definite meaning, just as the erotic partner remains unavailable to the other. This is necessarily so, if he or she is meant to continue to be the object of desire.

But the erotic field isn't the only semantic field we should recruit for 'reading' the Glass. There is another important aspect, the aspect that the Large Glass also implies a position in the aesthetic theory. When we analyse the Glass, as we have done, an analogy may occur: the structure of the aesthetic judgement is analogous with an erotic relationship, too. Within the scope of the analogy one could say: reflecting upon the Large Glass in an *aesthetic* way leads us to the experience that the object of art as well as the object of erotics need to stay out of reach and both have to retain a certain resistance against our will. Both have to retain the structure of infinity, an infinity that always has to be produced anew. But for this purpose neither a mechanism must be applied nor a technology acquired. A symbol of these relations should represent 'something possible' that 'necessarily' remains 'unfinished'.

Have these ideas really materialized in the individual presentation of the Large Glass, in its individual form? Which aesthetic effects and which intellectual structures can be found to connect this sense with the Large Glass? I will sketch this in the last part of this essay.

Taking a look at the sphere of the Bride you can see two single forms, the Bride and the Milky Way, I use the names from the Green Box here. There is no context, foreground or background. The figures we see do not follow the laws of Renaissance Perspective and therefore do not lead us to interpreting the surface as three-dimensional space. It is only the colour of the figures that makes them appear sculptural. Both figures can be called, 'free main figures', Duchamp states, in so far as they themselves determine how to be interpreted. The Bride and the Milky Way are suspended, but their being suspended gives rise to a completely different aesthetic effect than the one caused by the Bachelors in the lower part of the Glass. Both free figures seem to be suspended rather than hanging, as do the bachelors.

The aesthetic effects of the Bachelors' forms are completely different. They are constructed in accordance with the tradition of perspective. Their aesthetic effect depends on imagining this frame of construction, that's why they are not 'free' in an aesthetic sense. They appear to have a common structure, which allows to infer a single common law of construction that applies to all of them: the

Bachelors' forms are surrounded by a distinct, clearly visible seam, a kind of a welding seam. They differ only in extension. That's why they don't appear as individuals but rather as parts of a set. In the Green Box they are specified by their different professions. Unlike the Bachelors' machine the other machines run on the basis of a certain spontaneity following invented and somehow, 'extended' laws. The Waterfall, the Oscillating Density of the Bottles of Benedictine and the Emancipated Metal of the Slide Glider *cannot be analysed in logical terms.* The spectator gets to know these particular laws, upon entering the seemingly ordered world of the Green Box and if he imagines their effect. Therefore we could say: the machine doesn't run on words, but only on imagination. The imagination plays with the presentation and this causes an interest that is based on freedom, not on control. The Large Glass therefore is a symbol of this playful approach and of these ideas and 'so the bride, the bachelors, and by implication the onlooker as we'.[1] are suspended in a state of permanent desire', a desire which Duchamp as well as Kant held to be realizable only in art.[19]

But what are we meant to do with works of art that do not present an individual form at all? Are Duchamp's readymades such as his work 'Fountain', which he presented at the Society of Independent Artists as a work of art, not to be classified as art, because they are objects of everyday life and have a serial rather than an individual form? The aesthetic reflection of such a readymade can only awake our consciousness to the fact that the difference between a work of art and a thing of daily life never depends on a 'given form' itself. In the case of the readymades the aesthetic reflection creates no other content than this awareness of the constitutive limit, which can not be overstepped. Imagination here is taken to absurdity. We are forced to think about the essence and the concept of art. Vice versa, this approach qualifies the readymade as an aesthetic sign of this very theoretical reflection. But on the other hand, the concept of the readymade does not only demonstrate the logical limits of art, but also the limits of Kantian aesthetics. They clearly show, that art is not only an aggregate of things judged to be aestheticly valuable, but also a system which develops in a historical process. In this process, works of art and forms are seen in their relations and in their reference-making, like in the field of language the meaning of signs is determined by the current state of the system. Kant's analysis of aesthetic judgement does not take this dimension into account. It shows a limit that calls for being exceeded by a theory of art.

Notes

1. Immanuel Kant, 'Kritik der Urteilskraft'[Critique of Judgement] in *Kants Werke: Akademie Textausgabe*, Band V. Walter de Gruyter Verlag, Berlin, 1968; Immanuel Kant, *Critique of the Power of Judgement*, Paul Guyer. trans. and ed., Cambridge University Press, Cambridge/New York, 2000.
2. Arthur Danto, *The Disenfranchisement of Art*, Columbia University Press, New York, 1986.
3. Serge Stauffer (ed.), *Marcel Duchamp*, Regenbogenverlng Zürich, 1981.
4. Ibid., p. 30.
5. Ibid., p. 96.
6. Pierre Cabanne, 'Gespräche mit Duchamp' [Conversions with Duchamp]. Köln 1972.
7. Stauffer, *Marcel Duchamp*, p. 247.
8. Kant, *Critique of the Power*, p. 211.
9. Cabanne, *Gespräche mit*, p. 76.
10. Ibid., p. 105.
11. Kant, *Critique of the Power*, p. 227.
12. Ibid., p. 217.
13. Ibid., p. 219.
14. Ibid., p. 222.
15. Stauffer, *Marcel Duchamp*, p. 77.
16. Kant, *Critique of the Power*, p. 351.
17. Ibid., p. 316.
18. Jean Suquet, 'Possible', in Thierry de Duve, *The Definitively Unfinished Marcel Duchamp*, Cambridge, Massachusetts, 1992, pp. 88–133.
19. Calvin Tomkins, *Duchamp*, Owl Books, New York, 1986.

Contributors

BIJOY H. BORUAH is Professor of Philosophy in the Department of Humanities and Social Sciences, Indian Institute of Technology in Kanpur, India. His publications include *Fiction and Emotion: A Study in Aesthetics and the Philosophy of Mind* (1989). He has also co-edited *Persons, Mind and Value* (2000).

GOUTAM BISWAS is Professor in the Department of Philosophy, Assam University in Silchar, India. He is the author of *Art as Dialogue: Essays in the Phenomenology of Aesthetic Experience* (1995) and *Where Are You Going? An Excursion with Nietzsche*, in Franson Manjali (ed.), *Nietzsche: Philologist, Philosopher and Cultural Critique* (2006).

JONATHAN DANCY is Professor in the Department of Philosophy, University of Reading, UK, and the University of Texas, Austin, USA. He is the author of *An Introduction to Contemporary Epistemology* (1985), *Berkeley: An Introduction* (1987), *Moral Reasons* (1993), *Practical Reality* (2000), and *Ethics without Principles* (2004). He has also edited various works by George Berkeley.

SHARAD DESHPANDE is Professor of Philosophy, University of Pune, India. He is also associate editor of the *Indian Philosophical Quarterly*. His publications include *Philosophy of G.R. Malkan* (1997) and *Causation, Explanation and Understanding* (2001). He has recently edited *200 Years of Kant, Indian Philosophical Quarterly*, Vol. 31 (2004).

ANDREA ESSER is Professor of Philosophy at the RWTH Aachen, Germany. Her recent publications include *Eine Ethik für Endliche. Kants Tugendlehre in der Gegenwart* (2004) and 'Kunst als Symbolsystem: Nelson Goodmans Theorie der Kunst', in Ernst/Scholz/Steinbrenner (eds), *Kunst und Erkenntnis: Untersuchungen zu Nelson Goodmans Kunst-und Zeichentheorie* (2005).

MATTHIAS LUTZ-BACHMANN is Professor of Philosophy and Director of the Institute of Philosophy of Religion, Johann Wolfgang Goethe-University Frankfurt am Main, Germany. He is also Adjunct Professor of Philosophy at Saint Louis University, St. Louis, USA, and co-director of the DFG-Research Group on 'Human knowledge and the developments of societies'. He has recently co-edited *Metaphysics in the Twelfth Century: On the Relationship among Philosophy, Science and Theology* (2004), *Krieg und Frieden im Prozess der Globalisierung* (2005), and *Religion und Kultur* (2005).

GOENAWAN MOHAMAD, renowned poet, essayist, and journalist, lives in Jakarta, Indonesia. He was a Nieman Fellow at Harvard University, USA, and is Senior Editor of the independent magazine *TEMPO*. In 1994 he co-founded *Komunitas Utan Kayu*, a forum for literature and the arts. Among his publications are 'The Difficulty of the Subject' ('Kesulitan Subjek'), in *Diskursus, Jurnal Filsafat Dan Teologi* (2005), *Selected Poems* (2005), *Conversations with Difference* (2nd ed. 2005) and *Catatan Pinggir*, Vols 6 and 7 (2006).

MRINAL MIRI is a philosopher. He recently retired as Vice Chancellor of North Eastern Hill University, Shillong, India. He has published widely in professional journals both in the west and in India. The main focus of his interest is moral philosophy but his work ranges from mainstream philosophy to education, literature, and the arts. One of his recent publications is *Identity and the Moral Life* (2003).

BINDU PURI teaches at the Department of Philosophy, University of Delhi, India. Her areas of interest include moral philosophy and modern Indian philosophy. She has authored *Gandhi and the Moral Life* (2004) and edited *Mahatma Gandhi and His Contemporaries* (2002). Her recent publications are 'Zarathustra, Phronesis and an Alternative Understanding of Human Rights', in *New Nietzsche Studies* (2005/06).

A. RAGHURAMARAJU is Professor in the Department of Philosophy, University of Hyderabad, India. He obtained his PhD from the Indian Institute of Technology in Kanpur and was a Fellow at the Indian Institute of Advanced Study in Shimla. He recently published *Debates in Indian Philosophy: Classical, Colonial and Contemporary* (2006).

He also authored *Maidanam Lotulloki: Postmodern Parisheelana* (2003) and edited *Existence, Experience and Ethics* (2000).

MARTIN SEEL is Professor of Philosophy, Johann Wolfgang Goethe-University Frankfurt am Main, Germany. He was earlier Professor at the University of Hamburg and at Justus-Liebig-University Gießen. His most recent publications are *Sich bestimmen lassen. Studien zur theoretischen und praktischen Philosophie* (2002) and *Adornos Philosophie der Kontemplation* (2004).

HEIKO SIEVERS is Regional Programme Director for South Asia, Goethe-Institut/Max Mueller Bhavan New Delhi, India. He has served as Director of Max Mueller Bhavan Bangalore, the Goethe-Institut Lisbon and as Head of the Cultural Programme Department at the Goethe-Institut Head Office in Munich. In India he has co-edited *Structural Adjustment. Economy, Environment, Social Concerns* with S. Raghuram and V. Vyasulu (1995) and *Rules, Laws, Constitutions* with Satish Saberwal (1998).

HÜLYA YETIŞKEN is Associate Professor of Philosophy, Hacettepe University, Ankara, Turkey. She has also lectured at Mimar Sinan University, Istanbul University, and Marmara University. Her publications (all in Turkish) include *Women and Philosophy* (2004), *Ethical Possibility and Limits of Professional Norms* (2005) and *Kuçuradi's Ethical Views in Relation to Kant's Philosophy* (2005).

XIE DIKUN is Deputy Director and Professor at the Institute of Philosophy, Chinese Academy of Social Sciences (CASS). Among his publications are *About Fichte's Philosophy of Religion* (1993), *The Development of Humanities* (2002), *History of the West*, Vols 6 and 7 (2005), and *Philosophical Research in Modern China in the Past 50 Years* (3 vols, 2005).

4. He also co-authored *Mendelian Genetics: The modern fundamentals* (200?) and edited *Science, Evolution and Ethics* (2000).

Matthias Lutz-Bachmann is Professor of Philosophy at Johann Wolfgang Goethe-University Frankfurt am Main. Contributors was educated there and at the University of Hamburg, and at Jesuit schools in Germany. Contributors His research concentrations are both historical and theoretical. He teaches and publishes in *Philosophie* (200?) and *Allgemeine Philosophie der Kantianismus* (200?).

Janaki Sita is a Reluctant Programme Director for South Asia, Goethe-Institut Max Mueller Bhavan, New Delhi, India. He has served as Director of Asia Müeller Bhavan in addition, she is editor. In addition she is Head of the Cultural Programme Department at the Goethe Institut Max Office in Munich, in India her recent edited Structure, Literature, Bourgeois Movement, Social (2006) with "Partition and Asia" in Asia in (2006) and Public Culture Contemporary South Asia (2008).

Halil Yurttas, Associate Professor of Philosophy, Humanities Division at Koç University, Turkey. She has also earned a Master Sabancı University, Istanbul University, and Maximus University. Her publications call the self in history are John Stuart and Philosophy (2000), Jesuits, Sociality and Their A Phenomenality Study (2005) and Knowledge in John Locke to Kant to in India, Philosophy (2008).

X. Francisco Peyara, Director and Professor at the Institute of Philosophy of University Academy of Social Sciences (CSIC), Spain. He is the graduate from the Philosophy of Juárez (1988).